17 75

Methods in Analytical Psychology

An Introduction

D0807074

Methods in Analytical Psychology

An Introduction

HANS DIECKMANN

Translated by
BORIS MATTHEWS

Chiron Publications
Wilmette, Illinois

Originally published in 1979 as *Methoden der Analytische Psychologie: Eine Einführung.*
Copyright 1979, Olten: Walter Verlag.

© 1991 by Chiron Publications. All rights reserved. No part of this publication may be reproduced, stored in a retrieval system, or transmitted, in any form by any means, electronic, mechanical, photocopying or otherwise, without the prior written permission of the publisher, Chiron Publications, 400 Linden Avenue, Wilmette, Illinois 60091.

Translation © 1988 by Chiron Publications.

Library of Congress Catalog Card Number: 90-44750

Printed in the United States of America.
Edited by Kurt Hasselquist and Siobhan Drummond.
Book design by Kirk Panikis.

Library of Congress Cataloging-in-Publication Data:
Dieckmann, Hans.
    [Methoden der analytischen Psychologie. English]
    Methods in analytical psychology : an introduction / Hans
Dieckmann ; translated by Boris Matthews.
      p. cm.
    Translation of: Methoden der analytischen Psychologie.
    Includes bibliographical references and index.
    ISBN 0-933029-48-9 : $17.95
    1. Psychoanalysis. 2. Jung, C. G. (Carl Gustav), 1875-1961.
I. Title.
    BF173.D513 1990
    616.89'17 – dc20   90-44750
                                       CIP

ISBN 0-933029-48-9

Contents

Introduction

This introductory book on the methods in C. G. Jung's analytical psychology covers only part of the field, namely individual analysis, and hence is intentionally not entitled the *methodology* of analytical psychology. In addition to the individual analysis of adults, the methodology of analytical psychology also embraces methods used in child, group, family, and couples therapy. Granted, the analytic and synthetic work with individual patients has provided and continues to provide both the basis for all other methods of analytic treatment and the most important insights as well as furnishing new ideas for all other areas. Since this book is intended as an introduction, it makes claim neither to thoroughness nor completeness. It is intended to offer the beginner as well as the practicing analyst the opportunity to work out his or her position in regard to certain "essentials" that have to be confronted in every analysis. There is no long-term and deep-reaching analysis leading to individuation that will not, in one form or another, touch on the problems discussed in the various chapters.

I want to emphasize expressly that this book represents the position I have worked out; it is not a statement of a fixed system of rules. Whoever wants to find out what the analyst says or does at a given point in treatment will most certainly be disappointed since we neither can nor may impart that sort of technical precision in our discipline if we are to assure the individual the greatest opportunity for the free unfolding of his or her personality. In the countertransference the analyst must engage his entire personality as a subjective factor with its own individual specificity in the treatment. Thus every process of individuation is determined as much by the personality of the analyst as by the difficulties and problems of the analysand. For this reason I am convinced that, aside from fundamental questions concerning the problem of methodology and technique in analytical psychology in general discussed in the first chapter, this book reveals the specific features of my individual methodology which cannot simply be taken over by someone else lock, stock and barrel in the form I present them. But this book provides both the beginner and the experienced clinician the possibility of reflecting on certain basic methodological problems that one encounters again and again, and of taking note of the opportunities they contain.

For these reasons I also believe it is important to say at least a few words about my personal background out of which this book arose. In addition to my earlier training and practice of internal medicine, I have been in private practice as a Jungian analyst in Berlin since 1957. Since then, with few exceptions I have conducted only long-term, individual analyses with adults and adolescents. From the outset this area has held my interest which is just as lively now as it was at the beginning of my analytic practice more than 20 years ago. I have never regretted switching from internal medicine to the analytical psychology of C. G. Jung. For myself each and every individual analysis is still a thoroughly exciting and eventful journey into the new and unknown territory of another human soul. I have never gotten bored, although that by no means implies that there haven't been boring hours now and then. Although I tend toward being an introverted type, I am a relatively lively person, and if someone had predicted when I was 25 or 30 that I would spend the greatest part of my professional life sitting in an armchair listening to other people, I would have declared him mad. Today I know that this odd calling has brought me more fulfillment than any other area of medicine, ranging from surgery to internal medicine, both of which I initially practiced. The calling of the analyst is indeed something note-worthy. As Jung once phrased it, the analyst is, on the one hand, a highly trained and one-sided specialist in medicine who treats with only one method, and on the other hand he or she embraces the most universal concerns this world holds: the entire realm of humankind's soul and spirit. Precisely because this domain is so broad and endless, one fortu-nately never learns everything and again and again encounters something new and unfamiliar.

In addition to my private practice I am also active as teacher and training analyst in the division of analytical psychology at the Berlin Institute for Psychotherapy. Hence this book reflects not only my experi-ence in the analyses of my patients but also the background of training analyses, supervision, and the numerous seminars that I have conducted at the Berlin Institute during the past two decades. Consequently I have always stayed in touch with the difficulties and problems that beginning analysts have with very simple and banal practical aspects of analytic practice. Many of these issues have found their niches in this book. Whenever I have seemed at times somewhat too banal in my concern with various topics — as, for example, in my reflections on dealing with patient's late arrivals for appointments — I have consoled myself with a bit of Indian wisdom: one can discover an entire world in each and every mundane grain of sand. Indeed we do hold the view that access to the collective unconscious and the transformative effect of the encounter with archetypal images is a central process in our analytical therapy, but opening this avenue can come about and work out beneficially only if one does not forget the everyday things and if one is capable of delving into the banal difficulties and misunderstandings in the relationship between the physician and the patient. Hence this book is based on practical experience, is intended for practitioners, and waives claim to all-encompassing hypotheses and theorizing. These are invoked only when they are necessary for elucidating the background of practical actions.

Since the Institute for Psychotherapy in Berlin is, as far as I know, the only institute in the world in which analysts of Jungian and of the neo-analytic schools are trained in relatively close practical collaboration, albeit in separate divisions and curricula, this book naturally reflects the ways I have come to terms with the Freudian and especially with the neo-analytic methodology. I have attempted to present both what distinguishes us and what we share in common, for, on the one hand, I have no interest in forcibly postulating differences that do not exist in the practical treatment of patients; but on the other hand I must emphasize that in some areas there are significant differences that rest not only on different theoretical premises but also on a different stance and attitude toward the patient and his or her illness. For us, neurotic illnesses arise not only from infantile beginnings that took root in childhood but also from the current conflict in which the patient finds him- or herself and thus also from his or her attitude to the society and its entire history in which he or she lives and works. Jung himself was one of the first to point out that many persons suffering from neuroses or psychoses basically no longer fit in with the level of consciousness of the social group surrounding them but rather have fallen ill precisely because they need a broader and more comprehensive consciousness and are not able to break through to it. Given this background we are inclined to emphasize not only the neurotically limiting, ill, pathological, and infantile elements in our dealings with our patients but also the archetypal realm of the healthy child which bears within it the prospective and synthetic possibilities for development and maturation and approaches us from the unconscious part of the psyche. This is a point of view that, in recent decades, has won through more and more and is also held by Freudians or former Freudians, as for example Erich Fromm and Karen Horney. Of course this does not go so far as to say that the salvation of the world and the cure of illness is to be expected solely from a change in social conditions, since every society is ultimately composed of individuals and sick individuals cannot bring forth a healthy society.

We are confronted here, in my opinion, with a dialectical process in which we cannot one-sidedly accentuate either the changes in or the individuation of the individual or of society. They condition each other and we cannot — as some authors maintain again and again — alter only the one side, but must work on both poles of this dialectical process. For good reason Jung placed the individual's search for meaning, the foundations of belief, and the task in this life at the focal point of individuation. On the one hand the question of meaning cannot be answered collectively; rather, each individual must discover a personal sense of meaning and task in life within him- or herself. On the other hand, it is also necessary to live in a society that makes this possible and, as far as practicable, facilitates the individual's discovery of meaning and task and the creative unfolding of his or her personality. We can only lament how little society actually does this in our overpopulated world where the profit motive, recognition, ambition, and hedonism are stressed. Consequently a methodology that truly aims at individuation must in no way lead toward accommodating the individual to these menacing shadow sides of our modern system of civilization.

Two topics that actually belong among the fundamental problems of method are not treated in separate chapters here. In a book on methods one would expect separate chapters dealing with resistances and with what has been called "working through." In rereading and revising the various completed chapters, however, I noted that a separate chapter on resistance would amount merely to a summary of references and reflections found throughout the other chapters. There is scarcely a chapter in which I do not investigate resistance and the system of defenses so that, in my opinion, a separate chapter devoted to this topic would be superfluous. The same could be said for "working through," which is actually the presupposition for all intensive analytical work. The ever-recurring circumambulation that strives to bring unconscious symbolism to consciousness and to grasp meaning, embraces and describes the process of working through. Of course I have not, as already mentioned above, treated individual problems exhaustively, but rather have selected particular aspects of some of the topics that seem especially significant in practice. This is quite noticeable in the chapter on dream interpretation in regard to the entire, detailed description of subjective and objective levels of interpretation, as well as the reductive and prospective viewpoints. Had I been concerned with thoroughness in this area, the chapter would have become a book in its own right. I have dealt with this issue in detail in two other books to which I would refer the reader interested in this topic (Dieckmann 1972b, 1978a).

In conclusion I would like to express my special thanks to those persons who have permitted me to publish some of the material from their analyses. Of course, all case descriptions have been disguised in order to preserve the necessary confidentiality, and frequently the individual example is a condensation of similar processes experienced by various patients. Moreover I owe a debt of thanks to my wife, likewise a practicing analyst, who undertook the huge task of reworking and correcting the entire manuscript, as well as to Mr. Joachen Stelzer, who compiled the bibliography. My thanks also go to Dr. Gertrud Roos for compiling the index and last but not least to my secretary, Mrs. Sigrid Wiegand, who bore the burden of typing and retyping the manuscript.

Hans Dieckmann
August 1978

CHAPTER 1

The Problem of Method and Technique in Analytical Psychology

In contrast to Freud's psychoanalysis which, from the very beginning up to the present day, has taken an intensive and detailed interest in the questions and problems of analytic technique and method, there are very few works in the field of analytical psychology concerned exclusively with these topics although very early on Jung (*C.W.* 7) pointed to their importance. Greatly oversimplified, Freudian analysis proceeds from the position that in the analytic setting there is a fundamentally correct, optimal method informing the behavior and experience of both the analyst and the patient, and that this is imparted to the patient at the outset of treatment as a system of instructions or rules. All deviations or nonobservances of these rules are conceptualized as resistance or acting out and interpreted to the patient at the time. Among the basic rules of "classical analytical technique," Rycroft (1968), for instance, included the following: five sessions per week, use of the couch, abstinence from giving advice, the prohibition of using medications and from interfering in the patient's way of life as well as the absolute insistence on the method of free association and restriction of all the analyst's utterances to interpretations.

Schultz-Hencke (1970), the founder of the neo-analytic school in Germany, gives considerably more differentiated, precise, and comprehensive directions concerning the correct analytic technique in his textbook of analysis. In forming the so-called therapeutic agreement at the outset of treatment, Schultz-Hencke mentions eleven areas of information or instruction that should be imparted to the patient. These include the "basic rule" concerning correct association and lying on the couch, payment, length and frequency of sessions, the patient's correct behavior in important life situations and decisions, and the rules mutually governing vacations. Even among Freudians and neo-Freudians, however, opinion is divided between those who defend this sort of classical analytic technique and those that attack it or do not think highly of it. One of the most prominent representatives of the latter group is Michael Balint (1965). In any event, this sort of psychoanalytic technique has led to an abundance of modifications, and these modifications encompass an infinitely broad literature in psychoanalytic publications covering practically all the classic psychoanalytic rules. Sprouting like mushrooms from the extraordinarily fertile soil of psychoanalysis we find also completely new methods that claim to attain better and more rapid results with entirely different techniques, methods that attain worldwide dissemination and are devoured by a popular readership.

Yet in view of this sort of situation we must ask ourselves if we aren't perhaps doing something fundamentally wrong when we approach the developmental and maturational processes of the psyche with the idea that there might be something like a standardized method and technique, as there is in surgery, a technique that is applied to the patient externally in order to bring him to an optimum of emotional development and health. A problem arises here: Is there indeed no other way? Do all our interventions and efforts in this area rest on our finding specific methods that prove to be good, correct, and successful that we can then apply to other patients, perhaps with certain modifications?

In order to answer this question I would like to make a seemingly rather unusual historical digression, considering alchemy, which experienced its finest flowering in the Middle Ages. The reader of C. G. Jung's works will be familiar with the parallels between the symbolism of the maturational and developmental processes of the psyche and alchemical symbolism.

Alchemy is an extraordinarily noteworthy, partly material and partly philosophical-spiritual movement that thought of itself both as science and as art. It arose sometime in the third century A.D., but it traced its real roots back to antiquity, principally to the teachings of Plato and Aristotle. For more than thirteen centuries alchemy fascinated the entire civilized world. Emperors, kings, and princes invested huge sums in it, and the most significant scholars of the times were also adepts of alchemy or were concerned with alchemical teachings. Only with the development of the natural sciences and the triumphal march of technology during the last three centuries throughout the world did alchemy gradually disappear, leaving only a few insignificant eccentrics who still exist today. One involuntarily asks whether this entire expenditure of effort was only a hoax, the nonsense and superstition of a dark, yet-unenlightened age. But let us also recall that people of the caliber of Albertus Magnus, St. Thomas Aquinas, Gebser, Fludd, and Paracelsus dedicated themselves intensively to this art and science. True, modern chemistry is indebted to alchemy for the discovery of many chemical processes such as the production of glass and for the invention of everyday laboratory utensils such as retorts. For the alchemists, however, these were only very insignificant by-products, like the modern cooking pots made from the same material as rocket nose cones that have nothing at all to do with the real goal of the undertaking or the process. Alchemy was more than "just" an incomplete, preliminary stage to modern chemistry.

The real goal that alchemy wanted to attain with the help of its science — and we should not forget that alchemy was a recognized science and existed much longer than many sciences we have today — was, first of all, the production of gold. Besides producing gold they talked about other, equally important goals, specifically of a *lapis philosophorum*, a philosophers' stone, of an anthropos, of a completely hermaphroditic human, and of a number of other, similarly "final" symbols in which the alchemical process was supposed to culminate. Significantly, alchemical treatises also made this statement: "*Aurum vulgum, non est aurum nostrum*" (Jung, *C.W.* 13), that is, "Our gold is not the ordinary gold." Thus again we must ask ourselves whether or not the production of physical gold, too, might not have been only a by-product or a symbol for something entirely different from what alchemy had in mind, something that the alchemists either could not or would not express in words or in definite concepts. Consequently we must seek to understand what meaning gold actually had for the alchemists in addition to the material value of the metal. In this connection it is important briefly to consider the theory of correspondences, a central concept of alchemical, or of pre-rational thought, for the latter also plays a considerable role in our analytical processes.

Pre-rational thinking in the form of correspondences is a form of thought that was so natural for the alchemists, as for medieval thinking in general, that they did not even describe it as a method but rather simply employed it. In contrast to the logical-deductive thought in which we have been uninterruptedly schooled since childhood, thinking in terms of correspondences has become so foreign that we usually become confused or uncertain of ourselves whenever we encounter it. Actually we find it spontaneously active today only in children and among the so-called primitive or primal peoples in whom the symbolic processes of the unconscious live on. When we do encounter it, we tend presumptuously to dismiss it as illogical and confused and to think ourselves far above it. We do this quite unjustly, for thinking in correspondences is a primordial stage, a sort of matrix, out of which the entire body of our logical-rational thought has arisen. Moreover, this primordial form of thought encompasses more than logical-rational thought which is only a segment of that pre-logical layer that still lives on in our unconscious (Dieckmann 1969). Often it forms the basis for our creative processes that extend right up to the formulation of theories in natural science, as Pauli (1952) demonstrated in the case of Kepler.

Thinking in terms of correspondences is a very "archaic" form of thought that proceeds from the idea that a specific primordial fact finds expression in the most diverse areas and manifests in the greatest variety of correspondences which, by analogy, can stand for each other. Hence this form of thought is not logical but rather analogical, and it operates mentally with the concept *sicut*, "as if," not with the word "because" as is the case with logical-causal thought processes. This is best illustrated with an example.

For thought in correspondences, fire = light = energy = sun = hell = dragon = warmth = love = hate, etc. In this series of analogies we see that not only the most diverse objects, such as sun and dragon, are identical, but also feeling states or ideas, as, for example, hell and energy. Alchemy as well as primal and early cultures grappled seriously with the relationships among such correspondences, specifically in regard to the correspondences in which a given primal fact could manifest in the various realms of spirit, soul, or matter, or in the domains of the four elements fire, water, earth, and air. Regardless how incomprehensible such series may appear to us today, series of which we have the impression that everything could really be everything else and the whole thing a nonsensical chaos, we must nevertheless admit that they contain very clear and definite forms of order that are revealed to whomever delves deeper into analogical thought processes. There are, however, many things that simply cannot correspond to each other, e.g., fire ≠ water, mother ≠ father, but daughter = mother = water.

We are indebted to the French structuralist Lévy-Strauss (1973) for having given a comprehensive description of this ordering principle in "savage thought" among primal peoples and to have demonstrated that one can, for example, lay down a system of classification on this basis in the plant kingdom that can be just as effective and even considerably more comprehensive and more precise than our Linnaean system. The need for order is one fundament of thought, but it does not aim directly and primarily at the practical or the utilitarian, so that we can always argue which system of order is the most useful. However, it is essential to keep in mind that there are also possibilities other than our system of order. Lévy-Strauss's (1973) book contains an abundance of examples, for instance in regard to the cultivation of plants, where the system of savage thought of natives can attain results that we cannot match with all our scientific means. Keeping these considerations in mind, it would be frivolous to spurn this other, "archaic" kind of thought as a primitive or outdated preliminary form, just as nobody would ever think of repudiating childhood or adolescence but rather ever and again expects something new from just these two stages of life.

As Bernoulli (1935) has explained, one of the fundamental correspondences in alchemy is the equation world = man = God. This signifies that a fundamental fact is expressed in these three existential forms. In their treatises the alchemists write: "Make use of this in order to know God, nature and your self" (Bernoulli 1935, p. 155). Thus we have here the beginnings of an answer to the question posed when we asked after the goal of alchemy. Alchemy as art and science is by no means a greedy search for a method of producing physical gold — which was only a wrong way followed by bunglers and cheats — but rather something much more comprehensive that can be described in three aspects:

1. As theory, alchemy is conceived of as a vast, all-embracing vision of the cosmos, as the idea informing the entire universe, as the analysis of mankind, as a phenomenon radiating from and created out of God, as the compilation of all analyzable knowledge in correspondences in all areas.

2. As a practice, alchemy is the attempt to prove these things experimentally and to realize them concretely not only in the realm of matter but above all in the human soul which is the real locus of becoming, the only place that really is accessible.

3. As a transcendental endeavor, alchemy's great goal is that of effecting liberation from this world after man has come to know and experience it.

If we ponder Bernoulli's summary, it becomes clear that alchemy was actually concerned with an intrapsychic process, with a quest and a search for man's individuation within a domain in which the things of the soul and the things of matter were still so intimately conjoined that each was reflected in the other. Consequently this secret art and science was not only the preliminary step or the matrix of the modern natural sciences of chemistry and physics that arose from the purely material side of alchemy — that is, from the alchemists' involvement with, manipulations of, and experiments on substance and matter. Rather, there was a second, psychological level that arose from the spiritual-emotional processes at work in the alchemists. It is from this other side that alchemy is also the matrix or the preliminary stage out of which our modern depth psychology and particularly the study of the unconscious has arisen. *Seccare naturam necesse est* is an incontrovertible premise of scientific research, and on this premise we have separated the originally unitary structure of the transformations in the soul and in matter that alchemy still embraced. In doing this, the soul now no longer retains any material quality and we no longer regard it as that subtle body which alchemy ascribed to it; and matter, too, no longer contains any qualities of soul, for whoever today would attribute soul to a lump of gold would draw a few condescending smiles at best. Hence the very separation that we need for the purposes of our modern epistemology has, more than anything else, brought about the decline of that ancient, unitary science, alchemy.

Only long after we are gone will later generations be able to say whether or not the separation of the physical-material from the psychological-spiritual was correct, or whether behind the separation there is still a unity in which matter and spiritual-emotional processes are identical, just as, contrary to the scientific ideas up until the beginning of this century, it has now been proven that matter and energy are identical. But for the time being that is only a secondary question since what is important to us is the fact that this separation corresponds to our contemporary state of knowledge, a state of knowledge with which we must work methodologically. For the time being we must leave open this lacuna in our knowledge of the extent to which the physical and the psychic are related or linked in a greater unity although in many places this question will be important to us, for example, in regard to the relationship between, or the transformation of, psychological problems into symptoms of psychosomatic illnesses that find expression in the substance of our bodies. Granted, reference, or the fertile and positive regression, to the old unitary science of alchemy can be very meaningful and move us to formulate important theoretical and intellectual hypotheses, such as Jung (*C. W.* 14) did in his theory of the *unus mundus* derived from the alchemist Dorn.

No alchemist ever reached the goal of producing the uncommon gold, the complete human being, the philosophers' stone, or the water of life. The goals toward which the alchemical process strives were and still are utopian. However, like all things utopian, they have the dignity of an essential cornerstone of our existence as Ernst Bloch (1976) has emphatically pointed out. Hence it is still utopian for us today to hope that a person can become fully individuated in analytic therapy or, what is even more horrifying, to "completely analyze" a person. Even if our methods aim at attaining individuation through assimilating the unconscious, we must recognize that we can accompany our patients only a few steps along the way, that individuation is a life-long process and that ultimately the methodology of analytical psychology can only nudge this process into motion again for those patients in whom it has stagnated. Everything analysis can show persons about themselves, about the unconscious parts of their psyches and underlying motivations represents only a fraction of the possibilities contained in the unconscious, but it is just this fraction that decides between health and illness in the majority of cases.

Just as alchemy had countless methods at its disposal and every alchemist actually had his own particular method, it is inappropriate and senseless for analytical psychology to propound a fixed methodology and hand it on to its adepts or students precisely because analytical psychology rests on the principle of individuation. From this point of view it might seem senseless to write a book on methodology at all. Through the experience of his or her own training analysis and through knowledge of his or her own personality every practitioner must ultimately find the method and develop the treatment style that corresponds to his or her personality and to the personalities of his or her patients.

Nevertheless there are certain fundamental ideas that have crystallized as methodological essentials with which every analytical psychologist works. Each of us works with the unconscious and hence with dreams and fantasies. Each of us must create the necessary conditions for setting an analytic process in motion, and certain techniques are part of it. Each of us works within the tension of transference and countertransference and needs an analytic space for the analytic process in analogy to the alchemical *vas hermeticum* in which the alchemical process takes place which, of course, does not mean only the external space, the consultation room. Each of us must take into account the ages of our patients and their differing typologies, and, to some extent, each of us works with specific, traditional methods developed by Jung, for example, amplification or active imagination. It is possible to speak and write of methodology only in the sense that one expounds and describes basic aspects of analytical methods while the contents with which the individual practitioner fills them out may lie within the range of his or her individual discretion.

Although I have said above that each analytical psychologist approaches the phenomenon of neurosis or the intrapsychic processes of development and maturation with certain, general methods, I do want to mention that, in addition to the commonly shared, general methods that each of us uses, each practitioner probably also has a broad, individual spectrum of techniques that is not subsumed under these general headings and necessarily cannot be considered in this book. As an example of this I would like to mention that for many years I have been interested in finding out the favorite childhood fairy tale from each of my patients and, to the extent that they have such a tale, I have utilized the mythologem around which the tale is structured not only diagnostically and prognostically but also as an actual method in the therapeutic process. In numerous publications (Dieckmann 1967a, 1967b, 1971e, 1974b, 1975, 1986), I have pointed out this phenomenon which I consider very important, and I would like to elucidate it briefly. (In two additional works (Dieckmann 1968, 1971b) I have also developed the methodology of dealing with this phenomenon in the analytic process.)

If one is on the lookout for it, a favorite childhood fairy tale very often turns up in many people's analyses, a fairy tale which they very much loved or which greatly fascinated them, often one that especially frightened them. Probably all of us who are involved with children are familiar with this phenomenon and know that children listen to certain fairy tales or stories again and again; or, if they are somewhat older, they read them over and over or play out the themes of the tale before the mirror. In the course of later development these fairy tales are forgotten and repressed and often reappear only after childhood memories have reemerged from the unconscious. I am persuaded that the fairy tale is an especially suitable vehicle for expressing those libidinal energies contained in the magical-mythological layer of the psyche and for clothing the archetype per se in a specific imago capable of giving a symbolic direction and meaning to drives and instinctual energies. More clearly than the pure myth, the fairy tale combines magical and mythical elements corresponding to way they are combined in the collective unconscious. Moreover, it is more personal, more closely related to the life of the individual human being than is the myth which is often played out only among gods or semidivine heros. Knowledge of a patient's favorite fairy tale provides not only diagnostic information, but also understanding of the intrapsychic dynamics that take place in the background of the collective unconscious in an individual. Working with these fairy tales within the analytic setting can also have a significant therapeutic effect. As a consequence of having identified with or been inflated by an archetypal figure from the fairy tale, the individual unconsciously undertakes the impossible task of living a myth, and there lies the problem of the neurosis.

As a consequence of the ego complex having identified with a part of the fairy tale, usually with the leading figure, the other personifications fall into the unconscious and, since they are unconscious, they are projected into the environment. These projections and the constellating power that the activated archetype exerts on the environment then cause the patient to live a fate that corresponds with almost ludicrous exactness to that of the hero or heroine of their favorite fairy tale, except of course, for the redemption that nearly always comes at the end of the tale. Then what is actually lived out through the unconscious is not a human being, say a real man or woman, but rather a hero, a princess, a poor swineherd, or a beggar who suddenly acquires fabulous riches, or an animus-possessed woman who, in a figurative sense, like Turandot lops off the head of every man who approaches her.

The possibility of resolving this problem lies in understanding the patterning of the mythical dynamics as parts of one's own personality and in liberating the ego complex from identification with these patterns. As a result of the process of recognition and interpretation in analysis, the patient must learn to experience the myth as a non-ego existing in the collective unconscious layer of his or her psyche. Indeed, in certain situations the patient can draw on those powers from the collective unconscious but he or she must not conform to them. Rather, the patient must liberate his or her individual ego by stripping away the features of the mythical figure. To the extent that I have been able to discover a fundamental, underlying mythologem in my patients' favorite fairy tales, I have found it extremely fruitful to work with the fairy tale images and symbols again and again at appropriate times throughout the course of the analysis and to impart to the patient the most comprehensive possible awareness and understanding of his or her own personal fundamental mythologem. The interested reader will find more extensive discussion of this topic in my other writings mentioned above.

Analytic use of the favorite fairy tale is an example of an individual method that certainly is utilized by only a small number of analytical psychologists; by no means should the reader make the generalization that it is a standard analytic method. Every analyst of the Jungian persuasion probably has a sizeable number of individual methods that he or she uses in analysis, whether developed from his or her own empirical experience or borrowed from other areas and scientific disciplines. There are a number of passages where Jung himself points out that knowledge of the basic Freudian tenets is indispensable in analytical psychology, particularly in working with the personal unconscious and shadow issues. This says something about Jung's openness to accepting useful influences from other schools and to incorporating them in his views. In the development of analytical psychology after Jung, however, things have changed somewhat in this regard. The investigations of Fordham (1969), Neumann (1973), and Kadinsky (1964) on ego development and the beginnings of a special theory of neuroses, particularly in the work of H.-J. Wilke (1969, 1978), H. Dieckmann (1966), and U. Dieckmann (1974), give us the possibility today of expressing many things in the language of the psychology of the complexes from viewpoints that differ somewhat from the Freudian point of view. However, that does not preclude that much is identical in both major schools, especially when dealing with the family romance. The openness of analytical psychology to the methods of other schools has remained thoroughly characteristic. Aside from the integration of certain Freudian positions already mentioned, there are also connections to gestalt therapy (Whitmont and Kaufmann 1973), to Adlerian theories, and even to certain aspects of

behavioral therapy (Plaut 1971) but which include the underlying unconscious motivations. Yet it is essential to emphasize that consideration of
all these other ideas can come about only by modifying and integrating
the corresponding basic ideas of analytical psychology. In the case of
many methods it is actually a question of a retrogressive process, as, for
example, in the instance of gestalt therapy where the elaboration and
emphasis on the method of interpretation at the subjective level in Jung's
analytical psychology gave the decisive impetus for the development of
the gestalt methods from which analytical psychologists have now borrowed and used individual, more highly developed elements. Something
similar holds true for Leuner's (1970) approach to using imagery. Here,
too, the method of active imagination discovered by Jung ("The Transcendent Function," *C.W.* 8) was the godparent; the meditative variations and, under certain circumstances, the experiences developed by
Leuner in this area flow back into the further development of active
imagination in the methodology of analytical psychology.

Many Jungians experience an aversion and a deeply ingrained distrust
of the idea of methodology and technique, especially the latter. Consequently, analytical psychologists have written precious little in this area
in comparison with Freudian psychoanalysts and Freud himself. Various
underlying factors have contributed to this state of affairs. Primarily it
seems to me also a question of typology, since the pioneers in the field
and the first generations that followed Jungian psychology were predominantly of the introverted intuitive type, as Bradway (1964) has shown in
her investigations. Jung himself had this typology. Although the intuitive
can in no way avoid using certain methods and techniques, saddling him
with a very specific system of method or technique is loathsome. It is
loathsome not because he or she is capricious or arbitrary and has a
tendency to move about in the realm of blurry concepts or mystification
(as the very ignorant prejudice of other types would often have it) but
rather because being pinned down in that sort of strict, prescribed manner robs the intuitive of the best and most creative possibilities available
thanks to his or her leading function. Einstein would never have developed his theory of relativity had he been restricted to classical physics by,
say, the methodological prescriptions of an international society. The
role that intuition and the intuitive type plays in higher mathematics and
physics is generally well known. Moreover, a deep and, in the broadest
sense, religious discontent arises at the very moment that the human soul
is equated with a technical apparatus. That contradicts human psyche's
need for the transcendent dimension that was already expressed in the
third of the above-mentioned aspects of alchemy as the precursor of
modern psychology. Here it is a question of goals expressed not only in
alchemy but also in many religious and philosophical endeavors: specifi-

cally, the goal of liberating the human soul after it has recognized and experienced the material world. To what extent this must remain utopian is a moot point; however, it is important that this religious-mythological and also very scientific need has guided mankind to the greatest spiritual and cultural achievements.

A further underlying factor contributing to the aversion to the word *technique*, especially whenever one is speaking of things of the soul, is the shift in meaning that this word has experienced in our understanding over the last hundred years. If one now asks the oft-quoted Man-on-the-Street what the term *technique* means, he will, for example, point to an automobile and define technique as something that is capable of producing or repairing a machine of that sort when it has broken down. But this is exactly how he does not want his soul to be treated. An entirely different image appears if we go back about 150 years to the time when our entire contemporary, modern technology did not yet exist. There we find, for example, in the *Neues Elegantes Conversationslexikon für die Gibildeten aus Allen Ständen* (*New Sophisticated Encyclopedia for the Educated of All Classes*), from the year 1837, the simple statement that technique is a theory of art or a body of precepts according to which an art should be practiced. Here there is no mention at all of science or of apparatuses; rather, technique refers to the way in which one carves a madonna, how one paints a picture or even, to remain within our discipline, how one practices the precepts of the art of healing a person suffering from an illness. The same holds true for the concept of method. Pierer's *Grosses Universallexikon* (Great Encyclopedia) (1843) designates method as the procedures by which reason combines information, either as it acquires or imparts it, such that various pieces of information exhibit an inner coherence and relationship. Here the differentiation is made between analytic, synthetic, dogmatic, apodictic, skeptical, and critical methods. Thus we see that technique and method were by no means so removed or separated from the creative shaping of a complete work of art at that time. It is only the modern technology of our century that has created this separation and planted it in the collective consciousness.

In a discussion with Fordham, David Kadinsky (1970), who has dealt very extensively with technological symbolism in his book *Der Mythos der Maschine* (Kadinsky 1969), formulates technique as a manner of working with things which has been acquired through training and practice and is exercised through continual repetition without conscious thought or feeling. Consequently it represents an acquired form of skill. Here the technician is seen as the opposite of the artist or the scientist. As an example, Kadinsky adduces the act of writing down a scientific work in which two different activities are separated: first, the creative activity of formulating trains of thought and, second, the unconsciously executed ability, acquired as a skill, of manipulating the keys of the typewriter in order to record these trains of thought. In this regard the *Oxford Pocket Dictionary* agrees with him; it understands technique as the skill of the scientist in using instruments and as that part of artistic work that can be reduced to a formula, as mechanical adroitness in art. Under the impression of these definitions there arises, in my opinion, a momentous shift of emphasis or focus from the psyche of the analyst toward individual techniques that are objectified and made independent, for example, as prospective and reductive interpretation or the methods of association and amplification. Then, through acquired skill and with the help of unconscious components of the person, these learned analytic techniques that have been objectified and granted autonomy can be used in the analytic encounter without the participation of the entire personality of the analyst in the process. Kadinsky attempts to resolve this problem by regarding the persona as a part of the complete personality of the analyst that cannot be separated from the person of the analyst so that using a technique always corresponds to a reaction of the whole personality. Consequently in the realm of analysis one does not end up with the infamous production-line work where one practices according to preestablished norms.

Now it seems to me important not to give unconditional ratification to the separation that has arisen in our collective consciousness between mechanical-technical, acquired skill on the one hand and creative-artistic shaping and forming on the other. As analysts we act fully within our rights to be constructively regressive whenever an important, specific developmental stage has been bypassed along the way and should be retrieved from the unconscious. The above-cited modern conception of technique from which the creative element is excluded or separated out is by no means generally valid. The *Neue Brockhaus-Enzyclopädie* (1973) unhesitatingly includes the creative element in the definition of the concept of technique. In the narrower sense *Brockhaus* understands technique as

> the creative production of artifacts, apparatuses and processes utilizing the materials and forces of nature while respecting the laws of nature. Hence for technical production the following are essential: the creative idea, knowledge of the laws of nature and of the materials and their properties as well as the possibilities of manipulating them, and finally economic and social need. (vol. 18)

Also according to *Brockhaus* (1973, vol. 12), method is understood as a planned (methodical) procedure dependent on the subject and the goal, the mastery of a technique for the solution of practical and theoretical tasks (working methods, technical methods, etc.), especially characteristic for scientific undertakings. In analysis we must clearly realize that the technical instrument with which we carry out the treatment is not an objectifiable method of prospective or reductive amplification or association, of active imagination or the like, that is separable from the personality but rather that we are in the remarkable and quite unique situation of having before us our entire psyche and consequently the totality of our own personality as the instrument of our analytic technique. All the previously mentioned individual techniques are not the technical instrument itself but rather only various forms in which we manipulate it. In this sense, association does not correspond to the chatter of a skillfully manipulated typewriter but rather is a specific form in which one personality encounters another personality as a whole, an encounter in which both are touched in their totality.

This also corresponds to Jung's statement that there is only a personal technique, an extract distilled from one's own experience of life and the analyses one has conducted oneself, the result of one's own *perigrinatio*. The latter does not absolutely have to be of great value to other people (Jung, *C.W.* 14 par. 310). The early Freud also took a similar stance when he wrote, in 1912, "This technique has proven to be the only practical one for *my individuality*; I dare not deny that a physician with an entirely different personality can be constrained to prefer another attitude toward the patient and toward the tasks to be solved" (*S.E.*, vol. 8, p. 376).

Becoming conscious of the way in which we are individually dependent on our "instrument" in theorizing, experimenting, and practicing analysis is absolutely necessary. In our discipline there are no generally valid, hard-and-fast rules according to which something is right or wrong and which can be learned in a corresponding course of exercises in the way that one can learn to play a piano. Rather, every analyst is compelled to develop a technique in the course of training and from experiences with patients that corresponds to one's own individuality, which of course does not mean that the door is opened to every intuitive whim and that an analysis can proceed without any method or technique whatsoever. On the contrary, the necessity of technique and method demands additional, intensified exertion and work on oneself. The training analysis where one gains knowledge of one's own personality is the necessary foundation and precondition for developing personal technique and method.

If previously we have said that the instrument of our treatment in analysis must always be the totality of our own psyche or personality, we must also realize that within the personal realm a technical maneuver can never take place separate from the personality without missing its mark.

In analysis there is no standardized "know how"; one cannot address a given situation with a previously practiced reaction purely via the persona. In analysis there are of course ever-recurring, similar situations with which one is familiar due to prior experience, but it is of very little effect to make the same response to a situation one once experienced with Mr. X when one encounters that situation with Mr. Y. I would like to illustrate this with an example.

There are many analyses in which patients raise the question: "How can I open up to you when you remain such a stranger and tell me little or nothing of your personal life while I am supposed to say everything that concerns or touches me personally?" Depending on the structure or typology of the patient concerned, this question can be phrased variously, for example, with depressive sadness or with resignation; it can be aggressively demanding or hysterically quick-tempered; it can be expressed in attempts at getting emotionally close or remain purely at a rational surface level without any emotion whatsoever. But even if one selects one possibility from those mentioned here, say the one where the accent falls on the patient's depressive resignation, no standardized interpretation is possible even if the analyst has had the experience of once encountering this situation with another patient with the same underlying constellation. Then there arises the paradox that can be expressed approximately in this form: "I know this route and have already traversed it once," as well as "I don't know this route at all and never found myself on it." This paradox must arise, since in all collective, common human identities the unique, individual personality is irreplaceable and the encounter with this unique personality at a specific point in time always presents something new regardless of the similarity of structures and circumstances. One can conjure up certain situations and form a picture of them and of their possible courses with the help of the imagination and thereby gain the feeling that one knows what is coming. But does one really know? Always it is a half-knowledge, for the ensuing reality will never coincide with imagination and nothing, in fact, takes place just as we expect or anticipate. As Proust says, "*Rien n'arrive ne comme on l'espère, ni comme on le craint.*" In his *Psychologie der Weltanschauungen (Psychology of World Views)* Karl Jaspers (1954) has said that an event becomes a reality only when one brings it into the agora. But in analysis and in similar situations the agora is always "different" and hence ever and again demands of the analyst a creative "technique" by which he or she will respond to it.

Finally, the problems of methodology also embrace the question of the end toward which method is actually supposed to lead, i.e., in our case the question of the goal of treatment. Freud once verbally defined the goal of treatment as the restoration of the capacity to work and to enjoy; the goal of treatment in Jung's analytical psychology is the capacity for conscious individuation. Both goals overlap in many places, for in most respects the capacity for conscious individuation includes the capacity for constructive, meaningful work and by no means excludes the capacity to enjoy. But stressing the capacity to enjoy does seem somewhat problematic, for individuation also includes the ability to bear necessary suffering and to process it creatively. Of course, that takes place in Freudian analysis also, just as does a process of individuation, a concept that is used more and more by Freudians today.

Nevertheless a certain skepticism remains, and in practice also a significant difference on many points. The pleasure principle is hostilely opposed to the assumption of difficult and painful life tasks and challenges. They can be done away with by classifying them as masochistic if they offer little or no real pleasure, but from the standpoint of individuation they can represent a high value. Here we also touch on the concept of adaptation to an existing social order, a concept which justifiably has *Whether or* become ever more problematic in our times. *Nolens volens*, a system so *not one*, firm and in part compulsively rigid as Freudian psychoanalysis must *wishes it* accentuate adaptation to the momentarily existing reality of the social system. It leaves little room for unadapted changes whose path is usually painful at the beginning and is not understood by the collective. Think only, for example, of the ridicule and derision to which environmentalists were exposed only a few years ago and how they were depicted as ludicrous. All the while these "little green men" (as they are called in Germany) who today are feared even by the major political parties were the first to recognize a truly serious and very threatening problem of our times and to come to terms with it against the opposition of our society's growth ideology. It is no wonder that the system of psychoanalysis, accentuating pleasure and work as an end-state, has led one of the prominent exponents of the neo-Freudian view (Heigl 1978) to postulate the following diagnostic tenet in the context of a psychotherapy seminar in a widely circulated journal of general medicine: "Whoever in the past has responded to demands arising in society with physical or emotional symptoms or with *disturbances in behavior* has a *severe* neurosis. This failure indicates a disturbance in the frustration tolerance of the ego, of its ability to cope with internal and external stimuli and *demands*" (italics added).

If one ponders this tenet, very unsettling questions arise: Who actually decides what is a normal level of demand? Obviously it is the society here referred to. Is it then a normal demand of our society when, for example, more than one third of the young people in the upper classes in West German schools suffer severe emotional illnesses and develop symptoms from the stress of *Abitur* points [points on the final exams for graduation from *gymnasium*] which are necessary in order to have a choice in their profession? Do they all have a *severe* neurosis, or does the school system and the society that supports it have a neurosis? Initially at least and under certain circumstances, is not that individual more mature and more differentiated if he or she begins to suffer in a compulsively hopeless situation that robs one of the possibility of fighting? Are all the millions of young people who in the past two decades have attempted to drop out of our achievement, consumer, and growth-oriented society, or who have actually dropped out, perhaps not less neurotic than those who have adapted to this society with a "severe" character neurosis?

The danger today is that we are headed toward a destructive abyss if we submit to the "typical demands" of the existing forms of society, be they East or West, and if we seek no new paths. Some day truly intelligent beings of the future will surely be right in calling us not homo sapiens but the "crazy ape" as a well-known American biologist and Nobel laureate (Szent-Györgyi 1970) already does. Individuation would be a path that could help us out of this dilemma, that could lead us to ponder actualizing our selves and thereby to realizing a relationship to our own inner nature which would then no longer be the beast or the brute we must suppress and destroy but rather the living river of life in all its phenomenal forms which we must not destroy either outside ourselves or within. Reestablishing this relationship and thus leading man to his wholeness and not to a one-sided perfection is the treatment goal of individuation. However, completeness also embraces suffering, illness, death, and creative non-adaptation to existing conditions. Thus no psychologist of the Jungian school can approach a patient with the idea that this or that bit of non-adaptation must be eliminated or that the patient has to realize this or that specific idea held by the analyst. The treatment goal and the future personality of the human being lies in the unconscious whose constructive and creative stirrings both the analyst and the patient must follow. Here, too, the old maxim holds true: *Natura sanat, medicus curat.*

On the other hand, of course, individuation is neither chaos nor a willful non-adaptation at any price in the sense of a falsely understood individualism. Individuation stands in direct opposition to this. We know that the multiplicity of psychic factors in the human being are universal and collective and the individual quality of the personality consists in the particular proportions of those factors which vary from on to person. Individuation does not consist in an egocentric orienta-
ward the given peculiarity of the individual but rather demands a
operation among all the universal factors present in the human
dividuation aims at creating a wholeness and at developing all
lities in an individual in equal measure. Consequently it typi-

cally stands in opposition to the overdeveloped specialization of our times, in opposition to persons who have command over only a very narrow sector of life where they strive for the greatest possible perfection. There are many detailed publications on the concept of individuation in Jung's writings and in those of his followers to which I must refer the reader since an extended discussion would exceed the limits of this book. However, it was necessary to point out differences in therapeutic goals, for a case that appears unsuitable for psychoanalysis can be fully appropriate for individuation, just as a very old person (one thinks of Bergmann's film, *Wild Strawberries*) or even a person dying of an incurable illness can still individuate.

CHAPTER 2

The Initial Interview

Preceding or at the beginning of every analysis there is always an initial interview or an anamnesis, depending on the "school" to which the analyst adheres. Aside from a number of scattered remarks by Jung, there are only a few works, specifically from the London school (Adler) and from some Americans (Singer 1976, Whitmont and Kaufmann 1973), that take up the problem of the initial interview. Frequently the latter also proceed, as does Gerhard Adler, implicitly from the fact that the patient has undertaken an analysis and then include what the Freudians call the "analytic alliance," "therapeutic alliance," or "working alliance" in their discussion. Viewed practically, however, we are faced first of all with making a decision: from among the great number of patients that present themselves to us we must discern whether or not the analytic approach is indicated for their illness or problems. Consequently it is necessary to make a clear distinction between the first interview and the process of introducing the patient to the analytic method. These areas are to be treated separately. Therefore two questions arise: first, does it make any sense at all to devote a chapter to this topic in the context of this book; and second, does the analyst not contradict a so-called "spirit" of Jungian analysis if he or she imposes a specific structure on this first meeting between physician and patient since, as we know, the essence of which is supposed to lie in the individual human being's free and creative unfolding and self-discovery?

In the conversations touching on this topic I have had with analyst colleagues from all over the world, I have ascertained that actually all of them do have some sort of first interview in which they attempt to answer essential questions of diagnosis and symptomatology. Consequently I am inclined to the opinion that this lacuna has to do with the hesitancy Jungians feel about letting themselves be pinned down to specific techniques and a closed system: I believe analytical psychologists are following Jung's view that the time for that sort of closed system in medicine is still far from ripe and that they also hold the view that specific, generally valid techniques do in fact tend to have the character of a Procrustes's bed which hampers the process of individuation more than it furthers it.

However, we are faced with the impossibility of indiscriminately and chaotically commencing analysis with every patient that schedules an hour with us. Like everybody else, we are compelled to ponder the patient's clinical picture in a differentiated manner and assess whether analytic treatment is or is not indicated. This problem is by no means confined to analytical psychology. Freudian psychoanalysis, which concerns itself far more intensely and to a far greater extent with generally valid problems of method and technique, has a similar lacuna in the area of the first interview. Hence Argelander (1967) speaks of the initial interview as a stepchild of psychotherapy. Certainly there are more works on this topic since 1938 when Steckel (1950) devoted the first chapter of a book on the technique of analytic psychotherapy to the initial interview. Authors such as Deutsch (1939); Deutsch and Murphy (1955); Gill, Newman, and Redlich (1954); Sullivan (1951); and Frieda Fromm-Reichmann (1950) have addressed this issue. Nevertheless, the information is sparse, these authors differ in many points or emphasize various sorts of criteria and, moreover, use various designations such as "preliminary interview," "clinical interview," "psychiatric interview," or "associative anamnesis." The only exception in this area is Schultz-Hencke's (1970) "structured anamnesis" which is very uniformly taught and practiced. We shall return to it later.

Obviously we are dealing with a universal problem, a problem that concerns not only analytical psychology but one characteristic of the analytic endeavor itself regardless to which school the therapist belongs. We must be clear on this point: in most branches of medicine (except for psychiatry) there is a distinction between diagnosis and therapy in the vast majority of cases, and only very seldom do the diagnostic procedures to which a patient is subjected have any concurrent therapeutic effect. In psychiatric medicine the situation has an entirely different appearance since every diagnostic examination is always a therapeutic intervention that alters the psychic processes to a greater or lesser extent. These changes can be relatively minimal, but they can also be quite far-reaching as I will presently illustrate with two clinical examples. But changes are introduced in every case since, due to the analytic conduct of the interview — that is, due to the attention paid to the unconscious processes and their dynamics — the pathological psychic complexes are mobilized and the patient is thereby compelled to reflect on them and engage them to an increased extent. If one asks patients about their reactions following an initial interview with an analyst, what almost all mention is that the first meeting evoked more or less intense reactions in them and altered the clinical picture slightly in one direction or another. It is only the severely schizoid patients who now and again awaken the impression that the first interview evoked no reaction in them; however, in the course of a lengthy analysis — presuming that analysis follows the initial interview — it always comes out that extraordinarily deep and intense reactions took place in precisely these patients beneath their veneer of indifference. Two extreme examples will illustrate how extensive such therapeutic and other effects can be.

The first case is that of a woman who married an officer during World War II. The marriage moved along smoothly for the first year during the war. However, at the end of the war, when they began living together full time and took up the practical aspects of a normal married life, she was forced to recognize that he was bisexual and lived out his manifest homosexual tendencies. Moreover he had strong sado-masochistic traits that made living with him extraordinarily difficult for the patient. On the basis of a strongly ideological attitude of sacrifice she wanted to maintain the marriage at all costs. Over the course of the next two years she developed depressive moods and anxieties that gradually got worse and caused her finally to seek out an analyst. During the first interview the analyst cautiously asked whether her ideology of sacrifice was so constituted that she loved those closest to her more than she loved herself and not as in the Bible where it says "as oneself." This sentence had such a great aftereffect on the patient that during the time she was waiting to enter therapy she began to change her life. She initiated divorce proceedings against her husband, her symptoms vanished, and she became aware that there were other areas in her life where she had the right to look out for her own needs. After that she no longer needed therapy. Since I was in a position to continue to observe this patient for many years, I can confirm that she did not suffer from any psychological malady during the next ten years.

The next example comes from a study of a West German family by a team of sociologists; the study was presented at the Berlin Institute for Psychotherapy in 1976. The team started with one question: Could the theory of Freudian psychoanalysis, particularly the various intricacies and the working through of the Oedipal situation, be demonstrated within a so-called normal, randomly chosen family. In order to answer this question, the sociologists moved into the home of the family for several days, tape recorded all verbal expressions of the two children and of the parents, asked only a few questions and forewent all commentary. The end effect was that the previously intact family collapsed, the spouses got divorced and, as came out in the discussion, psychic symptoms appeared in all the participants. Opinions can differ whether or not in certain cases this result is to be conceived as positive — in the sense of a development of consciousness — or as an involuntarily naive destruction — in the sense of the earlier Christian missionaries who, without knowing what they were doing, destroyed the myth in which the primal peoples lived in order to bring them Christianity. In any event, however, this example shows that the mere process of observation suffices to set very considerable changes in motion.

These are extreme examples, of course, and in an interview conducted *lege artis* by an expert there are, as a rule, at most minor improvements or aggravation of the symptoms, and as a rule one can prevent a dangerous destructive process from getting underway. But in any event it is the peculiarity of psychological illnesses to react to every intervention and in far greater measure than is the case in organic medicine so that diagnosis in analysis always means that one is already doing therapy at the same time. In the positive sense this can lead the patient to more intense reflection and conscious confrontation with the underlying problems, but it can also have the opposite effect of strengthening repression and the formation of defenses.

A fundamental argument against taking a structured, biographical anamnesis rests on the consideration that as such it is an un-analytic procedure. Asking pointed questions and the unconscious pressure of the analyst's interest in obtaining as complete a picture of the biographical data as possible exert a high degree of control that holds the patient fast in the realm of consciousness and pays little attention to unconscious material. Consequently a situation arises at the outset which is unfavorable for undertaking analysis and can severely disturb the structure of the specific analytic relationship in its many ramifications. As it is practiced at the Berlin Neo-Psychoanalytic Institute, the "structured anamnesis" consists of a two-to-three-hour interview with the patient and the written results comprise four to eight type-written pages. This anamnesis consists not only of the subject's biography in as complete a form as possible including a detailed description of significant others and social development but also behavior and experiences in the realms of the various drives and the description of the situation where the subject was tempted or where he or she failed that precipitated the decision to seek therapy. As a rule serious problems are associated with this procedure. A patient suffering from a neurosis who visits an analyst for the first time usually is in a highly anxious or tense state and consequently is already too overstressed to present a multitude of accurate and relevant facts. In addition to this, very considerable lapses, errors, and distortions of memory are present in every case. In my experience most of the data taken in a structured anamnesis are corrected by the patient in the course of the analysis, and a second anamnesis taken at the conclusion of a successful course of analytic therapy would often present an entirely different picture than the anamnesis taken at the beginning. I would like to present two examples that address this issue.

A thirty-eight-year-old patient who suffered from paroxysmal tachycardia was referred to me by a clinic where a structured anamnesis had been taken. His first attack had taken place at a performance of Mozart's opera *The Magic Flute* and the patient still recalled the passage during which the attack began. It was the passage in the second act where the Queen of the Night sings the aria "The vengeance of Hell boils in my heart" and places the dagger in the hands of her daughter Pamina with the charge that she kill Sarastro. In combination with certain genetic facts and compulsive traits that the patient had, the first interviewer conceptualized his illness as an aggressive problem of predominantly neurotic compulsive structure. It was not until approximately the eightieth analytic hour that it came out that this attack had not been the first. Preceding this attack there had been two others that the patient had repressed and that show more clearly the patient's real problem which appeared most impressively in the circumstances of the first attack. Moreover, the circumstances of the first attack could be uncovered only gradually in the course of several analytic hours before it became accessible to recall. In the situation that initially triggered his heart symptoms the following elements were involved. The patient had attended a popular scientific lecture on heart ailments. During the lecture he suffered his first attack and had to leave the room when a picture of the open thorax revealing the heart had been shown. But in this same setting yet another small incident played a role, an incident that the patient had repressed very deeply: the lecture took place in the context of a supplementary training course, and in this course there was a woman participant for whom he felt feelings of love for the first time in his life. He had also, albeit quite timidly, made some attempts to approach her and had obviously built up an illusionary fantasy that he would not be rejected by her. Precisely at this point in the lecture where the heart symptoms were triggered his neighbor whispered to him that this young woman had become engaged to someone else just the previous day. After careful inquiry it turned out that the patient had initially told himself the young woman wasn't so very important, and only when he heard of her engagement had he really recognized how much he was in love with her. True, the patient did have some compulsive characteristics, but the core of his neurosis, as came out more and more clearly in the course of his analysis, lay in a positive mother complex with a close psychic and physical mother–child symbiosis that persisted in the unconscious and was accompanied by severe separation anxieties. Thus it was basically a problem of relationship at a depressive level, and the problem of aggression lay rather in his inability to free himself from being held fast by the mother figure. Between the first attack and the second (which followed two weeks later) and the precipitating circumstances — that is, the third attack at *The Magic Flute* — there lay a period of time during which the patient's actual external circumstances changed, which of course always plays a considerable role in judging the given situation of temptation or failure.

The second example, a woman, was diagnosed, following her anamnesis, as hysterical but with a relatively favorable prognosis. Precisely because of the intensive questioning about details of her biography during the anamnesis, the patient concealed a sensitive delusional system that had grown up around a masturbation complex. Being subjected to the anamnesis had mobilized the figure of her watchful mother in her from whom she had always had to conceal and hide her drive wishes. Not until the one-hundredth treatment hour did she succeed in revealing this sensitive delusional relationship system into which the analyst was already solidly interwoven as a forbidding and persecuting figure. Naturally one can object here that even in a first interview conducted along strictly analytic lines the patient would also have concealed this complex; but it is not probable that it would have been concealed so consistently and for so long since this was her real problem behind which lay the pressure of intense suffering and a considerable need to communicate.

The problem of asking questions in taking the anamnesis plays a very significant role in the first phase of analysis. Many patients shy away from openly answering questions lying within the domain of certain complexes and precisely on these issues tend rather toward concealment and negation which they maintain with feelings of great guilt, often until late in the analysis. In contrast to this, it has often been my experience that patients share much more from the outset in an open analytic situation than they do when the analyst asks pointed questions.

Consequently the question arises whether it makes any sense at all from the standpoint of analytical psychology to undertake something like an "initial interview" or if it isn't more correct to leave the beginning of treatment completely open and to enter the analytic situation wholeheartedly from the outset with the expectation that during that first hour it will become clear whether or not the case is amenable to therapy and an adequate diagnosis is possible on the basis of the information volunteered. Current conditions in West Germany permit this approach in the instance of analyses paid for by state health insurance since the first five sessions can be reimbursed without completing the Expert Opinion Questionnaire. Only after the first five hours is an evaluation submitted on the basis of which the decision is made whether or not the state health insurance will authorize and reimburse continuing long-term analysis.

Thus there is a pause so that, to a certain extent, the first sessions can be regarded as a sort of trial or mini-analysis, and it is to be assumed that within this period of time the analyst can compile sufficient data and facts to answer the queries posed in the Expert Opinion Questionnaire.

In individual cases this sort of procedure is thoroughly appropriate; but it has the disadvantage that an initial analytic interview extended over that length of time very frequently, if not always, creates a considerable transference-countertransference bond between physician and patient, the resolution of which, in certain cases, is an emotional shock for the patient if he or she is found unsuitable for analytic treatment. This outcome can, for example, increase the risk of suicide. Nor is this situation free from danger to the analyst himself. Again and again we find that even experienced analysts get involved in hopeless cases against their better judgment on the basis of transference and countertransference bonds that have arisen in this way because they are often of the opinion, not altogether unjustifiably, that they can no longer leave the patient in the lurch. This danger is avoided by having at most a second interview after mentally digesting the first interview and the information obtained in it.

The necessity of making an in-depth diagnosis in psychological terms and dynamics, and the elimination of the cases not suited to analytic treatment, demands that analytical psychology hold an initial interview before the actual treatment begins. Consequently the problem we must face is not whether an initial interview should be conducted or foregone, but rather how the patient can be given the opportunity for the greatest possible disclosure of the autonomous dynamics of his or her psyche in this situation and, simultaneously, also how the doctor can obtain the necessary facts of the patient's history and current condition.

In 1966 the problem of the initial interview was the topic of discussion for several sessions of the Berlin Study Group for Analytical Psychology and a number of initial interviews were conducted according to the postulates that the group had developed. At the time we proceeded on the basis of a provisional distinction between two main areas: 1) the analyst's observations of the patient; and 2) the content of the patient's statements. In regard to the analyst's observations, value was laid first on the patient's appearance and behavior, second on the transference and countertransference relationship that arose, and third on easily observable symptoms, e.g., depressive or manic mood, blushing, difficulties in concentrating, linguistic problems, tics, etc.

The second area, the content of the patient's communications, was planned so that initially attention was paid only to what the patient spontaneously communicated. In all events, we intended to avoid disturbing the patient's spontaneous self-disclosure. No questions were interpolated; rather, questions thought to be important were asked at the end of the interview. Five points were worked out that were compiled in the protocol. The first was symptomology: in addition to the symptoms easily observable, what does the patient spontaneously say of himself or herself, and what observable or suspected symptoms does the patient not mention?

Next we considered the length and the differentiation of the symptoms, as well as the delineation of the syndrome character of the symptoms, e.g., compulsive thoughts and actions. Here, too, our questioning was limited to the material spontaneously shared and we avoided asking about further peripheral symptoms.

Third was the situation precipitating the condition. Likewise here we left it to the patient to describe what had brought him or her into treatment, since patients do tend to avoid painful questions or to answer them in a non-utilizable way. We also forewent asking for unnecessary details. What we considered important was what appeared most significant and prominent to the patient and how he experienced himself in the corresponding situation. In the event that the patient mentioned no precipitating situation for the symptoms, we simply noted this lacuna in the protocol. In no case was the patient asked about the precipitating situation as such; rather, we pondered whether or not a precipitating situation could be ascertained from the patient's remarks. From the standpoint of analytical psychology this was regarded as the expression of the unresolved polarity of the ambivalence conflict.

Fourth we assessed the current life situation. Here, too, the description was left to the patient, and particularly significant points were noted, especially lacunae (e.g., that the patient did not speak of marriage or about his or her financial situation). Above all we wanted to avoid the danger of getting a "report" devoid of the essential psychic dynamics.

Fifth was the genesis of the conditions. We entered into this only if the patient spontaneously mentioned it or if reference points appeared in the course of the interview making it possible to speak of genetic material. Our special interest here was in attending to family issues in the sense of constellating archetypal patterns. What problem predominated in the family and was no longer only personal? Moreover, we did not accord interest exclusively to the early years of life; rather, we paid attention to the way the patient had worked over the experiences of the liminal situations of development as he or she had related them (such as entering school, puberty, etc.).

Taking these viewpoints into account, we then conducted a series of initial interviews. We found we were able to arrive at a differentiated diagnosis in regard to symptomology, typology, and structure without ascertaining all the possible facts by asking a minimum of questions.

Moreover, we were also able to answer the prognostic question concerning the patient's suitability for analytic therapy. We decided against differentiating the prognosis further since not only in individual cases — as I have reported elsewhere (Dieckmann 1962) — does this sort of favorable, average, or unfavorable prognosis seem to be very questionable but also because statistical investigations in this area show no relevant results (Dührssen 1972).

Early in 1967, Argelander's (1967) very detailed work on the initial interview appeared corroborating many of the positions we had developed. It is my opinion that we do not have to distinguish ourselves from the Freudians at all costs, especially on those points where in fact there are no differences and we can accept Argelander's technique of the initial interview and his distinctions. Ultimately the Balints' (Balint and Balint 1961) description of the atmosphere of the initial interview belongs here too, an atmosphere that demands a certain perceptual capacity on the part of the analyst that can be developed only in the course of extended work with unconscious phenomena. As the Balints describe the process, the physician's first goal consists in creating an atmosphere in which the patients can express themselves or at least reveal enough of themselves that the physician can be certain of having formed a relatively reliable judgment of the patient's condition and capacities for entering into human relationships. His second goal is that of deciding whether or not anything can be done in this case, and if so, what. Third, the physician wants to help the patient to see that the evaluation and recommendations proceed logically from what took place in the initial interview — and that they correspond only to what has happened in the patient's life and still continues to take place. From the patient's viewpoint, the initial interview should offer the impressive experience that here is being given the opportunity to open up, to be understood, and to get help in seeing past and present problems in a new light. With this new insight the patient — and this is the second goal — should be able to decide, as far as possible, what the next step ought to be and how the decision should be carried out.

The individual case examples published by Argelander demonstrate very impressively how the clinician can arrive at a differentiated diagnosis and formulate the patient's psychodynamics and prognosis by employing the open technique, even with relatively retentive patients and the meager contents of their communications, as, for example, in the case of the taciturn patient.

In regard to the initial interview as characterized above, we need only discuss those points on which we differ from the Freudians on the basis of our concept of individuation, not only because we employ a somewhat different terminology but also because our fundamental position is different and because of the specific or different questions or interests that would arise for us in the initial interview.

Concerning the first point, it seems particularly problematic that Argelander proceeds from some assumption of normative behavior and hence his observations place particular emphasis on conspicuous deviations from the assumed norm. The point of view that Jung stressed again and again — namely that neurotic illness also has a socio-political character and, in certain circumstances, contains a failed attempt at conscious development beyond the collective norm — has been taken up today by others, in part in the extreme, as in the instance of Laing (1969) and Cooper (1972).

Consequently it seems questionable to place so much emphasis on an assumed norm right at the beginning of analytic therapy in the first interview. From our point of view it is more of the essence to comprehend what dominants of the collective unconscious are in a conflictual relationship with unconscious material or with the tendencies of the unconscious and the extent to which these two poles are separated in the patient's psyche. This immediately gives rise to the question of the degree to which the attempt at a symbolic union of opposites is present in the symptomology or in the perceived unconscious material. For example, in the first interview with a woman patient expressing (excessively pronounced) feminist convictions, the analyst should not simply ask what is being defended against with this ideology and thereby classify her as deviating from a norm. Rather, we should ask ourselves what (perhaps most unjustified) patriarchal position in the collective conscious is the woman's unconscious femininity battling?

In this context I understand the term "collective dominants of consciousness" to mean the intrapsychic process in the patient herself and not a general, collective situation. In this regard we should clearly recognize that the personal father is only a "copy" of the contents of certain social images and that he carries them as the representative of society in Erich Fromm's sense (Fromm 1936). According to our concept of the psyche, a specific facet of an archetype that should be described in a similar manner stands behind the problem of the father and the man. The same hold true for so-called striking deviations from the behavioral norm, say in the area of homosexuality or in choice of partner (e.g., young man–older woman), that should not be logged as deviations from a behavioral norm but rather investigated as to their archetypal aspect. Moreover it happens that, in their particular shadings, many complexes express themselves not as something noticeable or as deviations but rather precisely in the sense of good adaptation, sometimes even as adaptation to the situation of the initial interview. However, such normative behavior itself suppresses the individual tendencies and needs of the *principium individuationis.*

Inquiring into so-called lacunae poses an additional problem in my opinion. Argelander reports the case of a patient who, in describing his familial situation, completely excluded his father and who, when the analyst intervened, reacted with positive reflection and a certain "aha" experience. But those sorts of interventions in the first interview can also turn out negatively and are not without their dangers and problems. On the basis of his conflicts and especially his professional situation, the problem of money very distinctly occupied the foreground for one patient who reacted by breaking off the interview when I pointed out to him that he had made absolutely no mention of his own sources of income and his own way of dealing with money. Aside from the question of whether or not a patient who reacts to that sort of intervention with exaggerated sensitivity is or is not a candidate for therapy, this kind of occurrence does clearly show what psychodynamic explosiveness can be released by inquiring into lacunae and that in doing so a significant psychic process is set in motion before it has been determined whether or not the patient is a candidate or can be accepted into therapy. In our experience, greater psychodiagnostic or prognostic reliability by no means necessarily follows from filling lacunae of this sort. For example, it can be more important for the diagnosis if a patient with an authority complex completely omits describing his or her personal father. This exclusion may show us how strong the depersonalizing tendency of this complex actually is, as well as indicate the extent and quality of this person's relationship difficulties with authority figures. Omissions themselves have a high degree of significance and, if it appears necessary to fill them in from the standpoint of documenting insurance reimbursement, they can be inquired into later when the patient is accepted for treatment and the psychological evaluation has to be submitted, provided that the initial interview does not exceed two sessions of 50 minutes each.

In conclusion I would like to present a preliminary model embracing viewpoints according to which we could conduct an initial interview. It covers eight discrete areas that I will discuss in detail below. Further, I will describe the basic structure of the corresponding interview summary.

1. The patient's appearance.

At least since the appearance of Kretschmer's historic book on body structure and character (Kretschmer 1922) we all know how strong the relationship is between anatomy and the psyche. In regard to the anatomical components of appearance it does not suffice to distinguish only the asthenic, the athletic, and the pyknic types; rather, a description of the patient's appearance should include highly differentiated details. It is important, as we know from our analytic experience, whether a patient is large or small; how the hands, arms, and legs are formed; whether the hair is blond, black, brown or red, or balding; whether the patient wears glasses or is definitely near-sighted but does not wear glasses; what expression or cast of facial features he or she has, etc. Not unjustifiably did Freud once compare his case histories with the act of creative writing, and the analyst should be schooled not to exhaust such descriptions of personality in only a few lapidary utterances that say little. To the anatomical appearance we would then add a description of the persona, worn, so to speak, for external appearance, including particularly the sort of attire and perhaps also other articles brought along, such as purses, etc. It makes a significant statement when a college professor appears at an initial interview in well-kempt jeans or if the office worker comes wearing a yellow dress, yellow shoes, and carrying a yellow purse. The signal character of clothing that can usually be effortlessly integrated later into the corpus of psychological problems can clarify or underline many things regardless whether it is conspicuous or inconspicuous. Here again it is not a question of showiness or abnormality but rather of the "how" that is presented for all to see here and now.

    2. The patient's behavior during the initial interview.

There is an ancient medical joke in which a professor explains to his students in their first lecture on internal medicine that two things are of great importance for the physician: first, overcoming the limits of disgust and, second, precise observation. The professor speaks of the physicians of earlier centuries who, before there were laboratories, were forced to diagnose the presence of diabetes from the taste of urine. "In order to practice this," he continues, "I have brought along a urine sample from a patient, and you will all pass by the lectern, dip in your finger, and taste the urine. Of course, I will be the first and give you a good example!" Having spoken, he dips his finger into the jar of urine and licks it. Obediently all the students march past the lectern and perform the ceremony. When the last one has finished, the professor explains: "Thank you, ladies and gentlemen; you have all proven that you have solved the first problem I mentioned, that of overcoming the limits of your disgust. But you are all still decidedly poor observers, for if you had observed correctly and closely, you would have seen that I dipped my index finger in the jar but licked my middle finger. That, none of you noticed."

    I have recounted this joke because, in my experience, the nonverbal expressions of the patient's behavior are observed and described all too little when one reads case histories, anamneses, initial interviews conducted by analysts-in-training, and the published literature. Here, too, as a rule, only those things are described that are strikingly unusual — as, for

Ginger
姜(jiāng)

example, the handshake of the patient who seizes the therapist's hand unusually tight and clings to it or takes it limply and immediately withdraws. I believe that there is a very great range of expression in shaking hands which, as we know, often makes a quite significant statement. Why does one not describe those sorts of expression as a matter of course just as one gives a detailed description of all the patient's behaviors observed as part of the initial interview? It is also a good idea following the first interview to reenact for oneself specific sequences of movement observed in the patient, for instance, gait or how the legs are crossed, or the way in which the patient sits, in order to get a better insight into the quality of experience associated with certain behaviors. From appearance and behavior alone it is often possible to formulate a quite detailed diagnosis without the patient having said a single word. Just as the experienced internist is able to say, "Here comes an anemic" or "Here comes an ulcer patient," we are also in a position to say, "Here comes an overly compliant authority complex with compulsive traits and an overly correct persona." Moreover, since we have very specific ideas about the underlying psychodynamics of such a complex, it is possible to make quite extensive statements about a person's problems without his or her having said a single word to us.

   3. *Transference and countertransference.*

   Transference and countertransference is a third area that can be explored without verbal expression from the patient. The publications of the Berlin Research Group (Dieckmann 1971a, 1973a, 1973b, 1976c) discuss in detail how differentiated an instrument of cognition we have in the analyst's careful observation of all the feelings and fantasies that arise within from the moment of first meeting the patient until the end of the interview. Such careful self-observation is a source of information about what the patient is experiencing. From this observational material of our countertransference reactions we can, as a rule with great certainty and clarity, discern the patient's transference and role models that, for their part, stand in relationship with his or her fundamental psychic conflict, e.g., the child fleeing trustingly into the opened arms of the mother, or the anxious boy fearing the stern father's punishment, or the bewitchingly seductive *puella aeterna* who coquettes with her animus, or the masochistically subservient patient who is humiliated by his shadow and offers it to a Great Mother or a Great Father imploring forgiveness. In any event, it is necessary to give a differentiated description of one's own feeling and fantasy world constellated by the patient and not to limit oneself to reporting whether the patient appeared nice or otherwise, or whether one considered him or her capable of contact and relationship. In doing this it is necessary — and actually this is almost always forgotten — to realize that there inheres in this process a powerful subjective factor and consequently that one must also take into account one's own personality and character structure about which one should have been enlightened in his or her own training analysis. Transference and countertransference are always constellations between two human beings, and as our experience with second case histories taken by training candidates shows, under certain circumstances a patient can present quite a different side of his personality to another analyst, just as the character of a second analysis can be entirely different from the first one. Of course it is not necessary and cannot even be asked that the first interviewer exhibitionistically describe his own personality and his own complexes in the initial interview. That is by no means the intention; rather, it is first and foremost a question of the analyst's ability to include these factors in his or her process of reflecting on the patient and of being aware that the patient often creates a very different impression with another analyst.

4. *Typology.*

The fourth point, the attempt to grasp the patient's typology, stands at the interface between pure observation and the inclusion of verbal expression. Here I intentionally say *the attempt* because we all realize that arriving at a rapid and differentiated grasp of a patient's psychological typology is not so simple a task. Often several treatment hours pass before one has some modest degree of certainty about the typology of the person concerned. On the other hand, we should not make all too much of these difficulties and be anxious about errors in diagnosis, but rather make a statement about the observable typological material following the initial interview. It was the experience of our Berlin Research Group that such a statement is entirely possible after a one-hour interview. In all cases we were able to agree relatively quickly on the attitude type since the extraverted and the introverted attitudes can often be clearly discerned from the patient's appearance or behavior. Almost always any additional information resulting from the content shared in the interview conformed to our initial assessment. The way the patient presents him- or herself usually indicates quite distinctly whether he or she is oriented more to the external object or to the inner, subjective factor. In this regard the diagnosis is, of course, more difficult when we attempt to assess the extent to which a person has been trained by personal history and the influences of environment to live out of his or her inferior function. This results in the primarily introverted person attempting to live as an extravert, and the primarily extraverted individual trying to live as an introvert. Although diagnosing this condition is not unimportant therapeutically, the methods presently at our disposal usually permit us to establish this only in the course of analysis, and in the initial interview it is possible only in exceptional cases.

Ascertaining the function types is more difficult; in particular, identifying the two irrational functions, sensation and intuition, is problematic. It is relatively simple to recognize, during the initial interview, whether a patient presents predominantly with the rational functions and orients his or her judgments in terms of right and wrong, as well as tending to work predominantly with thinking and to suppress feeling, or whether he or she is oriented more toward sympathy and antipathy, and includes and is oriented more by expression of feelings.

In contrast to this, diagnosing the significance of intuition and of sensation demands penetrating consideration of the entire material from the initial interview. The Berlin Study Group often doubted where the boundary between the primary and the secondary functions should lie except in pronouncedly typical, crass instances. Consequently in our diagnoses we started with the inferior functions that in many cases present much more clearly than the developed leading functions and forewent a clear distinction between leading and secondary functions.

As Jung (C. W. 6) has already explained in detail, the crassly one-sided types are extreme variants and we must learn to accept the appearance or the presence of mixed forms as the more common case. Nevertheless the attempt at diagnosing a patient's typology is very much worthwhile, for in this effort one also aligns the symptomology with the typology. Unfortunately the relationships between psychopathology and typology that Jung gave in the appendix to his work on typology are very intuitive and certainly do not hold true in many instances. For example, the wholesale judgment that one finds more feeling types among women than among men and more thinking types among men than among women does not hold true according to recent empirical examination (Göllner 1975) and may perhaps be understood as influenced by the times in which Jung wrote.

Following one of Wilke's (1974) suggestions, we should speak here rather of a problematic function than of a leading or a secondary function. In his studies of depressive patients, Wilke was able to diagnose feeling as the problematic function in the majority of cases. As I see it, I could extend the catalogue of problematic functions to include the remaining three neurotic structures (although I shall not discuss that in detail here since it would call for a separate study). I have observed that the problematic function is sensation for the schizoid with major lacunae in perception; that of the compulsive is thinking, although in this case thinking does not absolutely have to be the leading function since the compulsive's rigid and overpowering superego tends rather to be based on moralizing feeling judgments and not on logical conclusions. In the case of the hysteric, on the other hand, intuition should be regarded as the problematic function which, due to its pronounced changeability and insufficient endurance, plays a significant role. Jungians have tended to neglect this area of typology, and it would really be valuable if the correlation between typology on the one hand and structures and syndromes on the other were finally worked out in a more differentiated fashion, given the extensive case and clinical material presently available to us.

5. Content of the patient's remarks.

I want to preface my remarks on this point by saying that I consider it advisable to let the patient take the lead at the beginning of the initial interview and let the tension build, remaining silent oneself for a few minutes, rather than directing the patient with standard questions such as "What brings you to me?" or "How may I be of help to you?" or something similar. In my experience it seldom happens that a patient not begin to speak spontaneously when the analyst signals that he or she is not ready to direct the patient with questions. Through this approach the possibility arises in many cases of observing the initial problem, similar to the initial dream, that the patient brings into treatment. This can lie in the simple sentence, "Dr. X referred me to you," or in the description of relationship difficulties, or in describing symptoms.

What I think is essential here is which of three large areas the patient tends to accentuate in the course of his or her comments, i.e., whether more biographical material is offered, or the patient limits her- or himself largely to the current situation, or dwells predominantly on symptoms and their description and possible interconnections. Parenthetically, many works (some already mentioned) have said so much about the content of the initial interview that I do not need to enter into the details such as understanding psychic interconnections, theory building, etc. It goes without saying that one cannot forego posing questions in an interview situation, and it would be demanding too much to ask that. However, the analyst's questions should serve only to deepen his or her understanding of the patient's material and cautiously to build some bridges between the various areas of neurosis that are psychologically relevant. In doing this, however, it must be left up to the patient to chose whether or not to cross those bridges.

Further, the extent of unconscious material—dreams and fantasies, for example—that the patient is ready to present spontaneously in the interview seems to me relevant. In regard to this one can observe opposite extremes: for example, that a patient speaks almost exclusively of dreams and fantasy images while another completely excludes them. Here, too, it is certainly essential diagnostically for the subsequent analysis to find out during the initial interview the extent to which access to or cooperation with the patient's unconscious is possible at all.

6. Lacunae.

The sixth point in my initial interview is the description of the noticeable omissions or lacunae that appear during the interview or on subsequent reflection on the material. Often one can infer more from what the patient does not mention and what is omitted than from what is said. In any case, however, description of omissions provides valuable support for the diagnosis.

In order to do all this, one admittedly needs to have some idea of a certain model of how a complete interview might look, a model in which the psychodynamic areas are treated that are relevant for this patient and to his or her form of illness. Since often it is only the clinician with extensive experience who is able to do this, the beginner should simply keep in mind that the patient could have said something about biography or origin including the most important significant others, the conflictual situation that precipitated the illness, current life situation, and that the patient should have made some impression of the way in which he or she deals with the three major drive areas (orality, the strivings for power and possession, and sexuality and relationship).

7. The central complex.

During the initial interview the analyst should get some idea of the central complex the patient presents and of the likely appearance of its *archetypal core*. In doing this we should not complicate the situation by getting entrapped in the indeed poetically beautiful but practically unusable metaphor of the inner firmament of archetypes. Finding the more-or-less fitting one from among the billions of possibilities is so hopeless that one does best to forsake the attempt immediately. Consequently it is encouraging that one can reduce the entire range of archetypal problems to a few fundamental problems, for example, to the Great Mother or the Great Father. In doing this it is left to the diagnostic abilities of the individual and knowledge of the corresponding forms of the collective archetypal figures to identify the right aspects of the mother or the father archetype. I believe that when making diagnoses on the basis of complexes, one can limit oneself to speaking initially of the father and the mother complexes, the shadow, the anima, the animus, and the persona, and, in the instance of psychoses and narcissistic conditions, the Self. The breadth of individual variation is honored by describing the form, say of specific father complex; whether one can assume a Grand Inquisitor (E. Jung 1971) or a Jupiter tonans in the background makes a significant difference. A corresponding differentiation of the mother complex is already available in the first chapter of Erich Neumann's book, *The Great Mother* (1974). If we continually speak of Jung's psychology of the complexes, we should also make diagnoses in terms of the complexes, which, in my opinion, we have done all too infrequently, and we should also publicly champion diagnoses in terms of complexes, for example, in claims to insurance companies.

8. Tests and measurements.

The eighth and last point to mention only briefly would be that of tests and measurements that many analysts utilize at the beginning of an analysis. Aside from the specifically Jungian tests — the word association test, and the Gray-Wheelwright, the Myers-Briggs, and the Singer-Loomis type inventories — we should mention, especially for child therapy where one can hardly do without Sceno and Harwick, projective tests of which the analyst may or may not chose to make use.

In conclusion I would like to make a suggestion concerning the format for summarizing the initial interview. In my opinion, the summary should specifically cover at least the following six points:

1. Symptomatology with emphasis on the primary symptoms, i.e., the symptoms that have caused the patient to consult the analyst, but also a description of all other symptoms spoken of that could be observed in the course of the interview as well as suspected symptoms.

2. A detailed description of the appearance and the behavior of the patient, as was discussed in detail above.

3. A description of the verbal content of the interview including the transference and countertransference elements as well as the patient's omissions.

4. The results of the analyst's reflections on the patient's psychodynamics and the development of his or her neurotic condition including the precipitating conflict situation, insofar as the patient presented it.

5. A diagnosis that encompasses psychic structures as well as the typology and the above-described diagnosis of the complexes.

6. A prognosis that, above all, refers to the suitability of the patient for analytic treatment and, especially in our sense, the possibility of individuation.

CHAPTER 3

Frequency of Sessions

Following the initial interview the analyst must make three decisions: first, whether or not the patient is suitable for him or her to work with analytically; second, whether it would be better to advise the patient to undertake a different form of therapy; and third, whether or not to refer the patient to a colleague because of transference and countertransference problems. We know today that not all patients suffering from a psychogenic malady are suited to undertake a full analysis, as is the case, for example, in severely chronic compulsive neuroses, the majority of psychoses and additions, some of the perversions and degenerate conditions, etc., and that in those cases where analysis is not appropriate it is still possible to aim for an improvement in or lessening of the severity of symptoms by other psychotherapeutic means such as autogenic training, hypnosis, or gestalt, behavioral, or dialogic therapy.

It is not the task of this book to express views on the indications and prognosis for analysis, but I would like to point out the problems that arise from the specific transference and countertransference constellation in analytic treatment. On the basis of our present-day state of knowledge it does not seem to me appropriate to compile an apparently objective catalogue of those patients who are or are not suitable for analytic therapy, since the success or failure of therapy is always dependent to a large extent on the transference and countertransference relationship. In the instance of a favorable transference and countertransference situation, one can often successfully treat cases that others have considered untreatable or who, as a consequence of their illness — such as schizophrenics with many psychotic episodes, have been regarded as unsuitable for analysis. Of course, as in all cases, the opposite holds true here, too, and an unfavorable transference-countertransference constellation can contribute to a greatly prolonged treatment of a relatively minor neurotic condition with only meager success. Regardless how unpleasant it may be for the rationally oriented science of our times, the decision as to the quality and the productivity of the transference-countertransference constellation and consequently the indications for undertaking an analysis are subject ultimately not to factual, objective, rational criteria but rather must be made by the analyst's intuitive and feeling functions since only these two functions offer the possibility of judging and comprehending the transference-countertransference constellation qualitatively, with the inclusion, of course, of all the other information that was gleaned in the initial interview.

I would like to illustrate this point with an example that I described in detail elsewhere (Dieckmann 1962). The case was that of a relatively undifferentiated patient who worked as a postman and was suffering from a psychogenic gastritis, compulsive ruminations, sensations of choking, sleep disturbances, and a pervasive lack of energy. Before he came to me for treatment, he had spent six weeks in in-patient psychotherapy and had been discharged with the following report:

> The physical examination identified no significant pathological conditions. Organically, the clinical picture gave the impression of vegetative distonia. The psychiatric evaluation identified the presence of *constitutionally determined psychopathology with severe, exogenously determined faulty emotional development that had manifested early on.* Inhibitions in more or less all drive areas were impressive, but essentially the patient had major difficulties in connection with the issues around ownership and possessions. The patient had extraordinary difficulties recognizing his maladaptive behaviors; he had practically no awareness of the areas in which he fell short. Consequently the initial steps toward correcting his maladaptive behavior were extraordinarily laborious. The patient did not appear suitable for analysis. (Dieckmann 1962, p. 274)

Since the patient (who already had experienced many hospitalizations) had heard of analysis from fellow patients in the clinic, he nevertheless sought me out.

In the initial interview a positive feeling-toned transference and countertransference constellation developed between us which also did not lack a dynamic tension. Moreover, since he was suffering greatly, I decided to accept the patient into therapy although I had reservations that were expressed in reference to a constitutional component. Surprisingly the treatment developed extraordinary intensity and became very dynamic, and the patient very quickly gained access to his unconscious. Since he was able to avoid all rationalizations and to actualize the prospective possibilities offered by the unconscious directly thanks to his typology, which we need not discuss in detail, he was free of all symptoms after only forty-two analytic hours and had experienced significant transformations in his mode of experiencing and in his behavior. I had the opportunity to observe this patient for nineteen years following his treatment and during that entire period no neurotic symptoms reappeared.

I believe this case gives a very clear example of the extent to which significant changes can be achieved through a suitable transference constellation even in instances that initially appear to be hopeless. Likewise it shows how questionable the attempt at a so-called objective prognosis is in the realm of analytic treatment.

If the analyst is clear about his or her intention to accept a patient into analysis, and if, after due reflection, the patient also agrees, the question then arises as to how often the patient is to be seen. But before I discuss this question in detail, it seems important to refer briefly to the time the analyst needs for due reflection.

After gaining an impression of each other in the initial interview, both the analyst and the patient should once again ponder whether or not they want to work together. At least one night should intervene between the initial interview and the agreement to commence therapy, particularly for the analyst, since sometimes warning or alarming dreams can arise that call attention to features that have initially eluded conscious perception. The good old maxim of sleeping on it before one makes a decision certainly holds true in regard to accepting a person into treatment since, as we know, in agreeing to treat a person the analyst often must work together with this patient for many years and the success of the collaboration rests on the analyst's inner ability to accept the patient. The patient should also be made aware that he or she can take time to decide whether to chose this analyst or to go to another of his or her choice.

The problem of the frequency of sessions necessary for carrying out an analysis has led to controversy between Jung's analytical psychology and Freud's psychoanalysis, especially in the early years, and hence to divergent standpoints. In 1935, Jung, in his essay, "Principles of Practical Psychotherapy," wrote

> All method of influence, including the analytical, require that the patient be seen as often as possible. I content myself with a maximum of four consultations a week. With the beginning of synthetic treatment it is of advantage to spread out the consultations. I then generally reduce them to one or two hours a week, for the patient must learn to go his own way. (C.W. 16, par. 26)

Jung's attitude of leading the patient as soon as possible to a synthetic analysis and to collaborative work on emotional problems, expressed also in the rhythm of the frequency of analytic sessions, is significantly different from the demand of classical psychoanalysis according to which four to five sessions per week are necessary throughout the entire analysis in order for the patient to work through the transference neurosis. The patient's collaboration, i.e., his or her self-analysis that takes place between the individual analytic hours, is, to be sure, a central problem of every analytic treatment. In contrast to other customary forms of medical treatment in which the patient remains to a great extent passive and gets prescriptions for the appropriate medications or brief hospitalization after having described his or her complaints and having been examined by the physician, analytic therapy demands a large measure of collaborative work on the patient's part. Every analytic therapy depends on such collaboration not only in the session but also between analytic hours, and it is necessary to lead every patient onto this path, regardless how dependent and helpless he or she may be initially. On the other hand, self-analysis alone is not possible and leads to undesirable results, as Karen Horney (1942) pointed out in detail. Consequently the art of analytic therapy, especially for the Jungian, depends on finding the right point in time at which the patient has attained sufficient ego-stability to be able to shape and carry out independent collaborative work between sessions productively, and on reducing the frequency of sessions.

Moreover, one should not ignore specific problems having to do with the patient's day-to-day life. As a rule, analytic therapy proceeds on the condition that the patient's occupational activity is not to be interrupted or curtailed. Hence, extensive occupational demands from which patients cannot immediately free themselves, in addition to analysis in their "free time," can lead to situations in which the stress of various deadlines and appointments endangers the success of the analysis if one rigorously and perfectionistically attempts to hold sessions too frequently. Also, many patients do not live in the same locale as the analyst and sometimes must travel relatively long distances for each session. This situation certainly will not change over the next decades in spite of a relatively great increase in numbers of analysts, since the number of established analysts will certainly always trail the needs of patients, measured by the numbers of patients and the percentage of mental conditions that need analytic treatment. The distance factor necessarily leads to deviations, and in many cases necessitates a reduction in the frequency of sessions which is not at all desirable, for example, at the beginning of treatment.

However, my experience with situations of this sort in which analyses had to be undertaken and have been conducted with two hours per week, or sometimes even with two hours on the weekend, are by no means worse than the results of analyses that commenced with three or four sessions per week. Those patients who accept a considerable time invest-ment in order to be in analysis are usually much more highly motivated and consequently work more intensively on the self-analysis part of the collaborative effort between sessions. Moreover, one very often finds that they develop the necessary autonomy, since between times they are, for all practical purposes, not in a position to get to the analyst except in situations of dire need. Doubtless Jung correctly saw the problem that lies in conducting a long analysis with frequent sessions insofar as the analysis itself can reinforce the patient's dependency and impede the restoration or rather the discovery of his or her own autonomy.

The analyst's own situation is a third reality factor. Unless the analyst has a sizeable compulsion neurosis, there are practically none who can guarantee patients that they will be there uninterruptedly in the long run four or five times per week, excepting vacations that have been previ-ously discussed. Analysts, too, get overworked, get caught in profes-sional bottlenecks, have personal problems that can make them miss appointments, and can also fall ill. Cahen's so-called "absento therapy" arose out of just these sorts of personal exigencies (Cahen 1976). It proceeds from the idea of introducing a period in which only self-analysis continues and no sessions are scheduled following a period of intensive analytic therapy. Cahen has practiced "absento therapy" with a monthly rhythm and reports quite astonishing results with this method.

Taking all these considerations into account, I must nevertheless say that as a rule I commence an analysis with at least three, and at most four, sessions per week and maintain this frequency relatively strictly throughout the first phase of treatment. Only after the patient has attained sufficient ego-stability do I reduce the number of weekly ses-sions to two. In exceptional cases I would make do with one session per week since the continuity of the analytic process is not, it seems to me, adequately maintained even with persons who are accustomed to work-ing relatively independently. Moreover, too many external events and changes take place in the patient's life in an entire week and flow into the analysis so that the on-going work on the unconscious can no longer be assured in the form that seems necessary.

In his well-known work on ritual, Erich Neumann (1953a, 1976) pointed out the great importance of rite and rhythm in those situations in which the ego is exposed to unconscious contents that have, in part, numinous qualities. Already among primal peoples at the very beginning of the development of culture, rite forms the protection absolutely neces-sary so that initiants can approach a primordial experience whose libidi-nal power and charge very often exceed that of the conscious ego-complex. Consequently, those sorts of rituals are most scrupulously observed not only in the realm of religious ceremonies and celebrations, as Neumann discussed, but also, as Jung described in his experiences of Africa, in common palavers and business dealings. Scrupulous observance is vitally necessary and, as often described, offenses against rite are dealt with very severely, under certain circumstances even at the cost of the life of the offender. This is understandable insofar as the inner affective and emotional energies that are mobilized in a person in a primordial experience can endanger the entire community if they are not given a form through rite which enables the individual to have the experience but which also prevents being overwhelmed by affects, falling into a mad frenzy, and endangering others. In the very stable systems of civilization that we have introjected early in life we seldom experience such mad frenzies, but even among us the mobilization of unconscious complexes in the absence of an analytic *vas hermeticum* leads to blunders, to affective and emotional destruction in the *Umwelt* of the individual concerned, and often to irreparable damage. For these reasons, the necessary protective measures include, in addition to set times for sessions, also the recommendation that the patient make no vitally important decisions during the course of analysis without previously having thoroughly discussed them. (In a subsequent chapter on ground rules I will discuss the necessary protective measures in detail.)

Maintaining consistent session times also forms part of the necessary rite, the meaning of which is to protect patient and analyst from being inundated by unconscious contents. It seems very important to me that we treat the problem of frequency of sessions not only under the shibboleth of the patient's dependency or autonomy but that we be clear about the archetypal, rhythmical background. Only when we understand the archetypal, rhythmical background and, through practical experience, have become conscious of the sizeable energies with which we have to deal when the unconscious archetypal core of the complex has been mobilized will we understand how necessary it is, under certain conditions, to muster the rigor to maintain the protective rhythm. I would like to illustrate this point with a case that turned out badly.

Toward the end of the first third of her analysis, a patient who had already attempted suicide a number of times prior to analysis, got into a situation that, for her, typically triggered suicide attempts. Since she had already achieved a certain degree of stabilization, she did not have to see me immediately, as earlier had often been the case, but was able to live with the problem until her next scheduled appointment. However, when she next saw me, she decompensated in a manner that I felt was ominous and I decided not to conclude the hour at the customary time but rather to keep her there and to cancel the two patients that were to follow. In all, I spoke with this patient for something more than three hours, and during this time I succeeded to some extent in calming her so that I could let her go home. Nevertheless that night she made a relatively serious suicide attempt that necessitated a four-week hospitalization.

Although the analysis developed exceptionally well following her discharge, this experience has remained a vivid memory. I have had to reflect on and discuss it a great deal. Today I believe that it would have been better to let the patient go at the end of her scheduled session and not to have altered the ritual. I must also mention that I had scheduled her for an additional session the following day. At that point I think my own anxiety overtook me, that I credited the patient with too little stability, and moreover, that I intensified her guilt feelings which always play a major role in the psyche of a depressive insofar as I neglected other patients for her sake and made too much of my own time available although she herself urgently and absolutely desired it. Of course I cannot say whether it would have been possible to prevent her suicide attempt; but I can state that I have fared better as I have gained experience and as I have more strictly observed the rhythmic boundaries necessary in analysis than I did in earlier times when, following the notion of flexibility and variability, I was inclined to reschedule appointments, grant extra sessions, or cancel sessions that would not absolutely have had to be missed.

It is certainly necessary, as Hubback (1974) also points out, to be sufficiently flexible in terms of appointment times during those phases in which the patient regresses into preverbal developmental stages where few possibilities of conscious regulation exist. At those times the patient finds himself or herself psychically, at least for the time being, in the developmental phase of the infant who is not yet able to wait and for whom the positive mother responds to his or her world of urgent impulses with short-term attention. If, on the basis of a theoretical concept of autonomy, one expects the patient to tolerate too much tension at those times and forcefully insists that he or she do so, situations can arise in which the negative side of the mother archetype — which is already dominant in such a patient — will be further fixated by a rigid analytic stance. Yet I am fully convinced that three to four analytic sessions weekly are quite enough for mastering these problems and additional sessions will be necessary only in exceptional cases. It seems to me that the greater dangers often lie in being inundated by the energies of this preverbal aspect of the child archetype, in delaying the development of a frustration tolerance (if not making its development impossible), and in evoking a demanding attitude often unbearable for both sides. Sailing between the Scylla of the one and the Chrybdis of the other of these opposites and running aground on neither belongs among the most difficult analytic situations. Moreover, in attempting to do this is it also absolutely necessary again and again to keep clearly in mind and to come to terms with the reality of the extent of the aggression that this sort of difficult patient can mobilize in oneself. Here again the dialectical process Jung (*C. W.* 16) demanded so insistently is necessary, a process that makes the psychotherapist aware that every complicated treatment of such an individual is a dialectical process in which the physician as a person participates just as much as the patient does.

We have yet to ponder the point in time at which the frequency of sessions can be reduced and the more synthetic or constructive aspect of the analytic process begins. Earlier I pointed out that a certain stability of the ego structure must have been attained before this can happen. The concept of ego-stability, generally used somewhat vaguely by analysts, must be more precisely defined since a very specific point in the stabilization of the ego-complex seems to me significant in indicating the possibility of beginning the synthetic phase of analysis. It must also be mentioned here that the distinction between a more regressive, analytic phase and a more synthetic phase in therapy has the aura of something pointedly theoretical. In practice this does not occur with such sharpness since, first of all, from the beginning of analysis, synthetic tendencies arise from the unconscious along with the regressive and disintegrative elements and take place in consciousness as well as in the ego-complex. The second point to emphasize is that there is no second, purely synthetic phase in therapy in which regressive, analytic processes no longer take place. On the contrary, they absolutely must take place, since they form the prerequisite for the possibility of synthetic processes. If we make this distinction at all, it is a consequence of the practical experience that, following a pronouncedly regressive phase of considerable dependency, most patients can attain a certain degree of autonomy. Depending on the clinical picture, the point in time when this occurs has considerable variability and the possibility for greater emphasis on the "self analysis" appears along with stabilization of the ego.

The question that takes precedence over all others in this connection is whether or not there is a specific point in time at which we can say that the patient has achieved a sufficient stability of the ego-complex so that we can reduce the frequency of sessions. In 1921, Jung defined the ego as a complex of representations that forms the center of the field of consciousness and appears to experience itself as having great continuity and identity. As Jung wrote,

> I also speak of an *ego-complex*. The ego-complex is as much a content as a condition of *consciousness* . . . for a psychic element is conscious to me only in so far as it is related to my ego-complex. But inasmuch as the ego is only the centre of my field of consciousness, it is not

identical with the totality of my psyche, being merely one complex among other complexes. (*C.W.* 6, par. 706)

(Parenthetically I want to mention that Jung had already used the concept of the ego-complex in 1907 in his work, *On the Psychology of Dementia Praecox, C.W.* 3.) The above-quoted definition from *Psychological Types*, however, leaves out the account of unconscious and preconscious components of the ego-complex, as well as, for example, the dream ego and the ego-automatisms. Likewise, this definition does not clearly differentiate the ego-complex from those contents of consciousness that are not part of the ego. Jung later formulated a revised, more detailed definition of the ego-complex which states that the ego-complex is thought of as a factor to which all contents entering consciousness must be presented (*C.W.* 9ii). Not until 1955 did Jung also include unconscious and preconscious components in the ego-complex (in *Mysterium Coniunctionis, C.W.* 14). The definition in *Aion* (*C.W.* 9ii) according to which all contents capable of becoming consciousness must be related to the ego-complex in order to enter into consciousness, also implicitly includes the ego-functions to the extent that they are the preconditions for rejecting psychic contents from the ego-complex or for incorporating them via perception, memory, organization, language, defense mechanisms, and the controlling and organizing functions of consciousness. Hartmann et al. (1946) already proposed this definition of the ego in terms of its functions and Fordham (1969) adopted it, compiling in all eight different ego-functions.

The eighth and last ego-function mentioned by Fordham (1969) — that is, the capacity of the ego to relinquish its controlling and organizing functions — seems to me the most important when judging whether or not to move the analysis more into the synthetic dimension. Jung also devoted a great deal of attention to this capacity, for it plays a special role in his study of individuation. The conscious ego must learn to let other powers emerge and to accept them, powers that arise from the Self and that are represented by archetypal images. In an early work (Dieckmann 1965) I pointed out the ways in which the integrating processes of the ego-complex functions in dreams and how necessary it is that the threshold of consciousness be lowered or become more permeable if the integration process is to take place. The healthy functioning of the ego-complex's capacity to forego control temporarily over a stable boundary between consciousness and the unconscious and to admit and engage unconscious contents by loosening the firmly structured organization of the ego and placing it in question, in favor of opening consciousness to new possibilities and other modes of experience and behavior, is the precondition for the patient's autonomous and constructive collaboration in the analytic process. Here the accent lies, of course, on the word "temporarily," for the stable ego must always be capable of again assuming or exercising its controlling and organizing functions. When this is not the case, we encounter the well-known phenomenon of inflationary inundations, the mere exchange of positions, or the uncritical acceptance and incorporation of unconscious material. In my practical work, creating a sufficiently healthy level at which this capacity of the ego-complex functions has always seemed to be an important and decisive indicator for reducing the frequency of sessions in order to confirm and strengthen the patient's autonomy. There are a number of signs that indicate when this condition has been attained or is beginning to appear. I will mention only a few of them here.

It is generally customary in analytical psychology to encourage the patient to record dreams and to keep a sort of dream diary. I usually suggest this to most of my patients at the beginning of analysis. In another context I have discussed in detail why I consider this procedure meaningful and analytically valuable (Dieckmann 1978a). Of course I abandon this suggestion in those cases of severely disturbed patients whom one cannot yet expect to undertake work on the unconscious on their own or in those cases in which that sort of suggestion would disturb or block dream production. As a rule, the patients to whom I make this suggestion at the beginning of analysis write down their dreams as a sort of "homework" task for a rather long period of time. Since they are not yet in a position to establish a meaningful and fruitful relationship to their unconscious, they experience writing down their dreams as an annoying duty. There often follows a phase of opposition or rebellion in the sense of a protest and of the beginnings of some autonomy which patients express by recording their dreams either irregularly or not at all. Only after this third phase has been traversed does a condition arise in which the patient can develop a lively interest in the content of his or her own unconscious and realize that actively engaging those contents is personally meaningful and valuable. Here lies the point of transition to the beginnings of genuine autonomy for the ego-complex, and with the help of the ego-functions mentioned above, the patient is able to deal with the lowering of the threshold of consciousness and the reestablishment of the boundary between consciousness and the unconscious. Naturally this is only one example. One could say similar things about other forms in which patients work with fantasy contents. There is a similar sort of transition also in that phase of analysis in which the patient more actively engages the passively-experienced fantasy images and begins to work on them in the sense of doing active imagination. The same holds true for the acquisition of the ability to amplify elements or symbols of one's own dreams, to see developmental processes in one's dream series, and many other skills.

Speaking very generally, one could say that, fundamentally, reducing the frequency of sessions and the transition to a more synthetic or constructive form of analytic treatment can be made if the patient has learned to deal with his or her unconscious contents in a sovereign manner and is no longer helplessly delivered up to those contents or must defend against, suppress, or repress them as at the beginning of analysis.

At this point I would like to mention briefly the problem of the so-called "trial analysis" that a number of colleagues recommend in cases with questionable prognoses. The term "trial analysis" refers to the practice of patient and analyst contracting for a specific number of analytic sessions (usually twenty to thirty) at the beginning of treatment in order to decide if a productive analytic therapy can be undertaken and whether or not an adequate transference-countertransference constellation has arisen during this time period so that analysis can be continued. This period of time is also supposed to serve for more precise clarification of the extent of the clinical picture.

I do not regard this approach highly and in those cases where I have taken it, I have had consistently bad experiences. From the beginning the patient is maneuvered into a pressured situation and responds to it either by strongly mobilizing defensive systems and an unconscious denial that is often very difficult to penetrate, or with an excessive degree of industry that is just as deleterious and deceptive as the other response.

Moreover there is something fundamentally dishonest in this arrangement. When I have worked analytically twenty to thirty hours with a patient and have entered into an analytic process with him or her, I am, thanks to the transference-countertransference constellation, no longer in a position suddenly to leave this patient in the lurch and to say after the twentieth or thirtieth hour that there is no point in continuing treatment and that we must terminate. The freedom to decide after twenty or thirty hours of a "trial analysis" whether or not treatment should be continued lies entirely on the side of the patient and it is utterly unnecessary to concede this freedom since it is, at any time, the patient's right to terminate the analysis. In doubtful cases where the question arises whether or not analysis is indicated for a given patient, it makes more sense to extend the initial interview over a number of hours until it has become clear whether or not the case should be accepted. In this regard one should not slavishly restrict the time for conducting the initial interview to one or two sessions.

It is nice and often popular to use metaphors from other areas of medicine, but a psychoanalysis is not an abdominal operation for which one can do a biopsy in order to decide whether or not the condition is operable, and the metaphor simply doesn't work in this context. This does not exclude the possibility that, in the interest of the patient, the analyst can terminate an analysis or even must do so if it seems that the analysis can no longer be continued. But for this there is no need of a "trial analysis."

CHAPTER 4

Couch versus Chair

For a long time the methods of Freud's and Jung's differing schools have been associated with couch and chair. Corresponding to the fundamental notion of analytical psychology — that is, the states of tension created by the great pairs of opposites — Jung preferred and championed a dialectical method in which patient and analyst sit opposite each other. In the classical, orthodox form of Freudian psychoanalysis, the patient's use of the couch was an absolute prerequisite just as the patient sitting opposite the analyst in the chair was *de rigueur* for classical, orthodox Jungians. Today we know that, viewed analytically, the patient's lying or sitting position derived from the profoundly personal motivations on the part of the founders. In this connection we recall Freud's statement that he couldn't tolerate patients staring at him for an entire day, while for Jung, a stance opposing Freud as a father figure surely played a background role in his preference for sitting face-to-face with the patient and his emphasis on the equal rights of both physician and patient. In spite of this, we cannot simply dispose of the reasons in favor of using the couch or the chair as rationalizations for these sorts of underlying motives. If we attempt to formulate a methodology that makes as much sense as possible, we are well advised to elucidate clearly the reasons for the differing attitudes so that we can decide when it would be better for the patient to lie down or to sit up.

The proponents of the supine position proceed on the premise that this posture more closely resembles that of normal sleep, encourages relaxation, and consequently evokes a drowsy, meditative condition which reduces the level of ego-control and facilitates the flow of free associations. The flow of free associations from the id, when ego-control is diminished, is recognized as a cornerstone of psychoanalytic technique since unconscious material is supposed to emerge better and more easily under these conditions than in a situation in which the analyst and patient sit *vis-à-vis*. It is assumed that in this manner it will be possible to let repressed material enter consciousness in the session. If the analyst is also removed from the patient's field of vision by sitting behind, the patient's flow of free associations will not be hindered by the analyst's personality, and hence in the transference-countertransference constellation the "anonymous analyst" will better and more distinctly serve as a projection screen for the patient. Such is the underlying rationale.

If after long experience one ponders a great number of patients treated both on the couch and in the chair, one very quickly finds that one is dealing with illusions when grappling with these two ideas. Every patient who consults an analyst brings along a relatively great amount of anxiety, whether consciously or unconsciously. For the duration of the analysis these anxieties prevent the patient from being able to surrender to the unconscious in a drowsy, meditative manner. But dissolving these anxieties, an essential and central element of the whole analytic process, is never totally successful in any analysis. In the extreme cases of anxious, overly compliant patients, one experiences a caricature of the associative process as they attempt to lie desperately relaxed on the couch and give forth an uninterrupted stream of banal, conscious, psychological platitudes. The latter are very often introduced with the words "perhaps," "it might be," "certainly," or something similar. For example: "Perhaps I'm only saying this because I really think something else," or "It might be that I do that because my mother always did it," or "Certainly I behave toward my girlfriend that way because I am afraid of sexuality." This sort of defense against the unconscious and attempt at overcoming anxieties almost always involves compulsive structural elements and consequently is found most clearly and distinctly in compulsion neuroses.

defenses

The other hoped-for advantage—that of excluding the personality of the analyst—is pure fiction. As I will discuss in more detail in subsequent chapters, the presence of the analyst's personality is precisely the element that plays a central role in the analytic process regardless how much information the patient acquires about the person of the analyst. Removing the analyst from the patient's field of vision very often intensifies the paranoid component of the patient's anxieties and consequently access to the real unconscious is made more difficult.

Freudian psychoanalysts also recognize these problems, and more and more heretics are appearing who question the orthodox arrangement. Obviously the effectiveness of this arrangement is, as Jackson (1962) once expressed it, limited to those analyses that need only flow through the analyst's persona and take place completely within a professional relationship. Among the Freudians it has been especially Fairbairn (1958), Glover (1955), and Balint (1965), who have expressed doubts about the use of the couch. According to Fairbairn, the advantages of using the couch consist predominantly of rationalizations and he sees an essential disadvantage in artificially creating a traumatic situation in which the patient is regressively placed in a situation wherein he or she lies screaming alone in the cradle. Glover refers to the dangers of the impersonal analyst and points out that this attempt could lead to stabilizing the patient's defensive systems in such a form that the patient could make the analytic situation as impersonal as possible and consequently would not get near his or her own world of feelings and affects. Balint pointed out in particular that the severe neuroses which are associated with what he terms primary disturbances call for entirely different analytic techniques than the classical couch arrangement can provide.

The advantage of sitting face-to-face in analysis rests on the theoretical conception of analysis as a dialectical process in which analysand and analyst collaboratively look for a synthesis from the constellation of unconscious material. In this endeavor the analyst reveals his or her personality to the patient visually and thereby becomes vulnerable, but also in a more personal and closer manner than in the artificially experimental couch arrangement. Moreover, the patient is not drawn into an infantilization *vis-à-vis* the analyst; rather, he or she at least has the possibility of sitting across from the analyst as a person with equal rights and of dealing with the infantile side of the Self with greater distance since the adult ego-component is not so strongly identified with the infantile component or inflated by it. Sitting in a chair also has the advantage that it gives the patient a better emotional grip than does lying on the couch; this is important in those states of impending decompensation in which the patient functions initially on a more archaic level in which sensory modalities other than the optical stand in the foreground. This can have a fundamentally pacifying effect and thus, particularly in psychoses and borderline cases, considerably facilitate access to, and the creation of, a relationship with the unconscious. The advantage of conducting analysis on the visual plane lies in this: the patient gets an answer to what he or she expresses in the emotions read in the analyst's face. Moreover, the patient is again in the position of making some statement about the inner events that the analyst's emotions constellate within, be they correctly or incorrectly interpreted. If we proceed from the doubtlessly correct assumption that the analytic situation is a model for all relationships that have possibilities for development, there is greater opportunity to work through projective misunderstandings and to withdraw projections face-to-face than when the analyst is not visible.

But this situation has disadvantages as well, and it is important to be aware of them. As mentioned above, the chair can provide not only a necessary and comforting mooring when the patient experiences the possibly necessary therapeutic regression into the archaic realm; it can also be a hindrance and a constriction that slows down the aggression. The

sitting posture is very often used as a defense against submission anxieties and then continues to remain a security system to which the patient
can continue to cling unnecessarily for a long time. A further danger lies
in the possibility that a conversational situation can arise that corresponds more to a chat, discussion, or intellectual exchange. This hinders
the flowering of fantasies, and analysis remains on a superficial, conscious plane. One must be aware that this sort of situation can be sus-
tained not only by the patient and his or her systems of defense but also
by the countertransference defenses of the analyst who, as we emphasized earlier, is placed in a significantly more vulnerable position and
who can protect himself with his own defenses against fantasy material
that is incompatible with his feelings.

When we survey the arguments that speak both for and against the
orthodox psychoanalytic situation of lying on the couch as well as for
and against the orthodox sitting posture of analytical psychology, it
rightly appears to the unprejudiced eye at first glance as though in each
situation one had to pay for certain advantages by accepting certain
disadvantages. It might be easy to conclude that it actually makes no
difference whether one treats the patient lying down or sitting up, as
though it were not so important whether the patient could see the analyst. Thus it would appear to be purely a matter of subjective choice
whether one did analysis with the patient sitting or lying, a choice that
altered the ultimate effectiveness of the analysis in no way, since the
advantages and disadvantages of both approaches were approximately
equal.

That, in my opinion, is a fallacy. Insistence on one method unnecessarily restricts the technical possibilities available to the analyst and
grants too little space to the patient's developmental and maturational
potential. Neither does it correspond to the principle of individuation
championed by Jung which forbids the imposition of collective schemata
on the patient or on the analytic situation. According to Gerhard Adler
(personal communication), Jung's analytic style never had that repressive
element of orthodox methodology. With Jung, the patient could sit,
squat on the floor, sketch, paint, look at books and pictures with Jung,
or even go for a walk with the analyst, an approach that Zulliger (personal communication) has taken with great success when working with
young people. Zulliger, who doubtless has an unusually high intuitive
capacity for empathy with young people, approached a sixteen-year-old
at the beginning of treatment by cleaning his rifle (which every Swiss
citizen has in the closet) as they sat together in the garden where the
sessions were held. The teenager, whose attention nobody else could
arouse, began to show some interest in cleaning the gun and started
joining in. Thus the first emotional contact was established. With this

symbolism or symbolic approach the analyst intuitively grasped the unfocused, aimless, aggressive potential in the background of the patient's psyche and thereby initiated the analytical process.

It is clear that even Freud was by no means so orthodox as his followers, for Laforgue, who knew Freud personally, once told me in conversation that, when he was quite old and treating a young woman patient, Freud very angrily hit the pillow under her head with his fist and said to her with much affect, "Your entire resistance only comes from your not permitting yourself the fantasy of loving a man as old as I am!" Whether or not this personal anecdote is true, it nevertheless gives a picture of the personal vitality and liveliness that Freud must have had in his dealings with his patients. Freud's analysis of the "Wolf Man," written by the patient himself, reveals this in many places (Wolfman 1972).

Unfortunately, followers often tend to turn the founder's thoughts on method—which arose from both his personal equation as well as his lively dealings with others—into a rigid, self-sufficient principle without being aware that it is their own anxieties and uncertainties that cause them to cling to principles instead of reacting as human beings. Through their intentional and artificial frustrations they often turn the analytic process—difficult for the patient in any event and in many places frustrating—into something resembling sadistic torture that is rationalized as fidelity to principles or to a method. Here one should always keep in mind Brecht's statement: "The raging torrent is called violent, but nobody calls the riverbed violent that constricts it" (1981, p. 602).

These reflections, as well as my own experience with patients' attitudes in analysis, have moved me to leave it up to the patient whether he or she lies down or sits during the session and then to examine the choice analytically. It goes without saying that postures other than lying down or sitting are possible and conceivable. For long stretches of her therapy, a severely limited borderline patient, for example, remained standing in a corner near the door of the consultation room and at times regressed to this behavior when she was completely ready to sit in an armchair. As I will discuss in detail later in regard to sitting and lying down, permitting the patient simply to do that without any verbal, interpretive limitation and not discussing it until later when she had overcome this condition turned out to be extraordinarily fruitful analytically. Now and then during his analytic hours another patient with a rather serious compulsion neurosis had attacks of muscle tension so severe that he wanted to stand up and pace back and forth but he did not dare to do it. When I told him that in antiquity very profound intellectual discussions had taken place in Plato's academy while the participants walked about among the columns and that consequently that school of thought had been called "peripatetic," he heaved a sigh of relief and began to walk back and forth in the

*et
Jack
woven
into
work*

consultation room as he spoke during those hours. Thus the entire process that had previously been blocked by his having to suppress his motoric tension which consumed all his energy got moving again. By pacing, he was able to symbolize the anxieties that had evoked his states of tension arising from the unconscious and thereby to come to terms with them in a better and simpler fashion than would have been possible if one had demanded of him that he maintain a specific posture. But in this context I do not want to discuss special cases in greater detail since the patient either sits in an armchair or lies on the couch during most analytic hours. Rather, I would like to offer a few examples that elucidate how the free choice of couch or chair can be turned to analytic advantage.

I would like to preface the discussion of the following examples by pointing out that the seating in my consultation room is arranged so that the patient lying on the couch can see me by turning his or her head slightly and under no conditions do I sit so that I am invisible to the patient or can be seen only by contorting the body. In spite of all good will toward the concept that the analyst is or should be a screen upon which the patient projects, I consider the danger of an ultimately paranoid and depersonalized relational structure between patient and analyst to be too great if visual contact is prevented on principle. Likewise, since they are so important to me, I would not like to forego the nonverbal, visual signals that are much more clear and distinct and can be observed more easily and more accurately face-to-face. As it is, in analysis we tend to neglect the nonverbal in favor of the verbal. Possibly the analytic situation offers a continual temptation to do so, and precisely from the standpoint of sensory modalities we are often not conscious of the great degree to which we as human beings are oriented to the visual mode. I have pointed out in several publications (Dieckmann 1972b, 1974c, 1978a) how the prejudice prevails throughout the entire body of literature that dreams are almost exclusively visual and that the other sensory modalities are neglected, beginning with the dreamer's recall, although other modalities are clearly present in the dream and can be reproduced if asked for. Thus the various ways in which a patient looks at or does not look at the analyst — how anxiously, devouringly, aggressively, hatefully, rejectingly, disdainfully, humorously, with superiority or inferiority, reticently or demandingly — can be of great analytical significance. These ways of looking serve not only as an important signal and mirror of one's own bearing or as a means of monitoring the effect of one's own statements and interpretations; changes in the ways a patient looks at the analyst are often the first indicators and heralds of deeper transformational processes within the analysis. For example, a patient often loses an anxious, defensive look several sessions prior to being able to realize this internally or verbalize it. Certainly Freud was right when he said that it is decidedly difficult to let another person stare at oneself hour after hour. This manner of being looked at is particularly difficult if the look in the patient's eyes has unconscious aggressive, devouring, or incorporative qualities. But when one has learned to bear this situation with equanimity, it is, as I know from personal experience, incomparably more fruitful than sitting outside the patient's field of vision.

Now I would like to give some examples in order to pursue a few additional basic questions. Although I will be expounding on a few typical cases and situations, I must emphasize that in each instance we are really dealing with strictly individual issues and no hard and fast rules whatsoever can be derived from the examples cited, e.g., that with this function type, group of symptoms, structure or behavior one could always, as a rule, proceed thus and so.

The first case is that of a 28-year-old sociology student who sought treatment because of severe depressive moods combined with disturbances in his capacity to work and the prolongation of his studies. Typologically the patient was an introverted feeling type with a very rich, vital, and lively experience of his inner world and a number of creative possibilities that he could not realize. His auxiliary function was intuition and he very quickly grasped interrelationships, which remained in the realm of possibilities. The patient was the youngest of four siblings. After entering school, he had developed a quite inadequate extraversion as an adaptation to his social environment and to his predominantly extraverted family, thanks to the influence of his very authoritarian, compulsive father (who was an engineer), and his relatively unrelated mother. For the most part, his extraversion exhausted itself in his playing the clown. Initially he received recognition as class clown, later as buffoon at student parties where he continually made a joke of himself and, in his quest for recognition, misused his potential intuitive and creative powers. Moreover, in the choice of academic discipline, obviously made out of a certain degree of identification with his engineer father and from his own search for social status, he was dependent primarily on his inferior thinking function so that, for all practical purposes, he could not live in accord with his own nature. Characteristically his depression had begun after puberty in conjunction with an unhappy love relationship in which he had sought to impress the girl primarily with extraverted mannerisms and pseudophilosophical thought, which his girlfriend did not put up with for very long. The atmosphere of dealing with him also had something rather schizoid-unrelated about it. Since he had not been able either to make an identification with his hated father or to effect a regression to his very cool mother (who, moreover, was seldom present as a person in the family due to social obligations), he fled into an archetypal fantasy world of the Great Mother in which primordial mother figures with large breasts and plump, soft bodies predominated. In this fantasy world he moved about with great wit and skill so that he could thoroughly fascinate an observer without ever letting the other person get close to his own, real, personal world of feeling.

Following the initial interview and my agreement to take him into treatment, the patient made a beeline for the couch in the first treatment hour, lay down facing away from me and rolled himself into a ball like a porcupine. From this position he inundated me with a veritable torrent of fantasy images from the realm of the Great Mother intermixed with childhood memories that he believed were expected in analysis. He did this so skillfully and grippingly that I listened with interest as if I were at the theater. With a downright protean adroitness, however, he deflected every attempt on my part to obtain a little more precise information or to offer an interpretation; as he did this, everything that he had previously depicted changed entirely; where one had seen a raven just a moment ago there was suddenly a colorful bird that simply flew away out of one's hands. Now and then he related bits and pieces of dreams that could not be distinguished from fantasies, nor did he himself really know whether he had actually dreamt it or fantasied it.

After I saw how fruitless my attempts to say a word, let alone make any connection with him, had been, I let him simply go on talking although I was fairly certain early on that this patient was fully capable of maintaining his defensive attitude for well over 200 hours or more without any great difficulties. In the twenty-third hour I seized my opportunity to interrupt him when he related a dream or fantasy fragment in which I or a peripheral, indistinct shadow figure resembling me, was standing on the edge of a junglelike landscape. He knew the difference between the analytic schools and had voluntarily chosen to come to a Jungian analyst. I explained to him that I was most astonished that he had come to a Jungian and immediately taken the couch, and moreover, that he had assumed a posture in which he completely excluded me from his field of vision as though he were with a Freudian. From his knowledge of the literature, I continued, he certainly had to know that Jungians preferred the chair. His answer was thoroughly typical. He told me that he could imagine that maybe I was not a proper Jungian, and further that there was a mat for shoes lying at the foot of my couch which implied that my patients used the couch. Moreover, he had the feeling that he got deeper into himself if he excluded everything external and turned completely inward. "Oh," I said, "but is that what you are really doing?" Thereupon he fell silent for the first time and finally said, somewhat disconcertedly and irritatedly, "Of course!"

When he appeared for his next session he sat down in the armchair, looked at me with a very anxious, relatively rigid, orally incorporative glance and reported first that he had been extremely anxious about coming to his session and still felt very anxious in contrast to his previous sessions. Then his violent aggression poured out: I was forcing him to sit in the chair and thereby was sabotaging his whole analysis; he had had such marvelous experiences of himself in previous hours but there was no way that could happen if he were sitting; he had to look at me continually and pay attention to the face I made and anyhow the way I had behaved was completely unanalytic since I obviously wanted to manipulate him in an authoritarian manner and wasn't going to grant him the freedom to unfold and develop.

It was very apparent that in the transference I had now obviously taken on the role of the hated, authoritarian father, and from this hour forward he began to come to terms with this figure which now became personal and also more related. A little later he was able to see that his persisting in the archetype of the Great Mother as a little child curled up like a porcupine had predominantly the character of flight from both parents and from every personal relationship whatsoever. I believe it hardly would have been possible to make this patient so distinctly aware of his problems if I had not given him the possibility of presenting them in this way during the initial phase of his analysis. If I had forced him to comply at the beginning with a specific system of rules concerning his posture (either sitting or lying), that would have lead to a significant intensification of his anxieties and hence also to a greater degree of rigidity in his defenses.

This is an instance of a patient who was anxious about sitting and consequently chose the lying posture spontaneously. If the patient is given the possibility of choosing whether he or she will sit or lie, most patients elect the posture that arouses less anxiety, although of course there are exceptions to this. Methodologically it is essential that their choice be made the object of analysis. The opportunity for choice initially creates a situation at the beginning of analysis in which already-existing anxieties are not unnecessarily intensified by not forcing the patient to assume a posture that mobilizes additional anxieties. Moreover, this approach makes it possible to take the patient's inability to sit or to lie as an object for analysis. Those exceptional cases in which patients plunge into the more anxiety-provoking situation can also be addressed analytically. Compliant behavior—in analysis "one sits in a chair" or "one lies on the couch"—emerges more clearly this way. In regard to this, I proceed from the assumption that nowadays every patient who consults us has already heard something or other about analysis and has some degree of knowledge about analytic method gleaned from the newspapers or illustrated magazines. If this happens not to be the case, then the patient's lack of experience or information is again an object of analysis.

The patient's fear of sitting in analysis can derive from a multitude of underlying causes. It can, as in the case presented above, be due to anxiety about personal relationships in general, but with the figure of the authoritarian father in the background. It can manifest as anxiety about eye contact, as anxiety at having to be adult, as anxiety related to mobility and expansion, as anxiety that one can more easily be attacked, or something similar. The point of these reflections is not to compile as complete a list as possible of those anxieties due to which the patient avoids sitting. At best, such a list could have only superficial character since, in addition to the anxiety-provoking situations, we would also have to consider the personal background out of which the anxiety arose and which perpetuates it. The point in time when one tackles this problem is indeed important. Aside from the preconditions that are necessary for making an interpretation (see Chapter 12, Interpretation), I am guided first and foremost by unconscious material that arises. In the case mentioned above, I discussed a session in which I appeared for the first time in the patient's dream or fantasy, admittedly only vaguely as a peripheral figure (Dieckmann 1965). From the prospective viewpoint I utilized the patient's fantasy in order to bring myself into his field of vision (Dieckmann 1972b). Doing this enabled the patient to give up his defense, to overcome his anxiety about sitting, and to begin to come to terms analytically with the father imago. At the same time he recognized how great his childish dependency and his aggressive, defiant reactions still were, since he experienced my simple, questioning amazement as coercion or as a command to sit up.

The second case is that of a 45-year-old woman with compulsive symptoms. She was the only child of relatively well-to-do parents and the darling of her father who died prematurely when she was thirteen. The entire family atmosphere in which she grew up had a distinctly compulsive, solid middle-class character. Order, cleanliness, punctuality, and justice were the headings under which life was subsumed. Sexuality was excluded. At home nobody spoke about it. Her mother referred her to the literature for her sexual enlightenment, and her menarche was tersely explained in medical and rational terms. After completing a business training curriculum and a brief period of work experience, she married and had two children, a son and a daughter. Just like her depressive, self-sacrificial mother, she, too, was incapable of experiencing sexual feelings in the marriage. When the children were older, she took a part-time job as a business secretary. Her symptoms, which had predominantly agoraphobic and claustrophobic character, commenced when a somewhat closer, personal relationship developed between her and one of her bosses and she had to repress emerging sexual impulses. She was a very matter-of-fact, diligent woman, dominated by her father-animus, who was generally valued for her reliability and hard work.

In analysis she took the armchair although she had no inkling to which analytic school I belonged. Her animus cooperated and worked hard and diligently, punctually delivered the necessary number of dreams and led her to some insights and knowledge about herself so that there was really nothing about the analysis to cause complaint. Starting the 120th session, dreams began to accumulate in which her dream-ego started to move about with less anxiety, more expansively and lazily. She began to struggle with her accomplishment-oriented animus and to discover the healthy, unconcerned child in herself. Following a birth dream in the 138th hour in which she gave birth to a baby boy, she was able to fantasize how nice it would be to be rocked in a cradle. When I drew her attention to the couch and pointed out that it was, after all, something like a cradle for adults, she dismissed my comment. Five sessions later she reported a dream in which she dreamt that I had invited her to tea in a very relaxed and comfortable atmosphere. Then she expressed the wish to see how it would be to have a session on the couch for a change. She lay down for about five minutes, then sat up again and said, "No, that won't do," and again sat in the armchair. The remainder of the hour passed in a somewhat tense silence.

When she came to her next hour she explained to me with some hesitancy that she had to make a confession. The previous time when she had lain on the couch, she had experienced sexual sensations. That had been so embarrassing and unpleasant – and of course that wouldn't do at all – that she had quickly taken the chair again. I replied that she would unnecessarily confine herself by doing that; after all, she could simply enjoy those sensations. As a woman she even had the advantage that I would not even notice it if she did not want to tell me. That made sense to her. Again she lay down on the couch and during the next phase of her analysis her entire world of repressed sexual fantasies and experiences welled up. Her fantasies and experiences had been associated with passionately incestuous wishes for her father, correspondingly tabooed.

It is especially clear in this example that the fear of lying on the couch was linked with her fear of sexual surrender as well as with her taboo wish to be loved physically as a woman by her father. At this point it should be noted that without ever having expressed it verbally, her father would surely have preferred a son, and in rearing her he had, to some extent, treated her as a boy. This gives us cause to ponder what would have happened if I had demanded that the patient use the couch from the beginning. I am certain that, without a doubt, she would have done so without ever noticing that she felt any anxiety. Lying on the couch would have been the father-animus's way of doing analysis which would have been correct, right, and in order, and which she would have fulfilled obediently like a good daughter. Sexuality would have been repressed, just as it was when she was sitting, and a reinforced defensiveness against the loosening character of lying down would have set in. In the course of 120 sessions this attitude would have become well established — routine is difficult to breach — and it would not have been so easy to loosen up as in the situation that actually took place. On the other hand, if I had acted as an "orthodox" Jungian and continued to let the patient sit in the chair after the previously repressed world of feeling knocked on her door, its unfoldment would certainly have been more difficult and more circumstantial and would not have entered into the analysis so clearly and dramatically.

CHAPTER 5

Fee and Methods of Payment

A male patient in his early forties brought the following dream to his fifth session:

I am in a subterranean passageway that gangsters have built in order to break into a bank vault. The passageway is supported with shorings like a mine shaft. I cower behind one of the shorings while several gangsters carry great sacks of money and jewelry past me out through the passageway. Obviously they have already broken into the vault and are carrying out their loot. I am terribly afraid of being discovered and shot by them.

The following situation preceded the dream: the patient had entered analysis because of psychosomatic symptoms, anxiety states in stress situations, and an excessive degree of nervous restlessness. He was a relatively well situated businessman, owner of a small firm, and, although he knew that analysis was a very drawn-out undertaking and that we had initially agreed upon three sessions per week, he had not asked how much his treatment would actually cost. Even during the session in which he related this dream he did not at first connect this problem and the dream. Only in response to my asking whether there might be a connection did he have an "aha" experience and was then very puzzled that he, as a businessman, had forgotten to ask the price. At the same time he recognized that during his five sessions he had spoken uninterruptedly and with great agitation for the entire hour against a background of deep-seated anxiety without ever once giving me the opportunity to say a word. The dream showed very drastically, almost without need of commentary, how his neglecting to ask this important question in the present situation had initially constellated a high degree of underlying, unconscious anxiety that he would be looted and plundered.

Above and beyond this, the dream also points to the patient's funda-mental problem: at a continual hectic pace and in a perpetual drivenness to accomplish, he continually let himself be looted and plundered, on the one hand by others and on the other hand by his excessive acquisitive-ness. Consequently his own personality had gotten lost in the shuffle and could only look on helplessly as these shadow aspects acquired more and more libido. For all practical purposes this patient had no capability whatsoever of doing anything for himself. He had the manager's typical weekend neurosis: without exception he felt bad when he could not work on days off and was unable to take a vacation. In this connection he arranged very curious situations. When he finally did decide to take time off, he missed his flights or returned from his vacation spot after a day or two on some sort of pretext. If he stayed, he had to struggle with major depressive moods for at least the first week. Hence the problem of this dream continued to inform long stretches of his subsequent analysis and the impressive looting motif was brought up again and again at appropriate times in order to remind him where and how his own ego fell victim to this process of being robbed.

This dream contains the important archetypal motif of the treasure which the dreamer loses to the shadow. Later we will discuss this motif in greater detail in connection with the issue of money. But first I wanted to use this example to make it clear that the patient must engage actively in the analytic situation when the analyst waits and offers the patient no instructions at the beginning (here in reference to the issue of money). This approach has the advantage that sensitive motifs can surface rela-tively quickly in a drastic and, for the patient, cogent form. Certainly this problem would not have been constellated in this extraordinarily clear form if I had taken the initiative in the first session to negotiate a price or tell him what I demanded as a fee. One is well advised to wait until the patient takes the initiative to address this area and only then to reach the appropriate agreement with him.

It is an old, common medical usage to adapt the fee for treatment to the patient's ability to pay. This is why fees for medical services embrace a rather broad range between the lowest and the highest rates. From the earliest days of analysis it was taken as a sort of fundamental rule among all schools that the patient's material participation in analysis should be palpable and that this itself represented an important means in the ana-lytic process. Jolande Jacobi (personal communication) once recommen-ded to a Hungarian colleague who was treating a destitute patient for free, and who had written Jacobi because the analysis was stuck, that she should demand at least one florin per hour from her patient. When she did this, the analysis got moving again. The principle of the patient's material participation in his or her analysis has been, to a large extent, abrogated in Germany thanks to state insurance regulations that permit no financial participation on the part of the patient since the majority of patients are covered under state health insurance and thus have their analyses, like all other medical treatments, without personal expense. For these patients the arrangements concerning payment are limited to missed hours or to the continuation of analysis beyond the point where symptoms remit.

In the training analysis every analyst should have gained insight into his or her issues concerning money and should have worked through the underlying dynamics. On the basis of such personal awareness it is meaningful and necessary for the analyst to develop his or her own style of dealing with problems having to do with money. It makes little sense to formulate even general guidelines concerning how much, when, and how the individual is to pay. Likewise there can be no rules whether or not, as Frieda Fromm-Reichmann (1950) recommends, missed hours shall be paid for, or, as the majority of analysts handle it, how the fee for missed hours is to be paid according to specific agreements. The same holds true for arrangements concerning vacations, agreements about illnesses, etc. It is important only that an agreement be reached which, on the one hand, does not overburden the patient so that the patient's possibilities for development and expansion are not hindered and, on the other, that the analyst is satisfactorily recompensed so that latent unconscious aggression toward the patient does not accumulate due to an overaccentuated helper mentality and block the analytic process. Above all it is important that the analyst be clear about the character of money as a complex in the analytic process and also about the problem of money within the analytic relationship or in the transference-countertransference constellation.

An entire book could be written about the symbolic significance of money in analysis. Unfortunately, this has not yet happened since the problem of money and of dealing with it has so many shades of meaning and possible variations that it seems almost inexhaustible. Consequently we can treat this issue — and especially the question as to why the issue of money and the agreements and arrangements concerning money are so important in analysis — only briefly and incompletely.

In his book on dreams, Artemidorous of Daldis (1975) mentions money and expressed thoughts concerning the appearance of money symbolism in dreams. Some maintain, he wrote, that money and all species of coins signified evil things. Contrariwise, he had observed that coins of small denomination and copper money were the basis of ill temper and distressing conversations; silver money was the symbol of discussions concerning contracts and agreements involving important affairs; finally, gold coins were infinitely more significant. It was always better to possess less rather than more goods and money, he thought, because of the difficulties involved in administering them. Much money meant worries and cares, but if one imagined he had found a treasure of little value, that signified fewer difficulties. On the other hand, a rich treasure meant cares and heartaches, but often also prophesied one's death. Unless one dug up the earth, one could not find a treasure, just as one could not bury a dead man without lifting a shovel.

As we see, Artemidorous of Daldis regarded money quite skeptically and ascribed a rather dark significance to it in which he approached Luther's view of money as being associated with the realm of the Devil. Bornemann (1973) also took up this particular shadow aspect, seeing in the money complex a central negative phenomenon of contemporary capitalism that poisons the human psyche in the sense of the myth of King Midas. Midas, King of Phrygia, threw a banquet for Dionysus which so pleased the god that he promised his host the fulfillment of a wish. Thereupon Midas wished that everything he touched would turn to gold. The fulfillment of this wish then led to the horrible consequence that he could neither eat nor drink, neither make love nor keep himself warm, since all the objects — such as food, drink, women, clothing, etc. — immediately turned to gold as soon as they were exposed to his touch. In his exposition, Bornemann essentially follows Freud, who ascribed anal character to money, and describes the self-destruction of the anal character in the midas complex through his limitless greed for money.

It is indeed true that, as Freud described in his essay "Character and Anal Eroticism" (S.E., vol. 7), a relatively close relationship does exist between money and the anal phase. There are many etymological analogies between money (German, *Geld*), gold (German, *Gold*), and feces (German, *Kot*). On the other hand, however, Freud also agreed with later psychoanalytic theories, particularly those of Abraham (1969), Ferency (1916), and Jones (1919) who pointed out that only the retentive, withholding, and hoarding aspect of an interest in money follows from the anal character. By contrast, the acquisitive, incorporative aspect belongs more to the oral stage. Obviously, viewing this problem or symbol solely at the level of one very specific stage of libido development is too narrow. It also remains to be seen whether the very close connection between the interest in money and the anal character is not also subject to a certain time factor and whether the economic basis which informs the pedagogic superstructure of capitalism does not fundamentally contribute to promoting, deepening, and favoring compulsive structures.

Money has, of course, not always carried the high value and the great significance that is ascribed to it nowadays. Money and the value of money always come into being where a civilization arises that is no longer economically self-sufficient (as in circumscribed geographic areas or close-knit groups such as the extended family) and where the individual is subjected to specialization and dependent on barter or exchange. Hence money played a major role in the ancient Mediterranean cultures that were based to a great extent on maritime trade, a role which, as Norbert Elias (1969) has pointed out, substantially declined in importance in the early Middle Ages when trade was still undeveloped in broad regions and individual estates, villages, and provinces in large areas of Germany and France lived in nearly complete economic self-sufficiency on their own products. The amount of money in circulation during the early years of the Holy Roman Empire in Germany was, just as in France, extraordinarily meager and fell far short of what antiquity had known. Not until the 9th and 10th centuries of the medieval period was the collar harness invented which made the horse-drawn wagon serviceable for transporting larger loads by land. This form of transport was unknown in antiquity and because of the relatively simpler sea trade, antiquity did not have to depend on overland transport routes since the settlements, too, were situated around the Mediterranean Sea and at the mouths of the larger rivers. The moveable front axle was invented only in the 13th century as a consequence of the new harness, thus making wagons less cumbersome and capable of being steered around curves (*Brockhaus Enzyclopädie*, vol. 19).

I find these historical data important because of the fact that, wherever mankind is more deeply embedded in nature and lives off of nature in economically self-sufficient communities, money plays a relatively small role. The greater the degree to which we free ourselves from this condition and the more we separate ourselves from original realities, from the objective world surrounding us, the more the value of money takes the foreground as a means of exchange of wares regardless of the form it assumes. If we transpose this external situation into the intrapsychic realm, the symbolism of money becomes progressively more striking as consciousness increasingly separates from the primordial, instinctive facts of life and as the scale and the possibilities of human needs and ways of satisfying needs become more manifold. Money thus attains the symbolic character of disposable libido that liberates us from satisfying the momentarily compelling instinct. If we follow Jung's theory of libido as he has presented it in his essay, "On Psychic Energy" (*C. W.* 8), we find that the concept of libido is the psychic equivalent of the concept of energy in physics that is not bound to a specific domain or partial domain but rather can be expressed in appropriate form at all levels, not only at the anal. Here, therefore, money becomes a libido symbol in a very specific sense insofar as it is intimately associated with the archetype of the Great Mother.

In the images of the Mistress of the Plants and of the Beasts, this archetype personifies the unconscious inner world of nature out of which humankind seeks to liberate itself in the course of human development. But liberation and release from the mother archetype is, after all, something questionable and problematic in the last analysis. Our whole life long we struggle and labor to become independent, to attain freedom, and to get away from the mother so that finally we can return to her womb in the form of the grave as the last goal of all our entire efforts. Occidental culture has depicted this battle against the negative, possessive side of the mother archetype in countless hero myths wherein the hopelessness of overcoming the mother ultimately appears again and again. Thus Heracles' entire life and labors appear as a continual battle against the negative mother archetype, as an attempt at overcoming and at slaying the mother. This problem is most clearly expressed in the symbolism of his battle with the Hydra. But ultimately he meets his end in the Great Mother's Nessus's shirt. In this regard there is a certain difference between European and Asian culture to which Zimmer (1938) referred. Whereas the occidental hero is oriented toward overcoming and slaying the mother and then becomes entangled in an inescapable fate, the oriental type of hero is more often and more strongly oriented toward reconciliation and adaptation, a problem that I discussed more extensively in my interpretations of the tales from *Thousand and One Nights* (Dieckmann 1974a).

At this point let us again consider money. Its symbolism has a double aspect. On the one hand it is a means of liberation from the captivating, constricting, and development-preventing side of the Great Mother archetype; on the other, thanks to its being itself matter and consequently belonging to the Great Mother, it is an approach to and a union with the maternal world in its positive aspect which promises the fulfillment and satisfaction of needs. This relationship of money to the mother archetype has also been noted by psychoanalysts, and Desmonde (1957) described something similar in his work on the origin of money in the animal sacrifice. He offered the hypothesis that consuming the sacrificial animal corresponds to the longing to be united with the mother in ecstatic oneness, and that the first form of coin that replaced the animal sacrifice as an obolus was used with some of these motivations. Moreover, this ritual also represented the wish to revivify powers indwelling in the human being and to promote the well-being of humankind through the just distribution of economic goods. Admittedly, for the most part this takes into account only the one aspect, namely the regressive component of the longing for reunion with the mother; the progressive libidinal side that lies in gaining liberty and autonomy from the negative mother

archetype is expressed only in a very general and undifferentiated revivi-
fication of one's own inner powers.

Jung described this problem more clearly in *Symbols of Transformation (C. W. 5)* in the chapter entitled "The Dual Mother." Jung elucidates
both facets of the meaning of the money offerings to the mother. Offerings of animals and later of money dedicated to the Great Mother were
made at forks in the road or at crossroads sacred to her. The sacrifice was
made at the place where the paths crossed, where they interpenetrated
each other, hence it expressed the image of the union of opposites. Here
the mother is both the object and the essence of union as well as being the
image of departure, separation, and parting where the paths cross.
Chasm and well were also conceived as the portals of death and of life
where each person had to sacrifice his obolus instead of his own body.
Jung writes:

> In Hierapolis (Edessa) a temple was built over the crack in the earth
> where the flood subsided, and in Jerusalem the foundation-stone of
> the temple was laid over the great abyss, in the same way that Chris-
> tian churches are often built over caves, grottoes, wells, etc. We find
> the same motif in the Grotto of Mithras and the various other cave-
> cults, including the Christian catacombs, which owe their importance
> not to legendary persecutions but to the cult of the dead. . . . In olden
> times, the dragon in the cave who represented the devouring mother
> had to be propitiated with human sacrifices, later with gifts. . . . A
> substitute for the gifts seems to have been the obolus given to Charon,
> which is why Rohde calls him the second Cerberus, akin to the jackal-
> headed Anubis of the Egyptians. . . . The sacred cave in the temple at
> Cos consisted of a rectangular pit covered by a stone slab with a
> square hole in it. This arrangement served the purpose of a treasure-
> house: the snake pit had become a slot for money, a "poor-box," and
> the cave a "hoard." (*C. W.* 5, par. 577)

These descriptions very clearly reveal how money and the money offering
carry a double meaning: the separation from the negative-restrictive
death mother, and the movement toward and union with the positive,
life-giving side of the mother archetype.

It seems to me absolutely essential that we clearly recognize the symbolic, archetypal background of the money offering if we are to speak of
money and payment in the analytic process. All the rational justifications
given for private payment or the patient's financial participation in his or
her treatment are relatively superficial in the last analysis. For example,
the argument that the analyst must live from patients' fees no longer
applies to a staff physician or psychologist who conducts the analysis,
and the justification that the patient would be more strongly motivated if

he or she had to make some significant material investment in the analytic process is not valid. When we disregard the archetypal background discussed above and remain only on the rational level, the amount of time and effort the patient has to muster in analysis is just as motivating. Who will till his field year after year without the motivation of believing that finally something will grow on it!

Regarded from the viewpoint of the archetypal-symbolic background, money appears to be an extremely important symbol of those differentiated processes that are necessary in effecting the union of opposites, first in the realm of separation, and then of union with and integration in the mother archetype in the course of the analytic process. Viewed against this background, we must agree with Jolande Jacobi's observation cited above that analysis doesn't work without an obolus and that this obolus must be really and truly paid, for analysis can be regarded as an effectual process only if it does not remain caught up solely in fantasy images or sublime conceptions. Basically this is where the problems surrounding those "free" analyses paid for by insurance lie, for in the latter the patient gets stuck: he or she is taken care of by an anonymous Great Mother from which the sacrifice or offering of an "obolus" would set him or her free. Granted, we must also keep in mind that the original meaning of the act is not that of making a sacrifice of an animal, honey cakes, or, in later times, money to the person of the priest who kept watch over the sanctuary; rather, the offering or sacrifice was intended for the god himself, and the priestly caste's secondary enrichment thanks to the offerings is basically a debasement and distortion of the primary act. From this vantage point, the physician demanding money from the patient for analytic treatment is nothing but a capitalistic demand arising out of self-interest and the analyst should know this and rationalize away his self-interest neither by speaking of the extremely positive effect on analysis nor perhaps by holding the view that the patient can expect the treatment to run smoothly only if he paid as much as possible. For the patient and for his analytical process of maturation and development only the obolus is necessary, an obolus that, as we can see from the historical development, does not even have to consist of money but rather must be in the form of a personal material sacrifice, a sacrifice that does not even have to be made to the analyst but to something transcendental that stands between the patient and the analyst and that can be expressed through images of the great mother goddesses. Perhaps against this background we can find the explanation for the empirical fact that the great majority of "free" analyses have relatively good results. In these situations the human psyche apparently still finds a way of making a certain offering or sacrifice and consequently of working through the problem in a meaningful manner.

I must admit to feeling somewhat at a loss in judging this situation. In my own experience those analyses do proceed significantly better in which the patient participates materially, and those other analyses in which the patient even comes out financially ahead (as sometimes happens in Germany thanks to the complicated bureaucratic insurance and subsidy claims) show the most sluggish and worst progress. I have the impression that patients whose analyses are paid for by institutions remain within the archetype of the Great Mother in their individuation, i.e., the dependence on and attachment to the elementary character of the Great Mother (Neumann 1974) is preserved quantitatively and qualitatively to a greater degree than in the instances of patients who finance at least a part of their analyses themselves. Here, however, we must concede that the sorts of individuation processes that remain within the maternal archetypal field can also reveal specific forms of development and maturation. Correspondingly, the neurotic symptomology is influenced and can even be fully given up without being merely a passing remission of symptoms in the transference. This phenomenon is often found in the "natural" individuation of especially gifted artistic persons, as I have described in greater detail in the instances of Rainer Maria Rilke (Dieckmann 1958) and Marc Chagall (Dieckmann 1973c). But one should not underestimate the number of patients for whom this possibility is not relevant or sufficient. They consequently, in addition to the services covered by insurance benefits, need to take some financial part in their treatment in which they must take or complete the decisive, still lacking developmental steps, an experience that I have had not only with my own patients but also with cases under my supervision and which colleagues have corroborated. If these sorts of persons forego this part of their treatment, a large part of their symptomology persists, as a rule, or the risk of relapse is considerably higher.

The dynamics of the money problem that play so great a role in the transference, countertransference, and interpersonal struggles in analyses paid for out-of-pocket vanish almost completely in the "free" analyses paid for by insurance and appear in mild form only at those points where the patient must pay for missed hours. These dynamics are not replaced by the time invested, the travel expenses to and from sessions, etc., for the latter are the same in both instances. To the extent that the above-mentioned hypotheses do not apply, we must admit that we do not know much about patients who are cured without any financial participation on their part. Only future investigations will be able to show which criteria will discriminate between the forms of personally financed and state- or insurance-financed analyses. It would be far too early to make a statement on this today; rather, more comprehensive, comparative investigations will be necessary, and in our area they are especially difficult.

CHAPTER 6

The Analytic Ritual

At first it may appear somewhat odd if I speak of an "analytic ritual" where psychoanalysis is accustomed to being satisfied with very simple expressions like "working alliance," "analytic pact," or "ground rules." But I believe that in analytical psychology it is necessary to call to mind the background of the psyche and the archetypal substance of even the more simple methodological measures that play a role and are regularly employed in every analysis. I intend to elucidate the problems involved in detail, but first I want to make clear which agreements in analysis are, or should be, made explicitly or tacitly. Here I am concerned with a number of hints, suggestions, instructions or agreements that in part exert a considerable influence on the course of the analysis and on the individuation process, and by no means form only an external frame. I have already discussed a portion of my pact in the chapters devoted to frequency of sessions, payment, and the use of chair or couch. Besides the points already discussed in detail, there are a number of additional measures that are summarized under the psychoanalytic label of the "working alliance" and which are imparted to the patient at the beginning of treatment. Here we are concerned with the following areas:

First, the length of the session is stated (which must be at least fifty minutes in length according to West German state health insurance regulations).

Second, the patient is introduced to the method of free association, i.e., given the explanation that he or she should relax into a state of drowsy, free-floating attention and verbalize all thoughts and feelings that arise during the hour. Here the emphasis is placed on the word *all*, and the patient is instructed not to leave out anything, be it something seemingly nonessential, something very painful and unpleasant, something relating to the analysis or to the person of the analyst, or whatever.

Third, the patient is instructed that dreams are important in analysis and is requested to pay attention to his or her dreams and to tell them during analytic hours.

Fourth, the patient is told not to make vital decisions during the course of analysis if possible, e.g., marriages, divorces, career changes, etc. In case such decisions are absolutely necessary, they are to be discussed with the analyst and made by mutual agreement.

Fifth, the analyst and the patient reach an agreement about vacations so that, as a rule, their vacations coincide.

A detailed psychoanalytic description of this pact and of the ground rules including the previously mentioned problems concerning finances, couch and chair, etc., can be found in Schultz-Hencke's textbook of analytic psychotherapy (Schultz-Hencke 1970). It seems worth mentioning that many of my orthodox Freudian colleagues prefer to begin therapy in an open manner such as most analytical psychologists do, and that to a great extent it is the neo-Freudians who teach and employ these kinds of contracts and instruction in the ground rules. There is also a whole range of rationally cogent reasons why it makes sense to give this sort of "instruction" concerning the method of treatment and the formalities of therapy right at the beginning in order to make clear what is expected of the patient.

But regardless how diverse the national groups may be, it is not, so far as I know, common practice in analytical psychology to make this sort of contract or agreement with the patient in regard to the ground rules at or prior to the beginning of therapy although we also must come to certain agreements with the patient. As I mentioned earlier, I prefer a completely "open" beginning in that I initially assume that, given the contemporary state of general knowledge, the patient who enters analysis has at least some notion of analysis gleaned from the popular press. It seems to me completely senseless during the first hour or hours to impose a multitude of rules of behavior on a patient for the purpose of making a so-called pact or contract. The patient is already suffering under the extraordinarily high stress of a neurotic ailment and approaches the analyst with the usual projective anxieties; he or she is still a long way from being able to accept such rules, let alone understand the dynamics underlying them. Nevertheless we are constrained to enter into certain agreements with the patient and consequently it is wise to discuss the individual points mentioned here from the viewpoint of analytical psychology.

Concerning the length of sessions, it is, I believe, a common analytic standard internationally that the individual analyst sets the length of the session at something between forty-five and sixty minutes; the usual time lies between forty-five and fifty minutes. This follows from purely practical considerations since it is not advisable to let patients come immediately one after another, but rather to make a brief pause of ten to fifteen minutes for reflection between sessions. Since many analysts do not take notes during sessions, but jot down cue words immediately afterward (which is highly recommended) in order not to lose sight of the interconnections between individual sessions, a short break between patients also serves this purpose.

In practice, unfortunately, things always look somewhat different than in theory, however beautiful that may be, and due to the press of patients, many analysts frequently find themselves in a situation where analysands must be scheduled one after another and one is forced to note down cue words during the session. This does not change my fundamental belief that it is better to have a break of at least ten minutes between individual patients. On the one hand this is necessary in order to let one's feelings about the preceding session ebb, and on the other hand to let one prepare oneself for and attune to the next person. In any case, the beginning analyst should seriously consider this sort of break or pause. To the extent that one does not intend to treat patients in a technologized, analytically mechanical manner using one's persona but rather gets emotionally involved in the treatment process to a greater extent — as is necessary in a real analysis — one simply cannot survive without these sorts of breaks. Under the best of conditions it is difficult to shift rapidly from person to person and problem to problem in the course of a day. This sort of shifting of one's attention is something that can be learned only gradually in the course of many years, and I believe that an analyst needs quite a number of years of experience in order to become intrapsychically able to let go of the previous patient completely and relatively quickly and shift over to the next patient who is just arriving.

As I have frequently found when supervising analyses, the beginning analyst is often faced with the problem of not concluding sessions punctually which, of course, is a temptation when there are longer times between two sessions. Many patients have the tendency, for the most varied underlying reasons, to prolong their sessions. Often it takes a considerable measure of firmness and energy on the part of the analyst to conclude a session punctually. Of course, a punctual conclusion does not mean that one drops one's trowel like a mason when the whistle blows. But shortly before the end of the hour one should pay attention that the patient does not launch into a discussion of big problems or reports that demand considerable time, or, alternatively, one calls the patient's attention to the fact that soon the time will be gone and that only a few minutes are left. Vice versa it is better to stop two or three minutes early than to sit out the full fifty minutes at all costs.

Not at all infrequently the problem arises that the patient desires "double sessions." Generally I have not had very good experiences with double sessions; rather, I have found that lengthening the session benefits only the defenses, even in the case of relatively severely inhibited patients who are hard put to say anything during the hour. In the instance of these patients, lengthening the session usually only contributes to prolonging the healing process. An example of this would be a patient with a very severe speech impediment whom I treated. His speech impediment was so severe that during the initial treatment hours he was, as a rule, able to utter only some three to ten sentences, and that haltingly and with decided effort. It gradually came to light that this patient had an overprotective father who had relieved him of all those tasks where he had to speak. After he had left the parental home, his wife had assumed this role. His wife or his father had taken over even purchasing movie or theater tickets. Had I agreed to this patient's wish to lengthen the treatment session, I would without fail have fallen into the role of the father who continued to infantilize his son or to keep him entrapped in his inabilities. Only by strictly insisting on the usual session length and accepting that initially there would be many sessions that were verbally rather unproductive did I succeed in bringing the patient to the point that he could pull his efforts together in the analytic hour and relatively quickly improve his oral expression enough that sufficient verbal material came out in session. By treating the patient just like I treat every other patient, he escaped his special role in which he had felt like a Jew during the Nazi era (Dieckmann 1961).

Another case that I have discussed in detail elsewhere (Dieckmann 1967a) was that of a woman patient with a severe abasia. This patient's symptoms were so severe that she needed a relatively long time to climb the short stairway that led from my waiting room to my consultation room and was not able at some sessions at the beginning of therapy to handle the climb. Consequently at the beginning of her treatment I decided to extend her sessions into my breaks between patients since now and then only fifteen or twenty minutes remained after she had labored to climb the stairs. In addition to this, I held a number of sessions with her downstairs in my waiting room. My "meeting her symptoms halfway" proved to be very deleterious, for the patient reacted with a worsening of her symptoms. Her difficulties walking worsened rather than improved and moreover, now shifted to include her trip to my office so that it got later and later before she arrived, although she had regularly taken a taxi. Consequently I decided to discuss this problem with her and to point out to her that for therapeutic reasons we could make no more concessions to her symptoms.

After we had consistently held to our sessions so that therapy began only in my consultation room and the temporal limitation of fifty minutes was maintained regardless how late she came, her symptoms gradually began to abate and after about forty sessions she had improved to the point where she was able to make good use of practically the full allotted time. Of course, this had something to do not only with external measures but was associated with her becoming conscious of the problems that had led to her symptoms. But the consistent stance of not yielding to the symptoms did play an essential role. From the length of time it took her to climb the stairs from the waiting room to the consultation room one could almost measure how much resistance was present in the current phase of her treatment. When she finally became conscious that she could express protests and resistances in a form other than by using her symptoms to shorten her therapy sessions, the problem vanished completely.

A further practical problem relating to treatment time is that of the patient's frequent late arrival. Here we must distinguish between: 1) lateness as a symptom that is generally characteristic of the patient who inclines to be late not only for analytic sessions but for all other engagements, even if these are important and lateness is damaging; 2) whether we are dealing with a phenomenon that relates only to a particular phase of the analysis (which occurs quite infrequently); or 3) whether it is a question of being late only occasionally. An extraordinary variety of motivations may underlie each of these three possibilities and we do not have space here to discuss them in detail. In general, however, we can say something about them.

For the first group of patients for whom tardiness is a basic problem I think it is wrong to analyze this symptom immediately and prematurely and to insist that the patient come punctually for treatment. The latter approach has no effect whatsoever since basically such an insistence demands that the patients give up their symptoms which they simply cannot do. It wouldn't occur to anybody treating a patient with a duodenal ulcer to prescribe that from now on he or she should feel no pain. Usually it is best not to address the symptom directly but rather simply to accept the tardiness and consistently analyze the unconscious material just as in every other analysis. When the patient begins to come more punctually or sometimes possibly to relinquish being tardy altogether, one can include that in the analysis and point out that he or she obviously is capable of dealing with symptoms better. On the one hand, this avoids the situation in which, due to the symptoms, the patient feels additionally guilty vis-à-vis the analyst when the analyst reacts differently than do other significant persons who usually react to tardiness with at least underlying aggression. On the other hand, this approach makes it clear to the patient that the analyst is concerned with his or her symptoms and is trying to help gradually diminish them.

The second category having to do with tardiness related exclusively to the analysis should be handled as is any other form of acting-out resistance. Dealing with this problem falls essentially into the area of timing interpretations which I will discuss in the chapter on interpretation. Here also it is not advisable to bring this to the patient's attention too quickly; rather, the analyst should first have a clear understanding of the unconscious problems concealed behind the patient's lateness. Only when the problem is relatively close to the patient's consciousness can one address it.

In regard to the third category — the patient's occasional lateness — I do not consider it useful to treat every single instance of late arrival immediately and analytically and to attempt to get to the corresponding unconscious motive. Lateness to appointments, moreover, is part of normal human behavior, and vice versa; it can also be the case that when a patient begins occasionally to arrive late — as in the instance of a compulsive neurotic who throughout a long analysis has punctually rung the doorbell at the stroke of the hour — it signifies a relaxation of symptoms and is basically a sign of the process of healing and not a form of aggression masochistically directed against his or her own ego or an expression of oral inhibition. Only when a patient is frequently late does it make sense to call attention to the problem in the analytic hour. The problem usually clears up of its own accord when a stage of intensive and interesting collaboration on the patient's unconscious material arrives, as do other symptoms also. What I consider important is simply that the analyst not compensate for the patient's lateness even if it were possible to do so.

Of course, arriving late can grow to considerable proportions, especially in the first category. This often happens when the patient does not have to pay for the treatment himself but has insurance that pays, or when the patient is a housewife or a juvenile whose therapy is paid for by the husband or the parents. The most extreme case of this sort I ever experienced was that of a severely schizoid, neurotic woman patient who, among other problems, was also partially addicted to marijuana and who had a number of degenerative conditions. Since patients of this sort are especially sensitive to pressures exerted by persons in positions of authority and since she had already made several unsuccessful attempts at therapy, I resolved in her case — and her problem of lateness was so severe that sometimes only five or ten minutes of her session remained before she arrived — to put up with it for six months although her treatment was covered by a third party. In and of itself this is certainly not permissible, for neither policy holders or the general public pay the relatively high treatment costs for individuals so that they can arbitrarily squander treatment hours and not respect the appointments available to them. But in this exceptional instance that was the only choice because only by letting this extremely mistrustful and extraordinarily anxious patient have her way was it possible to create the conditions under which a transference could develop that contained a certain minimum of trust. Only when a degree of trust had developed did I reach an agreement with her that she herself would have to assume the costs of the therapy hour if more than half her session, i.e., more than twenty-five minutes, had passed before she arrived; if she was less than twenty-five minutes late, her sessions would be paid for by third party.

Although this agreement elicited intense affects and discussions from the patient, she was ultimately able to agree to it and to reveal a certain degree of understanding for my countertransference stance which no longer permitted me to countenance the situation. Subsequently the situation evened out. Actually she never exploited the agreement by consciously or unconsciously coming twenty or twenty-five minutes late; rather, for the most part she arrived considerably more punctually, but from time to time permitted herself to relapse into greater tardiness for which she then assumed the responsibility and for which she paid despite her own difficult financial straits.

In conclusion I should perhaps mention that in the "open" beginning to analysis that I prefer, I naturally do not tell the patient anything about the possible length of treatment. From their general store of information, by far the greater number of patients actually have some idea of how long a period of time analytic treatment demands. To the extent that this is not the case, there are a number of patients who notice this without its being explicitly discussed, and another group of patients who ask, which I generally do not consider very relevant analytically. The only important point is that the patient inform him- or herself in some manner concerning the amount of treatment time specifically available; the form in which the individual gains this information can be left completely up to his or her typology.

The second point to be discussed here relates to information concerning the analytically optimal behavior of the patient and the manner of verbalization. First of all, we should be clear about the fundamental issues involved. In the instance of every patient who consults us because of a psychic ailment, healthy communication between ego and Self along the ego-self axis is disturbed. Hence there also exists a disturbance in the patient's relationship to his or her own unconscious that finds expression outwardly in the multiplicity of disturbed subject-object relationships. Creating a healthy relationship between ego and Self, the optimal exchange of contents along the ego-Self axis and the creation of a threshold of consciousness that, to be sure, is permeable to unconscious contents, but that also protects the ego from inundation by the unconscious, is the therapeutic goal and consequently the precondition necessary if the process of individuation is to continue undisturbed without the help of ist. Hence a fundamental problem that runs throughout the se of therapy is that of enabling the patient to let unconscious contents arise during the therapy hour in an experiential fashion and to impart them with the appropriate emotional cathexis or to let the analyst also experience them. The most important precondition for this is the gradual development of a genuine relationship of trust between doctor and patient in the analytic relationship, a relationship of trust that enables the patient to share things that he or she would not say to any other person. Here one must not let oneself be deceived by a naive blind faith that tends to obscure certain other important areas; rather, it is a question of a genuine, deep, and real human trust between both persons that is, as we know, a plant that grows extraordinarily slowly. Thus one can actually never expect that patients will tell everything about themselves; rather, the ability to be really open is something that is attained only very gradually in the course of the treatment. Trust and openness of this sort cannot be created by technical artifices. I believe Freud was also aware that, especially at the beginning of analysis, it was futile to demand that the patient say absolutely everything, hold back nothing, and consistently produce free associations during the session. This procedure harbors two great dangers: first, it aids repression of inner events that call forth truly emotionally moving processes and processes of change where there does not yet exist a real relationship and condition of trust. It is precisely these decisive inner realms that do not enter the patient's mind during the session; for months or years they are consistently excluded from the analysis, and one can have the experience that they can be included only much later and with considerable feelings of guilt. Second, this approach encourages a split between verbal contents and the emotions as one sees most clearly in compulsively neurotic patients. In certain cases the patient says the most difficult, painful, and unpleasant things with ease, but the affect that belongs with them remains unconscious and usually cannot be brought to consciousness through interpretations that point out the absence of emotion. Admittedly, these patients do not hold anything back verbally, but nothing happens either, and the analysis remains experientially poor. It is limited at best to rational corrections of behavior that can, indeed, be very practical and also alleviate suffering, but ultimately do not remove the deeper cause of suffering nor consequently the lack of a sense of the meaningfulness of life.

Consequently, in accordance with the spirit of analytical psychology and of the individuation process, I prefer neither to give instructions of this sort nor to make demands. I content myself with what the patient spontaneously and voluntarily brings into analysis. It seems to me important that I, as analyst, take pains to create gradually an atmosphere between myself and the patient in which the latter has ever greater success in letting the unconscious also speak and, through appropriate interpretations of what transpires experientially between the patient and myself, to mediate to him or her the insight that it is most favorable to our analytic work if he or she can include and talk about everything that really concerns and moves him or her. There is hardly a patient who can fall into his or her unconscious and truly let unconscious contents emerge into consciousness at the beginning of analysis and often far into its course. For the modern person of our contemporary culture the overemphasis on consciousness is so strong that at best he or she experiences the unconscious as invasions or inundations. Everybody who comes for treatment must gradually learn how to look inward truly and to perceive what inner experiences are transpiring within. A chain of associations that derives almost always from the contents of consciousness is pretty much worthless for analysis. As an example of this far from unusual situation, consider the following.

At the beginning of analysis patients often report external events that have transpired between their analytic hours, events that are of little analytic relevance. If after a time one suggests to them that they look within and share what is happening there, one often gets the answer that they cannot discover anything or that it is a void. In my opinion it is wrong to explain to patients that a void of that sort does not exist but that a continual stream of thoughts and feelings is always flowing. It is extraordinarily difficult to learn to stop this flow even briefly; for example, it takes a yogi in India long practice in meditation to do so. The compliant patient will respond to such an explanation with additional, minimally relevant thoughts from consciousness; the less compliant will insist that such a void does indeed exist within. Hence it seems more appropriate to accept the void or the inner emptiness that exists, resting on the consolidation and rigidity of the patient's threshold of consciousness, and then to suggest that he or she fall into this void, or emptiness, and calmly wait and see whether something does arise after all. As a rule something does emerge to the extent that any disturbance in the capacity to surrender is not too great at that time.

Sometimes, of course, I make use of the method of free association, and I believe there are no analytical psychologists who do not do so and who restrict themselves solely to the method of amplification. The use of free associations does not, of course, mean that one lets them run on throughout the entire session; rather, the use of free association at certain points gives some hints or clues concerning unconscious material which, in turn, one can elaborate through amplification. Details on this, however, belong in the chapter on amplification and association.

The third point concerns the importance of bringing dreams into the analysis. Since working with dream material is methodologically of the first order of importance in analytical psychology, it is obvious that at the beginning of analysis one make clear to the patient in some form that the inclusion of dreams is extremely important. The form in which this information is given, however, varies from analyst to analyst as a function of personal style. There exists a very wide latitude of individual variation extending from the analyst's remark that the patient might bring along dreams, to instructing him or her to take note of them as regularly as possible, write them down, and discuss them, and how one best goes about all this. As a rule at the beginning of treatment, I wait to see whether the patient spontaneously brings in dreams. If after a few sessions the patient has brought no dreams and there are no acute, burning, and turbulent problems that absolutely must be dealt with in detail, I first mention to the patient that I am surprised that he or she has shared no dreams although he or she must know that dream work plays a relatively large role in analysis. Such an intervention is seldom necessary, for usually patients spontaneously bring in dreams from the first hour on, and bringing no dreams has definite, analytically important underlying causes that appear in this manner right at the beginning of treatment. In regard to the patient who maintains that he or she does not dream, we are now fortunately in a position, thanks to the extensive dream research of recent years conducted in sleep laboratories, to say with certainty that every person has three to four dream phases each night and that there must be specific unconscious reasons why the patient in question does not recall dreams. These unconscious causes must then be made the object of analysis. In two of my books (Dieckmann 1972b, 1978a) I have described in detail the methods by which one approaches dreams and how one can learn to retain dreams as fully as possible as well as how dreams are to be dealt with in the analytic process.

The fourth point to be considered is the issue of vital decisions in the patient's life. I think it is absurd and contrary to the concept of therapy to expect a patient to make no vital decisions during the entire course of his or her analytic therapy. On the contrary, as well as indicating a therapeutic success, it can, for example, be a necessary and vitally important step for a patient who has severe narcissistic wounding in the area of relationship if, in the course of analysis, he or she becomes able to form a solid attachment to a partner and perhaps also to marry. On the other hand, therapy should make it possible for a person who, to his or her own detriment and to that of the partner, clings to an intolerable relationship merely out of a sense of duty to liberate himself or herself. Of course, the same holds true for all other important areas of life, such as professional changes, pregnancies, the accumulation or the loss of wealth, construction or purchase of a house, etc. The sense and the goal of every analysis is that of enabling a person to make decisions and to assume responsibility for those decisions and for shaping his or her own life. If, due to over-cautiousness and excessive solicitude or even to a belief that they are better informed, analysts prevent this from transpiring, they infantilize the patient and only support the life-avoiding defensive organization of the neurosis behind which the patient, fearful of making decisions and of assuming responsibility, only all too gladly hides.

On the other hand the problem also lies in protecting the patient from the seriously fixating consequences that arise and that later impede the progress of the analysis and the possibility of free development of individuation through what Greenson (1967) calls acting out outside the analysis. As long as it is only a matter of acting out a part of the transference in an existing relationship that can again be dissolved, as in the example Greenson cites, this is not a great problem; rather, such behavior can be extremely fruitful analytically. It becomes more difficult if, due to anxiety about the libidinal transference, the patient forms a new, serious relationship with a partner—maybe even including marriage—right at the beginning of analysis, or, in the instance of a possibly still intact marriage, the patient transfers the positive libidinal components to the analyst and projects the negative transference on the spouse and then decides hastily and without reflection for a divorce that would not be necessary. The same thing happens when, for example, the inner child constellated by analysis is not recognized as the patient's own possibility of inner development but rather is acted out in the form of a real child. For example, only by repeated interpretation of her preoccupation with another child was it possible to keep a 32-year-old woman patient, who already had two children and was living in a very problematic marriage, from giving birth to the "analytic child" as a flesh-and-blood baby which, in her case, would have entirely overburdened her. Often with a woman around age 30 it is a very difficult and laborious analytic undertaking to discern and differentiate between her fears of a real pregnancy and her rightful wish to have a child, versus the extent to which her fantasies signify the inner analytic child that must not be confused with an external child. If the woman brings this into analysis as a conscious problem, it can be dealt with as such, and the differentiation mentioned can succeed while a hasty acting out outside of analysis can have unfavorable effects on the individuation process. When the patient has a corresponding "hook" in fantasies or in the actual living situation in regard to all these problems, it is important to recommend that the patient bring all these important decisions into analysis and to make the decisions after they have been discussed and analyzed in detail. But this recommendation, in my opinion, should not be a dictate, and above all the analyst should not chalk it up as a breach of trust if the patient does not follow it. Many persons commit arbitrary or reckless acts out of fear of authority and gradually must learn to assume responsibility for the consequences of their acts as well as for the negative consequences these acts might have on the analysis. Their problems are certainly not alleviated if the analyst reinforces the authoritarian stance of collective consciousness and of the superego.

Last, we should say a few words about vacation arrangements. I do not consider it a good practice to force patients unconditionally to take their vacations at the same time as the analyst nor to charge them in full for missed hours outside of the analyst's vacation. In my opinion every therapist in private practice can arrange his or her schedule so that financial difficulties affecting survival do not arise if now and then one patient or another takes a vacation. On the other hand, every analyst will have to work out suitable individual arrangements if patients have the inclination to use their vacation as a resistance and interrupt the analytic process too often. One must discuss with teachers, students, and other persons in similar professions that a consistent analysis is not possible if they are always on vacations that interrupt their analyses. Corresponding to individual style, every analyst has to find a particular arrangement extending from an agreement not to interrupt the analysis for longer than two weeks (except for the analyst's vacation) to a form that I prefer, namely taking the problem of the patient's frequent trips and interruptions as an analytic issue as soon as it arises. Of course, I also treat as the same sort of analytic problem the case where a patient regularly plans a vacation year after year too compulsively and consistently and always only at precisely the same time I am also away.

From all that has been said it follows that every analysis has need of the gradual construction of a system of relatively firm agreements. Only this system of agreements makes possible the fruitful work between patient and analyst in the analytic situation. In Freudian psychoanalysis it is called the working alliance (Greenson 1967), the "pact" (Schultz-Hencke 1970), or the therapeutic alliance (Zetzel 1956), the rational transference (Fenichel 1941), or the mature transference (Stone 1961). All of these concepts proceed from the condition in which, as Greenson (1967) puts it, the working alliance is a relatively rational, desexualized transference phenomenon freed of aggressions. This presupposes that the patient has the capacity to regress "to the more primitive and irrational transference reactions" but also is again and again capable of reestablishing the secondary process and maintaining a "rational" or "reasonable" objection relationship with the analyst. Consequently patients whose ego-functions are largely lacking or severely damaged need modifications in technique to the extent that the working alliance cannot be established with them initially.

We are now living in a time in which our rational consciousness is largely split off from the irrational and archaic background of psychic processes and from the unconscious as a consequence of the course of the evolutionary development of consciousness. Much that we regard as very rational and "reasonable" is fundamentally, as psychoanalysis has discovered, a rationalization that has arisen over unconscious anxieties and conflicts. Even analysis should examine itself again and again to discover how much of what seems rationally sensible rests fundamentally on deeper, irrational foundations and is perhaps created by these foundations relatively sensibly. It is to C. G. Jung's merit to have pointed out the importance of this irrational psychic background and its extremely wide-ranging effects on our rational consciousness, but at the same time to have drawn attention to the fundamental archetypal structures and patterns of order in the human unconscious that assert their rights when we take this background into account in a meaningfully "religious" way and which can be integrated, thereby granting life a more open, more natural arena than does the personalistic compliance with so-called rationality that has been learned.

Now we must pose a question from our viewpoint: Why does the analytic process have need of a specific system of agreements, and what might the deeper reasons be that make this sort of structure or order necessary? Here we are asking after the archetypal background of those things that are rationally subsumed under the concept of the working alliance or some such similar term. Let us attempt to visualize what happens in every analysis that penetrates to any depth, that does not run its course only via the rational and reasonable persona but in which both persons, the analyst and the patient, participate as complete personalities including their anima (their souls). Here two persons risk entering into a very deep, mutual inner relationship, a relationship that very often leads to the very last unconscious depths of one's personality and in which, as in every deep relationship of love or friendship, archetypal images of momentous emotional attraction are constellated from the collective unconscious. Here we encounter our own inner "gods," that is, those images that accompany the inner drive and instinctual powers and dynamisms that are more potent than consciousness and which were projected in mythologies and populate the heavens. Meeting these forces and powers has been, as humankind has known since time immemorial, a great and sometimes life-endangering risk. One of the most impressive mythologems illustrating this is that of the birth of Dionysus. As Kerènyi reports,

It was told that when Zeus came to Semele, this was not a divine mating. He had prepared a potion from the heart of Dionysos [the so-called "first" Dionysos], and this he gave to Semele to drink. The potion made the girl pregnant. When Hera learnt of this, she tried to prevent the birth. She disguised herself as Semele's nurse, and persuaded the unsuspecting girl to make a wish that Zeus should come to her in the same shape as that in which he came to Hera, so that Semele, too, might learn what it is like to be embraced by a god. . . . Led astray by her pretended nurse, Semele asked Zeus to grant her just one wish. Zeus promised to do so, and when his beloved wished that he would appear to her as he did to Hera, he visited her with his lightning. Vase-paintings show how she sought to flee from it. It was too late: the lightning struck her, and she descended into the Under-world. Zeus rescued from her body the unripe fruit, the child Diony-sos. (1951, p. 257)

There are numerous parallel mythologems which describe the danger to mortals of directly seeing the gods and of the possibilities of protection from being destroyed by that primordial psychic experience. Thus Jehova appears to Moses behind a burning bush or a cloud; Perseus looks in a mirror when he strikes the head from the Medusa; or the Image at Sais may not be contemplated unveiled. On the other hand the central element in all religions has always been that of placing human-kind in relationship with the gods and leading mortals to the primordial, transformative religious experience. As Erich Neumann (1953a, 1974) has discussed, the living ritual has offered the possibility of leading mortals to the primordial experience and simultaneously of providing them protection from being overwhelmed from the earliest times up until the present. In the earlier chapter on frequency of sessions I referred to this effect of ritual, albeit emphasizing its rhythmic components. Ritual commences in primordial times with the laborious and often dangerous passage through the labyrinth that ended in the subterranean cave with the divine images and symbols and extends to the rite of the Christian mass in which, as Jung described it (C.W. 11), transformation is sup-posed to take place through encounter, ingestion, and identification with the god. But wherever a living myth decays, ritual also degenerates. As Neumann in particular points out (1953a, 1974), two groups arise in this situation. One becomes self-absorbed in the protective function of ritual in a rigid, compulsively rational form and erects severe systems of order against which—as in genuine ritual—one must not sin on pain of expul-sion or of death, i.e., dogma arises such as we find unfortunately all too often in our analytic endeavors. The other group goes about seeking the immediate primordial experience without any ritual protection, frequently with the help of drugs and other highly dubious practices. Between these two extremes, however, individual rituals arise which possess far less of the magnificence, the imprint, and the accoutrements of the great collective religious rituals but rather, vis-à-vis the latter, produce a rather impoverished effect. We find these kinds of individual rituals today in the creative process, in emotional illnesses, and in the individuation process. On the basis of two case presentations, I have described (Dieckmann 1963) how the forces of creativity manifest in treatment when protected by individually developed rituals that correspond to collective rites found at primitive-archaic levels of consciousness. The appearance of such individually developed rituals in analysis can also often provide important methodological hints as to the form in which analyst and patient can approach decisive, transformative experiences. But here it is less a question of examining those sorts of individual rituals and their methodological applicability than of our gaining a clearer understanding that basically it is those very experiences which we subsume under such designations as working alliance, ground rules, or analytic setting. These have their archetypal roots in the formation of an individual ritual which, in a living and constructive form, lead both participants, analyst and patient, to the collective unconscious as well as protect both from inundation and the destructive inflation by the archetype.

It seems of the greatest importance and methodological necessity for every analytical psychologist to be acutely aware of his deep foundation. Consciousness of this foundation and awareness of the necessity of finding an "individual ritual" are needed if the individuation process is to become a real possibility and if one is to approach the archetypal imagos; moreover, the individual ritual also provides adequate protection, allowing both to undertake the dangerous descent into the unconscious and to reemerge intact following the night-sea journey. The entire system of arrangements and agreements that we must make with the patient rest on this foundation and have this as their true significance, and they should be formulated only in terms of these two facts or necessities. Thus the individual agreements and the "when, how, and where" of their observance do not ultimately rest with the creativity of the analyst's consciousness but rather with the creativity of the commonly shared unconscious process of imparting meaningful and goal-directed order. True, forsaking those paths that previous authorities have trodden and found passable is always a risky undertaking; but on the other hand, as Leonardo da Vinci once so beautifully put it, he who follows only the authorities is working only with his memory, i.e., with his persona and not with his common sense, or as we would add, with his anima. Ultimately the manner and the form in which the analyst arrives at a system of agreements with the patient must be left up to every individual analyst. But the analyst must be well aware of the fact that individuation is simply not possible without a ritual, an individual ritual that manifests on the rational surface as agreements that are kept by both parties. From what has been said it now follows that the ritual gradually arises in the initial phase of treatment. Hence it is something fundamentally different from a goal-directed "working alliance" that the analyst has drafted and that is ratified during the initial sessions.

CHAPTER 7

Methods of Working with Various Age Groups

Psychoanalysis has worked out a developmental theory extending from the early phase up to the sixth year of life, i.e., up to the onset of the latency period, to which all the later disturbances that arise in the course of human life are referenced. There are only a few authors — preeminently Erikson (1970) with his concept of identity — who have attempted to extend this model and carry it into the middle of life. Moreover, these attempts within psychoanalysis itself have been hotly contested and, for example, a concept like that of finding one's identity surely does not suffice to describe the differentiated experiences of transformation described in the "stages of life." The difficulty that arises again and again when we leave the primary foundations of the initial process of civilizing the human being in the early years of life is the appearance of the dialectical process between human being as a creature and the historically given transformations and civilizing processes. If we proceed only from biology, we can, as did Jung in his essay, "The Stages of Life" (*C.W.* 8), take the metaphor of the course of the sun and speak of human life as having a beginning with a course that gradually ascends until it reaches its greatest degree of completion at the midpoint, then commencing the descent, and finally, at the end, being swallowed up in death. All the tripartite or quadripartite divisions into childhood, adolescence, mid-life and old age, dying, and death that are still made by primal peoples correspond to this model. But from the viewpoint of the psyche, the human cannot be regarded only as an *anima naturalis*; rather, humankind is simultaneously, as the alchemists expressed it, an *opus contra naturam*. As such, humankind, not only as a group or a nation but also as an individual, is perpetually exposed to a continually changing civilizing process that is capable of superimposing itself upon the given natural conditions of the biological course of life or of estranging the individual from them. Perhaps especially during the last century and in our times, the developmental processes of social structures and consequently the dominants of collective consciousness have been sub-ject to particularly drastic changes which — if we understand the psyche as a self-regulating system — have, in turn, exerted a reciprocal effect on the unconscious and hence on the archetypal imagos. This comes out especially in the dreams of modern persons in whom the archetype of the machine (Kadinsky 1969) occupies a much more central position than in the dreams and fantasies of earlier generations, and with this, our mod-ern technical symbols such as the automobile acquire archetypal aspects (Dieckmann 1976b).

The developments and transformations in the civilizing process involve our evolution of very different forms of control over affects and emotions and, contrasted to earlier times, entail our having different ways of dealing with affects and emotions, ways that can change consid-erably within a single generation. A characteristic example of this are the various modes of child rearing that society has advocated. Whereas up until the end of World War II, severity and discipline stood in the fore-ground and were supposed to turn the natural child into the most civi-lized and diligent person possible, what followed was a liberalizing pro-cess which now demanded that parents suddenly develop quite different forms of control and ways of dealing with their own affects and emotion-ality in order not to disturb or hinder the "child's natural developmental process." Associated with this was the hope of achieving greater freedom for the individual and a higher level of creativity which, unfortunately, has by no means been the result. In recent times, by contrast, the idea that imposing frustrations and limitations on the child's world of wishes and needs is necessary in the civilizing process has gained ever wider acceptance and this again demands a rearrangement in the parents' emo-tional and affectual economy. Where previously a loving permissiveness was possible, the ability to say no must now be learned; and where earlier ideology advocated that the mother inhibit her aggression vis-à-vis her child up to the point of self-sacrifice, it is now again permissable for parents to defend themselves vis-à-vis their children.

Elias (1969), who has investigated the development of social structures in our culture, distinguishes a whole series of possible structural changes within a society. First, he describes two primary directions of structural change in society: a structural change in the direction of increasing dif-ferentiation and integration, and a structural change in the direction of decreasing differentiation and integration. Continuing, he states:

Above and beyond this there are, as a third type, social processes the course of which indeed alters the structure of a society or its individual aspects, but neither in the direction of a higher nor of a lower standard of differentiation and integration. Ultimately there are countless changes in societies without corresponding alterations of their structures. Granted, this falls short of doing justice to the rich complexity of such changes, for there are many sorts of mixed types, and often enough one can observe several types of change, even changes in opposing directions, in the same society at the same time. (Elias 1969, p. viii)

As Elias emphasizes, these processes of change take place not only within social structures but also within individual persons, for ultimately every society is made up of individuals who communicate with one another. If we want to do justice to the dialectical process between nature and civilization, we must let the socializing-civilizing processes of change and the biological model of stages of life overlap in order to arrive at a meaningful psychology of the various stages of life.

In doing this we must keep in mind that the individual phases of life with their continually changing tasks for the individual cannot be related only to early childhood in a reductively psychogenetic manner and that the ability to effect specific transformations is not simply dependent on disturbances that arose during the early childhood phase. Each of these phases demands the acquisition of genuinely new features and also, in part, quite far-reaching transformations within the structure of the psyche. Wilhelm Busch composed the verse "*Vater werden ist nicht schwer, Vater sein dagegen sehr,*" which rendered into English goes something to the effect "Becoming a father is no work, but being a father many shirk." This means that being the mother or father of a child calls for a considerable reorientation that cannot be borne only by the early identification with the personal parents or caretaking persons; rather, social processes of development must be given their due and, in order for civilization not to stagnate, one must again and again resort to archetypal material that offers the elements that compensate the momentarily existing dominants of consciousness. In this, the transition from being a youth to an adult who rears one's own children is after all not the only liminal situation in the course of human life, and just as crises appear here that demand the acquisition of new psychic resources, so do the crises of midlife, the process of aging, and finally the transition to death.

Of course, it is not the task of a book on analytic methods to elaborate a theory of development that does not yet exist. Granted, such a theory of development is implicit in the concept of individuation, about which I will have more to say later, but it has not yet been worked out in detail for the various liminal situations of life, and, perhaps due to the difficulties of the above-described dialectical processes of nature and civilization that take place in liminal situations, it may be very difficult to describe in terms of specific fundamental concepts. But it is the task of a book on methods to make reference to this problem and to pay attention to and to take seriously the various processes of transformation within analytic therapy. This necessitates a methodological flexibility that demands we treat a twenty-year-old differently than we do a fifty-year-old and that we approach the crisis situations of the various phases of life in different ways. Here we can repeat: Nobody can say what "one" should do nor how, where, and when one should do it; rather, we can discuss the problem in terms of various concepts and examples and then suggest that the analyst's attitude and stance must be flexible and diverse enough to recognize these sorts of differentiated processes and to deal with them accordingly.

The concept of individuation in analytical psychology implicitly includes the perpetual process of change and transformation from the beginning to the end of life. This concept, deriving from biology, carries a rather strong if not exclusive biological orientation in Jung's writings. In biology the *principium individuationis* designates the diversification of the general into the unique or particular, into individuals. In philosophy, too, Aristotle, Albertus Magnus, St. Thomas Aquinas, Leibnitz, and Spinoza took up the *principium individuationis* and described it as the existential ground of individual beings or particularities.

From the perspective of the deep psychological processes that analytical psychology addresses, individuation is the developmental goal of humankind. Jung defined it explicitly for the first time in 1921 in *Psychological Types* (*C.W.* 6). This concept can be found in essence in Jung's dissertation, "On the Psychology and Pathology of So-Called Occult Phenomena" (*C.W.* 1). Here Jung speaks of "spirits" as an expression of a future, larger personality. The definition of individuation that Jung gave in *Psychological Types* has led to profoundly differing views within analytical psychology, views that, in part, still persist. These differing views of individuation rest fundamentally on the sharp juxtaposition of individuation and collective norms. Hence it seems to me important that first we take a closer look at the definition Jung gave in *Psychological Types*. In one passage he writes:

> The concept of individuation plays a large role in our psychology. In general, it is the process by which individual beings are formed and differentiated; in particular, it is the development of the psychological *individual* as a being distinct from the general, collective psychology. Individuation, therefore, is a process of *differentiation*, having for its goal the development of the individual personality.
>
> Individuation is a natural necessity inasmuch as its prevention by a levelling down to collective standards is injurious to the vital activity of the individual. . . .
>
> Under no circumstances can individuation be the sole aim of psychological education. Before it can be taken as a goal, the educational

aim of adaptation to the necessary minimum of collective norms must first be attained. If a plant is to unfold its specific nature to the full, it must first be able to grow in the soil in which it is planted. (Jung, *C.W.* 6, par. 757ff)

I have cited this text because it contains the two opposites upon which the differing directions in analytical psychology rest. On the one hand, Jung states that individuation can only be undertaken when the initial goal of rearing, that is, adaptation to collective norms, has been achieved. That would signify that individuation can actually occur only after life's midpoint; in only a few special cases can individuation take place at an earlier time. Even in his early work, *The Life of Childhood*, Fordham (1944) wrote that individuation proposed a goal diametrically opposed to that of childhood. The goal of childhood was that of strengthening the will; the goal of individuation appeared when willing has been brought to a halt. Fordham qualified this when he wrote elsewhere that there were certain children who apparently also felt the drive to follow the path of individuation, if not from the beginning then at least from puberty; but they were the unusual exceptions. It is probably due to the influence of Jolanda Jacobi (1965) that the concept of individuation as a treatment goal was freed from its restriction to the second half of life and to a specific group of "elite" introverted personalities, and that this concept, borrowed from biology, was extended in the psychological sense to embrace the entire span of human life.

At this point I would like to consider the other aspect of the quote from Jung's *Psychological Types* invoked by those who advocate individuation as a process that runs throughout the course of life.

Individuation, therefore, is a process of *differentiation*, having for its goal the development of the individual personality. Individuation is a natural necessity inasmuch as its prevention by a levelling down to collective standards is injurious to the vital activity of the individual (Jung, *C.W.* 6, par. 757ff).

I believe it must be generally obvious and clear that, in the psychological sense, this sentence holds true for the child, for the entire process of ego-development, and for the origin of the ego complex. There are other passages in Jung's writings, e.g., in "Answer to Job" (*C.W.* 11), where he emphasizes this even more strongly. In these passages Jung speaks in metaphors of a process that extends practically from birth until mid-life and which commences where consciousness separates from, and comes into conflict with, the unconscious. Here only conscious and unconscious individuation are differentiated from each other. While unconscious individuation comes about as the spontaneous course of development and change in human life, conscious individuation can only take place where a reflective consciousness enters into relationship with the unconscious, and that in the form of an analytic process. Thus conscious individuation serves to deepen and to make conscious a process corresponding to a process in nature.

Following Jung's own interest in the process of individuation that occurs during the second half of life, analytical psychology initially distinguished only two great phases in individuation: that of the first half of life and that of the second. A central feature of this view of individuation was the typological reversal during the midlife crisis. It was thought that the extraversion of the first half of life, which actually is most often found in our culture, shifted to introversion in the second half. Hence Jacobi distinguishes two specific phases of the individuation process, that of the first and that of the second half of life. Her definition reads: "Generally speaking one can say that whereas the first half of life is, in the nature of things, governed and determined by expansion and adaptation to outer reality, the second is governed by restriction or reduction to the essential, by adaptation to the inner reality" (Jacobi 1965, p. 25).

In this statement Jacobi goes far beyond Jung's definition of the concept which opposed individuation to the collective psyche and to the processes of adaptation. Jacobi includes the processes of adaptation of the first half of life in the process of individuation. Jacobi sees the underlying archetypal and mythological images that inform the first phase of individuation in the first half of life (i.e., ego formation) in the creation myths whereas the familiar mythological motif of the night sea journey is supposed to apply to the second phase. Fordham (1969), Neumann (1973), and Edinger (1972) have likewise extended the concept of individuation to include the first half of life, but they also distinguish it from the collective mechanisms of adaptation.

In numerous articles and in his book, *Children as Individuals* (1969, p. 98ff), Fordham developed the notion that the ego develops out of the primary self. Introducing the concept of the self into child psychology signified something of a revolution in the thinking of analytical psychologists since Jung had initially referred the concept of the self to the later phases of life and to religion. In 1947 Fordham began to describe his model. He said that the first or the original self of the infant was uprooted at birth by the advent of completely new stimuli that inundate the psychosomatic unity. This ushers in a labile, "deintegrative stage" of the self accompanied by changes in orientation that initially involve the whole but later only parts of the person. These deintegrates of the self then play an essential role in ego formation, since that of their contents which reach consciousness are annexed by and integrated into the archetypally and structurally inherent ego-germ. Following this a more settled condition appears until the entire process is repeated in the next developmental step.

Fordham calls the underlying forces "deintegrative" and "integrative," and they are repeated during the *entire* process of maturation. Phases in which the one or the other of these processes can be observed are, for example, birth, the phase of breastfeeding and weaning, the changes taking place around the third and seventh months after birth, separation-individuation, the birth of siblings, oedipal developments, and later the vicissitudes of the adolescent phase with the creation of an initially rather stable maturity. According to Fordham, this initial maturity continues in a certain sense until the transition into later life where the series of deintegrations and integrations are repeated in the realm of the individuation process of the second half of life so extensively described by Jung. Thus Fordham extends the developmental and transformational processes beyond adolescence and concedes a relatively stable stage lasting from the end of adolescence until the beginning of midlife.

In contrast to Neumann (1973), who hypostatizes a shared mother-child self for the entire early postnatal phase and thereby explains a series of deep, participatory phenomena, Fordham assumes a separation between the infant self and the maternal self from birth onward. On the basis of more recent investigations by Spitz (1960), Klein (1962), Winnicott (1969), and Piaget (1969), ego formation begins in the first year of life, much earlier than the third or fourth year of life as Neumann had postulated. Without a doubt, analogies with Jung's archetypal theory are to be found in the works of the above-mentioned authors. Thus Spitz uses the notion of "organizers" during early extrauterine existence; the Kleinian school has the concept of unconscious fantasy that is at work from birth onward; and Piaget has put forward the theory of inborn schemata. All in all, these ideas imply a gradual justification of the concept of the archetype that has been sharply attacked from early on.

A similar concept concerning the development of the ego out of the Self, but depending more on Neumann, is that held by Edinger (1972), who speaks of a continual process of "ego-Self separation" and "ego-Self union." He, too, locates this process within the first half of life. In the process of ego-Self separation and ego-Self union, Edinger differentiates four stages beginning with the stage in which the ego-germ is still completely contained in the Self and extending to a stage characterized by the theoretically ideal separation between the newly emerged ego-component that is now linked to the Self only by the ego-Self axis. All states of ego-inflation and ego-separation appear in the course of psychological development throughout life and these four stages are experienced again and again as a cycle. They vary only in their intensity. Like Fordham, who accepts a period extending only from the conclusion of adolescence up to mid-life, this model does not include a so-called latency period, and the processes of ego formation and individuation are understood as a continual, ongoing process.

On the basis of my empirical observations and the experiences of my analytic work, I, too, have come to hold the view that there is neither a fixed latency period nor a definite relative stability referenced to specific years in the course of human life (Dieckmann 1976a). It certainly cannot be denied that both exist; but I am of the opinion that today these periods or phases cannot be assigned with certainty to definite years in the course of life; rather, it is a question of periods that, on the one hand, are determined by the influence of specific environmental stimuli and, on the other hand, by individual genetically given principles of maturation and development. We find analogues of this also in the somatic realm. Even if ten-year-olds have not yet entered puberty, they hardly have the same bodies as do six-year-olds, and the body does not know of any latency period between the end of the sixth year of life and the onset of puberty. Parts of the ego always stand in some relationship with archetypal processes and structures, for example, the larger part of perceptions, fantasy, movement, and the defense mechanisms. These all are basic elements of the personality upon which the ego rests and with which it must be in some continual, vital relationship via the ego-Self axis in the course of healthy development, just as it must be with the social environment and external reality that surround the ego outwardly.

It is superfluous to go into the early developmental phases up to age six that have been extensively researched and described in the psychoanalytic literature. According to all that is known to us today, the fundamental psychological structures are without doubt formed during the first six years of life; but in addition to the necessary adaptive tasks, creative processes of individuation with transformations and changes in the ego-complex extending into its very structure must take place between the seventh year and mid-life and then again from mid-life up until the transition into old age, dying, and death. For modern persons these creative processes of individuation are all the more important since we, in contrast to primal peoples or to early cultures, no longer have at our disposal the *rites de passage* into the various phases of life that, as collective tradition, facilitate the transition from one phase into the next for the individual still largely imbedded in biology. With the loss of the religious dimension that, at least to some degree, preserved a part of such *rites de passage* and that still knew of a certain hierarchy of generations, modern people have been largely thrown back upon their own and individualized. The phases of life with their necessary transformations of the ego-complex and of the changes in the inner attitudinal and experiental world have been obliterated, which has misled many contemporary persons to live "timelessly" and consciously or unconsciously coerced them at least to look young for as long as possible and to appear outwardly effective and perpetually successful.

Here it is necessary to interject a few brief thoughts on the concept of adaptation. Especially in psychoanalytic circles the concept of adaptation is regarded not only as a passive process of the individual's achieving adaptation to the collective and to the external world but rather also as an active process. According to this view, the active side of adaptation rests on the individual exerting an active influence on the collective and on the environment in order to adapt them to one's individual needs and intentions. This more creative aspect of the problem of adaptation — which is also understood as an achievement of the ego — transcends the usual, popular concept of adaptation. To the vernacular notion of adaptation — i.e., "I adapt myself to something" — is added the idea that "I adapt a thing to me by changing it." In my opinion the question now arises whether or not it makes sense scientifically to extend a concept in this form. In order to maintain clear definitions in the relations between subject and object, it can be more meaningful to describe the influences proceeding from subject to object in terms other than those used to designate the influences emanating from object to subject. Moreover, it seems to me that this approach partially blurs and relativizes the concept of adaptation, for the notion of active adaptation describes not only the individual, creative achievements of the individual. Rather, thoroughly collective processes also belong here that have fundamentally nothing to do with the *principium individuationis* and that very clearly have an underlying element of the individual's passive adaptation to the collective. A teacher, for example, who "adapts" a chaotic class to the customary school discipline in order to hold a moderately constructive lesson does indeed perform an act of active adaptation while the pupils in the class must passively adapt. But both teacher and pupils remain within the customary, standardized, collective-norm forms of adaptation, although the means that the teacher employs to achieve this end can display an extraordinarily meager creative component and rest merely on standardized and traditional pedagogic methods. Consequently it seems to me important to distinguish so-called acts of active adaptation from the principle of individuation actually describing the specific development of the individual out of the collective unity.

I would like to offer two examples that illustrate the difference between adaptation and individuation during the first half of life, specifically within the so-called latency phase and at the point of transition into puberty. From a certain point of view, these two phases are precisely identical with specific phases of socialization, namely the first phase extending from primary school age through high school and the second phase beginning with apprenticeship or college age.

The first example is that of a seven-year-old boy in first grade. He was a quite sensitive, very delicate child with lots of fantasy and by no means up to dealing with the law of the strongest which prevails in the primary schools in West Germany and especially in Berlin. As a consequence of his physical inferiority he developed some degree of anxiety. Regular nightmares with a very specific, recurring motif were the primary symptom. The nightmares presented a situation in which the child was alone in a desert and suddenly he saw himself face to face with a lion which he feared would attack and tear him to bits. It is fairly clear that the image of the lion had to arise here. On the one hand, it referred in part to his environment and personified his overpowering schoolmates; on the other hand, in regard to his inner world it represented the pent-up drives of his activity, of his continual fear and humiliation, and the inability to defend himself in this situation. I attempted to continue the dream with him as an active imagination and to look for a solution that gave the ego the possibility of mastering the danger. I asked him whether there was the possibility of dreaming about an effective weapon against the lion, say a gun for defending himself against the dangerous animal. At first the child seemed satisfied with this solution and pondered it for a while. But then he told me that this solution was completely unrealistic. He was much too small to aim and shoot the gun properly. So a gun would not help him with this lion. However, he volunteered that it would make a lot more sense if he dreamed of a hunter who would accompany him into the desert and if necessary could shoot the lion. Would that work? When I told him it would, he went home satisfied and his anxiety dreams ceased. Shortly afterward he succeeded in resolving his school situation in a manner that satisfied him. Since he was able to tell stories very well and interestingly, he began to tell them to the strongest and most rowdy boy in his class who in exchange protected him from the other boys.

The dream of the lion in the desert shows very clearly a certain part of what Edinger describes in his "psychic life cycle" (1972, p. 37ff). Again and again during the process of individuation in the formation of the ego-complex, a condition of "separation" between the ego and the self arises in which the ego sees itself torn away from its inner, stabilizing connection to the core of the personality and helplessly exposed to a hostile and desolate world. A very characteristic archetypal motif for this situation is that of the desert. A biblical amplification of this is the story of Ishmael, the illegitimate son of Abraham and his concubine Hagar. When Isaac, the legitimate son, was born, Ishmael and his mother were banished to the desert. Here the motif of the fatherless, illegitimate child appears who is exposed to the hostile world without protection and aid, which psychologically also fits the school situation. Only after psychologically regaining an archetypal inner father figure, independent of the personal father who in this situation is actually rather helpless and powerless, can a reconnection with the Self and thus also a restoration of the feeling of self-worth come about. Hence the dream contains a solution and the uncoordinated animal drive energies symbolized in the image of the lion remain initially split off and pass over into another figure in the service of the ego-complex. The hunter is also an archetypal figure who understands how to deal with the animal powers of nature and how, by killing and eating wild game, to turn them into introjects for humankind. In this form the hunter also appears in numerous mythological parallels, as, for example, Wotan in Germanic mythology, who had the nickname of "the hunter" and who protected people from the hostile, destructive, chaotic aggressiveness of the giants in humankind's eternal battle with them. With its function of organizing emotional contents, the ego-complex utilizes fantasy to assume the role of the symbolic process first appearing in dreams and fantasies and, like the nimble Däumling in the fairy tale, turns a part of our superior, internal strength into our helper. In this instance it is totally an individual, creative achievement that was tailored to the possibilities of the individual concerned and that one would no longer call a process purely of adaptation.

The second example has to do with the dream of a thirteen-year-old girl, something dreamt at the beginning of adolescence shortly after the first menses. Indeed, her parents had enlightened the girl in the most modern manner, but nevertheless the onset of her first period unsettled her and made her anxious. Shortly afterward she had the following dream: "I have given birth to a child, and the birth was without complications. It was a very small baby, much smaller than babies usually are, and looked strikingly foreign, a little bit Asiatic with large, almond-shaped eyes. Oddly, it was already able to walk and talk and was wonderously beautiful."

After this dream the girl was able to experience her menstruation and the development of her femininity as a natural, joyous process of which she was proud and which no longer frightened her. Clearly visible in this dream, dreamt at an important time of transition—the beginning of puberty—is the motif of the divine child, which Jung and Kerényi (1951; Jung, C.W. 9i) first described in detail and which likewise is a manifestation of the Self archetype. In this instance it symbolizes both the understandable and rationally comprehensible elements of pregnancy and birth as well as the incomprehensible mystery of womanhood and of human fertility in all its strangeness.

One can object here that in this situation it is a question not of something intimately individual but rather of a more collective process of inner adaptation to a collective, physical event. But we should recognize that, according to Jung's explicit description, individuation is by no means identical with a pronounced individualism. Self-realization even stands in direct opposition to what we commonly mean by individualism. The multiplicity of psychological factors in the human being is universal and collective. The individual quality of the personality, by contrast, consists of the particular ratio of components and can vary from person to person.

Since we are regarding individuation as the specific self-realization of the individual out of the collective, and since individuation takes place in connection with the ego's vital experiencing and shaping of the archetypal imagos, we must also ascribe the character of the *principium individuationis* to the process described above and cannot view this entire process only from the angle of the relation of the ego to the environment.

It also seems appropriate to mention an additional group of themes that play an essential role in the first half of life. I am referring to the relationship to and development of the persona. First of all I would like to mention certain features that contain the problem of the persona in relation to the concept of individuation.

According to Jacobi (1971), the healthy persona consists of three factors: the physical and emotional constitution, the ego-ideal (i.e., what one would like to be, how one would like to appear, and the effect one would like to have), and the ideal of the environment by which one would like to be seen and accepted in this or that form. If we ponder these three factors, actually only the third—that of the environment's ideal—is a purely collective defense mechanism such as we customarily understand the persona to be. The factors of both the individual's genetic constitution and the ego-ideal also contain, along with collective givens, pronouncedly individual features. The genetic combinations in the individual are compounded of nothing but collective factors as Jung has described them, yet they lead to a quite specific, individual mix. In many cases the same can hold true for the ego-ideal precisely since it is also composed of factors that arise out of possibilities intimated and sensed in the unconscious of one's own personality. Thus the development of the persona by no means stands only in a relationship of adaptation to the environment; rather, certain parts of it arise from the archetypal substrate of the collective unconscious in one's own psyche. Wickes (*The Inner World of Man*, 1938), who did profound analytic work with children and young people, also referred to this factor. She writes that the persona, which is formed according to a collective norm, can rest either on a collective, social ideal, or on an image from the collective unconscious. When identification with an inner ideal takes place, an archetypal image is probably active in the background.

In a detailed discussion of aspects of the persona, Blomeyer takes a stance opposite that of Jacobi (1971) who situates the development of the persona in puberty and conceptualizes it as an actual adult possession. Blomeyer argues that the persona indeed does experience an additional, developmentally determined degree of emphasis in puberty as in all threshold situations of life, "but that every phase of development has its individually and its collectively differing persona images and the persona is not only an adult affair" (1974, p. 17). According to Blomeyer, the persona and the ego begin to develop with the child's first expressions. The infant already imitates, adopts behaviors, makes identifications, and intermingles with all this its own, "individual" notes. This process goes far beyond a playful imitation. Thus Blomeyer consistently expands the concept of the persona in the direction of describing it as an organ of expression for the entire psyche and says that the persona is more than a mere mask, an official countenance, or an appropriate suit. Rather, as Jung also emphasized, there is something individual in the particular selection and definition of the persona that may not be taken off at will like a mask but has the more individual and organic character of a healthy skin.

If this is as Blomeyer has suggested, we must by all means include the development of the healthy persona in the process of individuation, and in the development of the healthy persona we must differentiate which factors correspond to purely adaptive mechanisms and which to the unique selection that contains something individual, as Jung also defined the persona concept in "The Relations Between the Ego and the Unconscious" (C. W. 7). If we regard our examples in this context, we are fully entitled to say that with and through the processes of individuation that have taken place, a change in the persona of the person concerned has also taken place. I have attempted to emphasize this in the changes in the individual's relationship to the environment. Of course, one could say that in all these examples fundamentally collective elements are contained in the persona and in the modification of the persona. If we take, for example, the case of the seven-year-old, the role of becoming a sort of "ringleader" through exercise of intelligence and wit is a completely collective form of relationship that can be learned externally. But what seems essential to me in this example is that, in the development of this aspect of the persona, a creative, individual accomplishment was involved which, moreover, has its special, individual quality in the form of telling stories in exchange for being protected.

I am treating this topic so extensively here because differentiating it within the methodology of therapy plays an essential role. If one understands these processes in a purely reductive manner—in the first case as, say, the child's fear of the overpowering father or the overwhelming mother—one devalues the outer and the inner real situation as illusionary, childish fears that cannot be of much help to the patient. By contrast, one does the situation greater justice if one conceptualizes this process prospectively in the sense of individuation and understands the fears and anxieties that appear as related to the necessary, new step in development. This enables the ego to master the real external situation constructively by integrating additional but different energies that initially express themselves in a purely destructive and anxiety-provoking manner. Methodologically the possibility of promoting or frustrating the developmental and maturational processes lies not only in the form of a possible interpretation that would have to take a more prospective viewpoint, but also in the analyst's whole stance toward and conceptualization of the situation and in his understanding of the process. The danger is that of leading the child into developing a purely adaptive mechanism in which the only view would be that he simply was smaller, weaker, and more sensitive and would have to take that into consideration and come to terms with the given situation. Let me also point out that the processes described here appear not only in the latency period and in puberty but also extend from puberty up until mid-life. I will discuss these issues separately later and they must be accorded their due. (Here I have omitted discussion of the problem of the development of attitude and function types during the first half of life; methodologically this should also be taken into account, but I will consider it in greater detail in the chapter on typology.)

One of the great crisis situations in the course of human life that we very frequently see in our consultation rooms is the problem of mid-life, its distinct transition into aging, and the descent of the arc of life. Granted, the years between ages 30 and 50 are generally taken to be the most productive and the most creative in the human lifespan; and yet, during those two decades a deep crisis always takes place, sometimes consciously but very often unconsciously, a crisis that today we refer to as the so-called mid-life crisis. During this crisis, neurotic ailments, psychosomatic symptoms, and, in the extreme case, complete psychological collapse frequently appear if the person concerned cannot master the crisis. Very early on Jung described this group of problems, and in 1931 he published his well-known essay, "The Stages of Life" (*C.W.* 8), in which he called for schools for adults that would enable persons to become aware of the unconscious psychodynamic factors involved in the process and better survive the mid-life crisis. Jung proceeded from the premise that, following the midpoint in life, a shift in psychological attitude should take place. The extraversion of the first half of life with its tasks of creating one's life should yield to an introverted attitude which would turn attention to the background of one's own soul and to the archetypal bases of existence. Jung devoted a great part of his opus to the process of individuation during the second half of life, and many of his followers have discussed the individuation processes of the second half of life again and again. Nevertheless, this theme has remained extremely unpopular up until very recent times. Only lately has it returned to Europe with the label "mid-life crisis" via a detour through America, and with it has come a flood of more or less popular scientific publications among which is the best-seller, *Passages*, by Sheely.

Jung described the three great tasks of the first half of life as: first, socialization and learning to live in the human community; second, the problem of relationships with members of the same and of the opposite sex (love, founding a family, and rearing of children); and third, establishing oneself in a job or profession that provides not only for the material necessities of life but also offers the motivation to work in a meaningful, productive, nonalienating manner. All these tasks lie more in the domain of extraversion, and in the mid-life crisis the shift toward introversion is supposed to take place. In this view certain questions remain moot. First of all, Wheelwright (1968) raised the question of how mid-life looks in the case of those persons who have lived the first half of life predominantly as introverts. Granted, they are a minority in our culture, but nevertheless they do exist in greater or lesser numbers. Obviously they would have to live more extravertedly in the second half of life.

A second, more important question, concerns the extent to which introverted processes — as Jung (*Memories, Dreams, Reflections*, 1962) described of his own experiences in his autobiography — are still meaningful and possible in our present-day civilization with its rapid progress and continually increasing hoard of people, and how far the tasks facing us in the form of an overpopulated world, total annihilation by the atom bomb, and the destruction of the environment demand at least a certain degree of extraverted engagement on the part of the more mature, responsible human being. It was not all that many years ago that a prime minister of Pakistan in his early fifties resigned his offices and went into the desert as a sadhu, a forest brother, there to dedicate the remainder of his life to religious meditation. Our world, which, in the last hundred years, has become extraordinarily more dangerous and has experienced a very large degree of distancing and alienation from every natural event both externally as well as internally, no longer permits that sort of retreat. Were someone among us to attempt to withdraw into the solitude of the forest as a sadhu, his attempt would be doomed to failure by the reality that that forest solitude no longer exists, as well as by the fact that Sunday tourists would so overrun him that he would never get to his meditations. Only a hundred years ago, in the age in which Jung grew up, something of that sort was still theoretically possible. In his story, "Old Protheus," Wilhelm Raabe (1977) describes the hermit Konstantinus, who withdrew for thirty years into the forests in Germany following a disappointment in love and who, after some puzzlement in official quarters, was tolerated without immediately being committed to a psychiatric institution. We cannot assume the philosophy and practices of the life of peoples who, like the East Indians, live essentially closer to nature. In a number of essays (e.g., "Yoga and the West," "Psychological Commentary on *The Tibetan Book of the Dead*," *C.W.* 11) Jung also expounded the view that the spiritual situation of India does not know the severe separation of science and religion that has existed in the Occident for some 300 to 400 years. The Indian is closer to his inner nature and knows it better than the European who is largely estranged from it and possesses only a science of nature. Precisely in this regard the lucid and highly trained consciousness of the occidental person needs no further reinforcement against the unconscious. Rather, we have too great a measure of superiority vis-à-vis nature both around us and within us, and what we lack is the conscious acknowledgment of our inferiority to nature from whom we must learn that we cannot do everything that we want. Moreover, through the historical process that the Occident has traversed in the development of civilization, a very extensive reshaping and control of our affectivity and emotionality has arisen that separates us moderns considerably from, say, the medieval person.

For these and other reasons I described three different types. One of them is the person who turns within toward his or her own inner world and follows the path of introversion (Dieckmann 1971a). As the second type I described persons who must resign themselves to recognizing that they have not achieved the goals set in youth. Lastly, as the third type, I discussed those persons who, blessed by success, come into positions of guidance and leadership. These three types are, of course, singled out only because they are so distinct. We must remember that, in practice and in dealing with flesh-and-blood people, we accent only one aspect or another. Basically all three types live in every individual. The increasing inwardness of older people is a common phenomenon. Each one of us must accept a degree of resignation in regard to the goals one set for oneself earlier in life. Seifert (1978) described the productive side of this resignation and its consequences as the precondition for new processes of transformation. Lastly, each of us will have been successful in this or that area and hence will be confronted with problems that accompany success. But I do not want to get into a description of specific typologies here. Rather, I would now like to turn our attention to the problems confronting modern persons at the midpoint of life, a phenomenon that we likewise face daily in our consultation rooms.

An initial problem is implicit in the question of whether or not it is correct nowadays to situate the midpoint of life between ages 35 and 40. Most people now live with the idea of attaining a greater age than did people in earlier centuries. In recent decades our civilization has overcome and reshaped nature in a manner never before known, and in almost all areas of life. Here I would like to mention only a few examples that I have discussed in greater detail elsewhere (Dieckmann 1976b). The example I shall take is that of speed, which enables us to move. Humankind has always faced the problem of overcoming distances. Human beings have always had to seek food, flee dangers, or leave regions that became unproductive or unbearable. Humankind has had to satisfy interests and an insatiable curiosity, corresponding to our mobility drive, our longing for what is distant and new. To accomplish this end, we, just like other animals, were restricted to our own body and to the speed and endurance of our own legs from our first appearance as a species up until the Neolithic revolution (approximately 4000 to 6000 B.C.E.) when domestic animals appeared. The possibilities of transportation were limited to what the human body could endure. In addition to the horse, the preferred means of transportation from that point in time onward, were oxen and camel caravans for moving goods and persons over longer distances. Transportation by animals was almost twice as fast as walking or marching. The models of Gawra show that two-wheeled and four-wheeled carts were already in common usage by approximately 3000 B.C.E. Around 1600 B.C.E. the first horse-drawn wagons with organized exchange stations appear, again nearly doubling the possible speed of travel to approximately 25 kmh. At first these were intended for the transportation of urgent and priority messages. The first regularly scheduled post coach traffic in England, which commenced in 1825, attained a speed of about 14 kmh. For transportation over longer land routes to come about, the rise of the great Western medieval kingdoms that controlled extensive land masses was necessary, in contrast to antiquity when major powers were grouped about the Mediterranean or along rivers where sea transportation was possible. Thus it was only during the medieval period that harness and shoeing for horses was invented, making it possible to exploit the full strength of these animals for the transportation of goods. Here, too, speed remained relatively low.

This means that approximately 3,500 years of human history passed without anything essential changing in regard to the speed with which distances were traversed. A sudden leap in technology and with it a fourfold to fivefold increase in the speeds up until then attainable came in 1880 when the first rapid, highly efficient steam locomotive was invented, achieving speeds of nearly 100 kmh. There now followed an almost terrifying increase. Only 58 years later, in 1938, this number was again greatly multiplied when air speeds of over 600 kmh were reached. Again only 28 years later, in 1960, rocket planes attained a tenfold increase in speed of 6,000 kmh, and space capsules orbit the Earth at a rate ranging from 18,000 to 20,000 kmh. Toffler's *Future Shock* (1970) reports on the changes that rapid mobility have introduced into the private sphere of the individual's life, especially that of Americans.

In this context a question arises: Can we expect similar leaps in biology and in the human lifespan such as technology has granted us in not only in the realm of speed but also in many other areas?

There remains little doubt that the development of modern medicine and the intrusion of technology into it have brought about significant changes in the area of human life expectancy. First of all, human life expectancy, viewed collectively, has increased by leaps and bounds through reduction of infant mortality in highly civilized countries, although not with the same rapidity as in the example of the development of speed. Developments in gerontology and prophylaxis against processes of biological deterioration and degeneration have likewise led to a prolongation of life expectancy for aging persons. But here certain limits are reached, and one can by no means say that we have succeeded in essentially lengthening the life of the individual beyond the biblical age. This is a fact to which we often pay too little attention; all our magnificent progress, all our medical refinements and technology, tend to blind us with regard to the fact that the limit of our life as individuals has remained the same as it was before. Granted, more people now are living into their 70's and 80's, but the individual does not live longer than was the case under optimal conditions in biblical times. In this context it is interesting that, according to investigations and statistical analyses (Jänicke 1977), the trend of average life expectancy which rose over the last century has reversed direction during the 1970s, especially in the highly-industrialized societies such as Denmark and Sweden. Stress, loss of the meaning of life, and toxic substances are waging a battle in which medicine is retreating. Referenced to the average life expectancy of boys age 5 (in order to exclude infant mortality), this retrograde movement amounts to 0.1 years in Denmark and 0.22 years in Sweden. In the Federal Republic of Germany the average life expectancy lies at 64.9 years for men and 71 years for women (again excluding infant mortality). These hard figures clearly suggest that after age 35 we no longer have a longer life ahead of us but rather that we have passed beyond the midpoint.

Almost everyone represses this problem. The real underlying, unconscious element in the process of repression is, on the one hand, the fear of death and, on the other, our society's distorted criteria oriented to achievement and youth. The human being has the tendency to erect defense mechanisms against the repressed problem; these are intended to prevent the problem from reentering consciousness. The simplest and most primitive is that of artificially prolonging youth and attempting to look outwardly younger than one actually is. Due to cultural influences, we find this phenomenon most clearly and most frequently among female patients. Many maintain the outer persona of the youthful woman into their forties and even fifties. This façade remains in place intrapsychically, too, and only dreams reveal how far the aging process has already advanced.

However, in our culture many other things are misused as defense mechanisms and these are much more differentiated and complicated than the simple, direct attempt at externally prolonging youth. Among these, for example, is the prolongation of professional training which plays a great role especially in the highly industrialized countries that are far advanced in the socialization process. Lengthening the period of mandatory schooling, for instance, raises the age at which persons marry, hence first births take place later. This in turn delays the time when children are finally mature enough to leave the parental home. In addition to this are the continually lengthening courses of study, whether university or technical school training or the ever more narrowly specialized courses of training in the area of technical and manual work. Our day and age finds it scarcely imaginable that in the Middle Ages there were university professors twenty years old. Granted, these delays in training and postgraduate study reaching into midlife are necessary in our society, but viewed psychodynamically the cost to the person concerned is that he or she remains intrapsychically in the position of the pupil or the student, i.e., that he or she can remain psychologically immature. Such a situation tempts one to yield to the self-deception that one is still at the beginning and on the path into life where "the real thing" is yet to come. Thus a "perpetual student" of this sort was worried and horrified by a dream in which ancient, shrivelled skin covered his entire body. Only after this dream did he begin to come to terms with his real age. I have discussed this problem in a more detailed case and dream example elsewhere (Dieckmann 1978d).

There are countless other possible forms of defense that I will not enumerate here, but of which treatment methodology must be aware. For example, there is a lot of talk about men around fifty who enter a second puberty. Usually they fall in love with a very young girl, throw out the old marriage, and start to live the first half of life from scratch with another woman who is perhaps in her early twenties. Doing this, they initially have the subjective feeling that through their decision they have tremendously rejuvenated themselves. But if one scrutinizes this for a period of time as to what is going on underneath the surface, one notes that in most instances the whole thing is an illusion behind which lurks an unpleasant reality. In cases of this sort that I have had opportunity to observe, these second marriages soon experience the phenomenon wherein the man does not become younger; rather, the woman he has married quickly becomes much older than she actually is because at least the attempt at an approximation must, of course, be made. It is simply easier to grow old and stoggy than to become young and capable again. Moreover, life lived and experiences gained are not transferable, and from this standpoint generational differences exist that can be bridged only with great difficulty if at all.

We encounter the same phenomenon in the workplace. Contrary to what is propagandized today in many books on the mid-life crisis, life's midpoint is by no means the time to undertake something completely new in order finally to get to the real thing one had wanted. Many changes in occupation or profession made during this period are decidedly false solutions to the real problem. People who think they can begin something entirely new at this age and thereby live out their real destiny all too often resemble those persons who attempt to bury their shadow. Indeed, they change their external position but they discover they are standing emotionally on the same spot. A successful manager in industry who happens to discover a love for healing often becomes nothing other than a successful manager in the area of health care, and an actress who suddenly discovers writing basically does what she had already been doing previously in the theater. The dangerous thing about these processes is that the change often brings a short phase of relative freedom from symptoms; however, the essential issue — i.e., maturation, individuation, change, and development of the personality as an intrapsychic process — is neglected in favor of nonessential externals. Every analyst would be well advised in terms of methodology to take a skeptical view of these sorts of impulses aimed at beginning anew in the middle of life and to work carefully through the patient's symbolic constellations which come from the unconscious and often indicate that the whole attempt at a new beginning is actually a flight from the aging process.

I believe that it is worthwhile for each one of us to indulge in a bit of reflection. What are the real tasks of the second half of life for a person living in our present-day civilization? We are an extraverted culture; likewise, our religion knows of and seeks God primarily "out there" or externally and not within ourselves. On the other hand it is important that — after we have fulfilled external tasks which have occupied us up until life's midpoint — we take time to introvert a bit in order to ask ourselves about the meaning and the value of our existence and in order to enter into relationship with the transcendent. This also consists of our leaning to understand things in a larger perspective, of extricating ourselves from the events of the day; especially in our age of fast living, it is important to ask no longer about hours, days, weeks, or years, but rather to ponder in terms of decades or even generations. This means that we ask after what is truly enduring. Much of the oft-cited but too little lived wisdom of age consists of the older person possessing just this ability, having developed a sense for differentiating between the transitory and the enduring. In the broadest sense of the word, *religio* means a "linking back," a "retrospective contemplation," and this in terms of the real values of our existence. Each of us has her or his own inner scales and hierarchies of values. These hierarchies of values, however, are not, or rather should not be, anything static that remains immutable throughout one's whole life. Life's midpoint should be the time when the individual human being can reflect upon and revise these hierarchies of values. Much that has been uncommonly valuable and important up to mid-life loses its significance and recedes into the background to make place for other values.

This process is something individual. Every person must find the meaning of his or her own life. This inner search for meaning, the time of inner reflection and of coming to terms with the deeper roots of one's life, belongs irrevocably among the tasks of the second half of life. Then there arises a different attitude toward the positions of leadership and the responsibilities already attained, an attitude that should reach beyond the events of the day, mindful of coming generations rather than solely concerned with fulfilling one's own drives, be they money, power, respect and recognition, or the like.

At the midpoint of life one's sense of time changes profoundly. While life still appears endlessly long to the youthful person, it begins to have boundaries and limits for the person getting older. Time is no longer something endless; rather, it becomes something one can count. But with this also comes a restriction of possibilities, a problem on which many persons run aground and concerning which many deceive themselves. For the person who truly and genuinely comes to terms with these problems during the second half of life, this time can become the most fruitful and meaningful period of life. Life can attain a new depth and significance. The setting sun of the course of life can, among other things, radiate more vitality and warmth than the rising sun. It is important that we relieve our patients of their fear of having to grow old and to die by imparting to them the knowledge that sunset can be just as beautiful as sunrise. Creating this beauty and fullness of meaning, however, can never be the task of the state or of a society; rather, it must always rest on the individuation of the individual human being. Individuation is a process that lasts until death. Consequently, analytical psychology as method is available also to the aging, the very old, and the dying, and can accomplish significant things, even if these patients do not yet seek us out very often.

CHAPTER 8

On the Methodology of Dream Interpretation

At the turn of the century, Freud and Jung made their sensational discoveries concerning the understanding of dream and fantasy contents and formulated their conceptualizations of the ways to make dream contents comprehensible to consciousness. It is remarkable that there has been no essential new breakthrough in either psychoanalysis or in analytical psychology regarding the understanding of dreams since then. This has come from a different quarter, that of experimental psychology and sleep research. By monitoring rapid eye movement, Kleitmann (1963) succeeded in establishing a relationship among the various dream phases. Although we can differentiate five distinct sleep phases with the help of the EEG, basically only two of them are of interest for our purposes: non-REM phases and REM phases. The latter stage of sleep reveals a mixed picture of alpha- and betalike EEG waves and is characterized by the fact that the majority of dreams occur in this stage. We know that isolated dreams occur in the other sleep stages, but dream activity is most intensive during the REM phase. In general we can assume that the adult experiences three or four REM phases each night and consequently has a corresponding number of dreams which can be recalled. In the course of human life we find an elevated REM phase during the late intrauterine period. At the age of four years it amounts to 30 percent of our sleep time; at the age of twenty it drops to 25 percent; and in old age (i.e., eighty years) it drops to 20 percent. That means that we spend about one-fourth of our sleep time dreaming (Bossard 1976). We also know that these phases are of special psychological and physiological significance for the healthy functioning of our psychophysical life. Sleep research–based studies of the psychophysical interface still have a long way to go and much to clarify, but we can say that total REM-sleep deprivation gives rise to severe psychological disturbances resembling psychotic states. On the other hand, experimental reduction of REM-sleep in depressive patients can result in an improvement in their depression. All in all, the experimental research confirms Jung's hypothetical conception that the "monologue" of the unconscious in our psyche continues uninterrupted during sleep and that dreams have an essential psychophysical function. Hence it is all the more astonishing how little value the average person attaches to this second life within despite all of depth psychology's work of enlightenment up until today. It is astonishing how quickly and carelessly the average person abandons dreams to forgetfulness although in them he or she has the most exciting and most interesting experiences which are presented with complete sensual and sensory qualities and take place as an objective reality in Jung's sense of the term (Jung, "On Psychic Energy," *C. W.* 8). Rather, it seems as though interest in the dream that came alive again around the turn of the century and very much held the foreground of interest among experts and analysts who worked with the unconscious is waning again even among them, and that many analysts now work with dreams only a little if at all. To some degree, increasing interest in group dynamics and in the focused treatment of current conflicts, in sociological problems, and in transference-countertransference phenomena have again pushed work with the dream and with its contents into the background. Perhaps this derives from a general dissatisfaction with the methods of dream interpretation available to us and to the question raised again and again by critics concerning the extent to which the results that our interpretative methods claim actually are valid and can be proven and confirmed. In light of these considerations, it may be important first to reflect upon the approaches to dream interpretation or the ways in which people have dealt with dreams over the course of human history.

We can distinguish three fundamental approaches. First, as is customary among many primal peoples or "primitive cultures," the dream is included as part of external reality, and, as we suspect it to be with children, no clear distinction is made between unconscious fantasy and reality. This can go so far that a person is held responsible not only for what he does in his own dreams, but also for what he does in the dreams of others. Lévy-Bruhl (1959) cites an entire series of reports of this sort which sound inconceivable to us. For the most part, they come from New Guinea and Borneo, and from the Linguas of the Great Tschako where it is quite customary that a person is punished for infidelity committed in a dream or likewise must make restitution of the goods stolen in a dream of another. Sachtelen states:

A man arrived in my village. He came from a place about 150 miles away. He demanded I compensate him for the gourds that I had recently stolen from his garden. Astonished, I told him that I had not been anywhere near his garden for a long time and that, consequently,

I could not have stolen his gourds. At first I thought it was a joke, but soon I was convinced that the man was serious. For an Indian to accuse me of theft was a totally new experience. To my rebuke he openly admitted that I had not taken the gourds. When he said this, I comprehended even less than before. I would have gotten angry had I not seen that he was completely convinced, and now, on the contrary, a lively interest in the affair overtook me. Finally I discovered it: he had dreamed that I had been in his garden one night and that he — concealed behind a few very large plants — had seen how I picked three large gourds and made off with them. He wanted me to pay for them. Then I said to him, "But you just admitted that I did not take them." Again he agreed, but suddenly added: "If you had been there, you would have taken them." Thus he revealed that he regarded the act of my soul (which he had suspected of being in his garden) as an act I had truly willed and that I would really have committed it had I been there in the flesh and blood. (Lévy-Bruhl 1959, p. 8)

In another case Roth reports that "In Muke (Borneo) I met Janela. As the reason for coming he said that a penalty had been imposed on his daughter in Luai because her husband had dreamed that she had been unfaithful to him. Janela had brought his daughter with him" (ibid., p. 94).

Lévy-Bruhl cites a great number of similar reports that seem incomprehensible to us. Thefts, infidelities, even murders, are ascribed to another person who has committed them in the dreamer's dream. For people in these cultures, it is really the soul of the other person that appears in one's dream and commits such acts for which one very naturally demands the other take responsibility in waking life. A person's soul is just as real as the flesh-and-blood person and as his or her acts in waking life. We are forced to ask how these kinds of cultures have been able to exist if we really do proceed from the idea that it is merely a person's suppressed images of wishes and drives that are depicted in the dream. Or is it perhaps that, in our own culture that so stresses rationality and with our deprecatory attitude toward the unconscious, we are so destructive to our own inner nature that we would exterminate ourselves in short order if we held each other responsible for what we do in the dreams of others? Obviously there are cultures that are by far less destructive than are we and that can function within this point of view.

The second approach is that the dream is a message sent from the gods and serves primarily as an oracle, i.e., it has mantic (divinatory) aspects. This viewpoint enjoyed its heyday in antiquity and was gradually abandoned only in modern times under the influence of the Renaissance and the rise of the natural sciences. In the mantic view of dreams, we already find the idea that dreams are encoded and that a decoding must take place. To a great extent the symbolism of the dream was understood collectively, and the ancient dream interpreters compiled dream lexicons on the basis of collective symbol interpretation. Of these, the first known to us is that of Antiphon of Athens from the 5th century. The best known dream book of this period is that of Artemidorus of Daldis; his book commands a very considerable understanding of the human psyche, even from the viewpoint of our current knowledge, already taking into account the conditions under which the dream was dreamt and the person of the dreamer.

Third and last, in modern dream interpretation the individual aspect stands in the foreground. Every dream and every dream motif or dream symbol is related to the individual's memories, life and family history, and conscious situation independent of the collective features which, of course, must also be considered. Here the same dream motif can have an entirely different significance for one patient than for another. In this mode of dream interpretation, the range of possible meanings dependent on the dreamer's personal, experiential world is much too great to be captured in any way in a dictionary; thus, encyclopedias of symbols or dreams now exist only in magazines or in the lay literature.

In contrast to what is usually maintained, the ego-complex commands a considerably greater degree of constancy and stability and by no means has the tendency to dissolve and dissociate in the dream. Rather, the ego-complex is concerned with preserving its functions in the dream-ego. This does not exclude the presence of very distinct tendencies toward loosening of ego-structure, and the dream is most suited to mediating suppressed or new experiential qualities to the ego-complex.

In an early work (Dieckmann 1965), I described these integrative processes in the dream-ego as well as changes in the manner in which the dream-ego experiences and behaves in analytic work. In that paper I came to the conclusion that most of the processes of change in analytic work took place first via the dream-ego through which they later came most easily into the realm of conscious changes. As a rule we again find confirmation neither for the wish fulfillment theory nor for the theory of compensation in the qualities of the dream-ego's experience and behavior; rather, the dream-ego attempts to maintain the continuity of the ego-complex in the dream. A fourteen-year-old girl dreamed that, while ascending a flight of stairs in a children's home, another child grabbed her and that she got into a terrible fight with the other child. In reality this girl did experience outbreaks of wild aggression as soon as someone else touched her. A patient who continually flees her or his own problems initially will not be a hero who faces the opponent but will flee in the dream, too. In a dream series I discussed in the article mentioned above, a woman patient with severe oral inhibitions initially dreamt of being in empty stores where she could buy nothing or get nothing due to other people pushing in front of her. Only in the course of extended analytic work did she finally come to the point that she could dream of buying and getting what she wanted in a store. A corresponding change in behavior in her waking life appeared promptly after having this dream. Likewise the sexually inhibited philistine, lying in bed next to his unlovely wife of many years, does not in reality dream of orgies with other girls. Rather, he needs extensive analysis and a corresponding emotional loosening before dreams appear in which he can experience sexuality with other women. Hence as a rule this indicates that a problem becomes conscious only when the dream-ego tackles and integrates it.

Now it seems to me that the continuity the ego-complex maintains both in waking life and in the dream offers a very great advantage methodologically. At this level there is the possibility of appealing to the patient initially in terms of the most clearly evident parallels between his or her customary modes of experiencing and reacting. Establishing similarities and parallels then leads, on the one hand, to the patient's discovering some familiar qualities in confused, meaningless, and incomprehensible dreams. On this basis the patient can then build the first bridges of relationship and understanding. It is well known that relationships are possible only when we discover similarities and familiar qualities, and that it is much more difficult and far more laborious to establish a relationship with something completely unknown and incomprehensible. Moreover, the ego-feeling with which the dream-ego is also very clearly cathected facilitates this process. On the other hand, the unusual, remarkable, and strange experiences, motifs, and symbols see to it that the loosening processes we desire in analysis can begin to admit the confrontation with the suppressed or repressed psychic material, or they enable the ego to deal with and to integrate the new acquisitions necessary in its current situation. From this vantage point, Jung's rule of thumb that we should work on the objective level of interpretation before taking up the subjective ("The Practical Use of Dream Analysis," C.W. 16) once again reveals another value and significance than that of merely coming to terms with significant others. If we initially regard the figures (except the dream-ego) and symbols that appear in the dream as objects, and if we concentrate on the dream-ego and emphasize the continuity of the ego-complex at the beginning of analytic therapy, then we give the patient a greater degree of security with which to move about in this inner world that up until now has been so incomprehensible and unknown. This is all the more important since, as we know, practically every patient that consults us suffers from some ego weakness and the analytic process always strives simultaneously both for ego strengthening and stabilization and for openness to and the possibility of confronting unconscious material. Precisely the lack of ego stability is the reason that we seldom get the patient's genuine collaboration in working on unconscious material and on dreams right at the beginning of analytic therapy. As a rule we first run up against very distinct defense mechanisms and formations with which we have to deal again and again in the course of therapy.

I would like to mention the most frequent and most common forms in which these defenses appear. For this purpose I will use the typological model, since in my opinion it most comprehensively embraces the ego functions and consequently also the defenses. Further I will use it to show how the continuity of these very same ego functions is maintained right into the dream world. (Here I am referring to the way in which the conscious ego-complex deals with dream material.) To date there exists no typological diagnosis based exclusively on dream content. In my discussion I will proceed initially and chiefly from the attitude types (introversion and extraversion) but in conclusion I will comment briefly on the function types.

In my experience the introverts' dreams and their attitude toward dreams can take two characteristic forms. One form characteristic of this attitude type is usually described by saying that the introvert lives more in a dream world than in reality. They move about in reality more or less as if in a closed system. Such patients often bring a multitude of extraordinarily lively and vivid dreams at the outset of therapy and move about in these dreams as if they were at home there. If they amplify them or freely associate to them, they do so in rich measure, but it is striking that whatever associations they have bear little relation to external reality. It is most characteristic of introverts that every dream motif reminds them of another dream, and this of yet another. In extreme cases it initially looks as though this attitude type is enveloped in dreams as in a cocoon and can move about in this cocoon in a colorful and lively way. Patient and analyst can often be swallowed up together in an abundance of exciting and inspiring amplifications — but nothing at all changes, and it almost seems as though life did not exist at all outside of dream motifs. If this form of defense is more pronouncedly evident, the interventions of the analyst intended to lead toward objective associations are useless. Consequently with these patients I let the process run on for a period of time until it is more than clear to both of us. Then I interpret it directly in order at the same time to discuss with the patient the extent to which he or she persists in this sort of regressive introversion in real life, the magnitude of perceptual lacunae vis-à-vis the environment and the degree to which the symptoms of illness might perhaps have something to do with this problem.

The second form of introverted defense is that in which dreams and fantasies have no relationship to the ego-complex and the latter is isolated. Most characteristic for these patients is the form taken by their daydreams. True, they do have fantasies, even to excess, that can lead to disturbances in their ability to work, but they really do not know that they are having those sorts of fantasies. They seem far distant or absent, and if one mentions to them that they were fantasizing, they return to reality and often must exert much effort to recall that they were having any fantasies at all of which, as a rule, they recapture only remnants. The situation is similar in regard to the dreams of these patients. Often they say that they have had long and detailed dreams, and that they remember having dreamed the entire night, but that they can recall nothing. Only when one asks them for details does it turn out that only tiny scraps are still accessible. It is characteristic of these patients that, when they recount these remnants, they insist they are quite inessential parts of their actual dreams which, however, they cannot recall. It is entirely possible that one gets no dreams at all from this sort of patient for extended periods of time. If so, the first task of analytic therapy is to clarify how it came about that they lost touch with their fantasies and what fears hide behind their defending against their own fantasy world in this form. It is typical for these patients that their defense against fantasies does not coincide with a simultaneous act of discrimination; rather, they value dreams and fantasies highly, hold them in high esteem, and like every introvert are convinced that, fundamentally, they are more important than external realities. Hence among these persons one usually finds a distinct regret that, in spite of all their good will, they cannot retain their dreams and fantasies.

The extraverted attitude type can also react to a corresponding disturbance in his or her relationship with the unconscious with both the mechanisms just described, i.e., by being inundated with dreams or by blocking them all out. However, in the instance of the extravert these defenses have a different quality. One finds the flood of dreams most often among those patients who have strongly hysterical components in their psychic structure, just as Jung initially described extraversion in cases of severe hysteria (*C.W.* 6). In the extreme case the patient can fill whole hours with often extraordinarily colorful, lively, but usually confusingly fragmented dream episodes, or bring in several pages of dreams recorded since the previous session. But these dreams stand like a kind of foreign body beside the ego-complex which is occupied with entirely different things and cannot do anything at all with the dreams. This plenitude of dreams is a defense to the extent that they so fill up the analytic hour that no time remains to come to terms with the problems and the inner stance toward the events of the outer world that they contain. For example, at the beginning of treatment a patient of this sort told me so much dream material that she succeeded in filling the first fifteen sessions recounting it. She became aware of the character of this defense only when I regretfully pointed this out to her; then the dreams diminished to a manageable quantity.

The blockage between the ego-complex and the dream appears differently in the extraverted attitude type than in the introvert. Granted, the extraverted patient does not recall dreams, or only meager scraps, but it is clear that the extravert is not lost in a fantasy world that runs its course alongside consciousness. Extraverts do not make the same impression as introverts whose soul has flown away like a strange bird, to borrow an image from the world of primal peoples. Rather, they are simply oriented exclusively to the external object. For these patients fantasies or dreams are nonsense just as they were for the large rationalistic groups in the last century. Since their psychic energy is so exclusively oriented toward the external object, they are in no position to pay attention to their dreams or to remember them. A large proportion of the patients who say, in the analytic session, "Indeed I dreamt something, but I forgot it immediately," belong to this type. During the first phase of his treatment, a patient I described in detail elsewhere (Dieckmann 1962) brought in only one-sentence dreams, if any at all; for example, "Swimming with lots of women in water." Only by consistently taking up the motifs contained in the dreams and by analyzing his resistance were we able to lift the barrier to his dreams, and in the further course of his analysis this patient, who was quite uncomplicated and uneducated, brought in quite lively and impressive dreams until his symptoms abated, his modes of behaving and experiencing changed, and he felt better. Then he stopped dreaming, or stopped observing his dreams.

It is quite clear that the forms of disturbance, in relationship to the unconscious, of the attitude types described here have clear correspondences to the narcissistic disturbances described by Kohut (1971). This is obvious since the attitude type is always based on the subject-object relation and every deep disturbance of that relationship falls within the realm of narcissism. (The lack of collaboration among the analytic schools is particularly lamentable, considering the many parallels between the ideal in analytical psychology and the conceptions of modern Freudians like Hartmann, Kohut, and others.) It is also clear that we are dealing here with either a partial inflation or alienation in Edinger's (1972) sense, and that the heart of the disturbance consequently lies in the realm of the ego-Self axis (Neumann 1954). This also explains that these disturbances between the ego-complex, on the one hand, and recall, understanding, and metabolizing of dreams, on the other, are by no means simple and easy to treat, but rather often continue throughout the entire analysis in severe cases. The analyst who loses patience and attempts to correct the situation with "behavioral directives" harvests a displacement of symptoms or a termination of the analysis.

Methodologically all these disturbances must, of course, be treated differently. As is usual in analysis, there is no general "know-how." Moreover, these various forms of disturbance in the relationship to the unconscious also have their own, individual, causal-genetic roots in each case. Although in our Jungian view, analysis should not be pursued purely regressively back to childhood, the childhood background must be known. The analyst must be aware why precisely this form of defense against the unconscious has arisen in each phase and how it came about that this was the psyche's only useful defense against a yet greater impairment. This insight into the meaning of the resistance then permits the analyst to tolerate it for the time being in the here and now and to avoid exposing a still weak and unstable ego that has not yet been sufficiently able to develop its functions to the influences of the unconscious for which it is no match. It is in complete conformity with Jung's discussion in "The Psychology of the Transference" (*C.W.* 16) that one meaning of the resistance lies in protecting the damaged ego functions and therefore that resistance must be respected. (Not without good reason is the Reichian method of persistent analysis of resistance hardly mentioned in contemporary analytic literature.)

Concerning the function types, we can state that each one also reacts in specific and characteristic form to the phenomenon of the dream. Space does not permit a detailed discussion of the type-specific characteristics of the dreams and of the approach of the ego-complex to the dream when specific typologies are dominant. Consequently I will limit myself to describing the typical and predominant characteristics of each function type.

Aside from the fact that the thinking type — like the sensation type — is irritated and vexed by the "senseless" and illogical structure of dreams, he or she is unique in excluding the emotions. As a rule the thinking type gives a description of the plot in which unclear or irrational elements that do not fit in are excluded. The analyst discovers elements, just like the feelings that accompany them, only when asking about them in the course of the hour.

Likewise feeling types often omit unclear or irrational dream elements that do not fit into the context of the dream. By contrast, their depictions of dreams are distinguished by extensive and differentiated accounts of feeling and sensory impressions. As an extreme example, I had a woman patient whose description of the feeling tone of a meeting with another person in a dream took up more than two pages and who delved into various detailed shades of meaning again and again.

N's

On the other hand, the intuitives' fascination with the unusual or indefinite stands out. Regardless whether they have more imaginative or more mundane dreams, they are impressed by what appears new, unknown, or unusual; the difficulty here lies in working through these elements with them. (It is certain that something entirely new will appear in the next dream, and should it turn out that it is not so new after all but the same problem in different symbols, they usually respond by withdrawing their interest.) In contrast to the more rational types, one seldom hears from these patients, at least in the early phases of treatment, the complaint that the analytic process proceeds too much by leaps and bounds, that too many diverse themes turn up in dreams, and that no problem gets properly dreamt or worked through to the end.

Corresponding to their typology, the sensation types present the factual material of their dreams. On the basis of my observations, the

ES

extraverted sensor typically relates dreams in which the external events of the day are repeated largely or entirely as realistically as they actually took place. The analyst can do something with this material only if he or she can move the sensation type to reflect on why the unconscious singled out precisely this event and no other; here the underlying problems are

IS

usually very much camouflaged. The more introverted the patient is, the more magical, mythological, or farcical the dreams can become; here, too, value is placed on the detailed depiction of objects, persons, or symbols. Thus the analyst can find out very precisely from the patient what clothing, for example, a certain person, say a magician, was wearing in the dream but get hardly a word about the effect of this figure on the dream-ego.

It goes without saying that all these characterizations hold true in "pure" form only in extreme cases. As in waking life, all four functions take part in every dream experience, and the auxiliary functions in particular participate in describing the dream in the analytic setting. The typological picture arises only out of a certain placement of emphasis and is especially distinct only as long as other functions have not begun to develop alongside the leading function in the analytic process.

As already discussed above, the ego-complex is obviously to be regarded as one of the most stable points in the dream. This is also necessary since the different sort of experience must be assimilated by or juxtaposed to an intact ego in order to be registered at all and worked through. As long as anything at all is experienced, the carrier of the experience is always the same ego (E. Lubac, cited in Siebenthal 1953, p. 239). Meyerson (cited in Siebenthal 1953) also sees no change in the unity of the ego from waking to sleeping but rather in the relationship to the ego; the unity of the personality, or as Siebenthal describes it, "one and the same identical ego experiences itself through the relationship to other psychic facts, but due to the loosening of relationships (dissociation, displacement) in the dream it simply experiences things differently (1953, p. 290). Now within the analytic process a direct loosening of ego-structures takes place under the protection of the transference and countertransference constellation. The ego-complex can relinquish defense mechanisms and more broadly develop just those functions damaged and constricted in the neurosis, can forego control and organizational structures, and can surrender ego-boundaries and admit new experiential contents. This corresponds to the parallel development of ego-consciousness and of consciousness in the dream, and to the observation that consciousness and the ego are most closely linked (de Sanctis 1896, cited in Siebenthal 1953, p. 289).

Consequently this gives rise, in my opinion, to methodological demand that more emphasis be placed on the dream-ego when interpreting and working through dreams and that the dream-ego be placed in the center of the developmental and maturational process of individuation. What the ego cannot do in the dream, it cannot do in waking life, and as long as it still must flee before certain experiential contents in the dream, the patient will be overtaxed if one demands that these experiences be integrated. A woman patient with severe disturbances in the area of heterosexual relationship dreamt during the first period of her analysis almost exclusively of men who overpowered, pursued, and raped her, and against whom she was helpless. This corresponded to the initial intrusion of the patriarchal uroboros into the dual union of mother and daughter (Neumann 1953b). Only as dreams appeared in which these male figures became less brutal, in which supportive figures were present, and she was able to confront her pursuers in the dream, did she also dare enter into relationships with men in her waking life. Up until that point in time she had erected a wall of defense against every man, a wall that could not be broken through.

The same holds true for the integration of feeling contents. A forty-year-old businessman, who led the life of a totally overtaxed and harried manager, dreamt: "I am in the house of Liv Ulmann (*Scenes of a Marriage*). I have a very affectionate, tender relationship with her. She leads me into her bedroom. I ask her where her husband is (in the dream, he is Hans Albers). She says he is on the way and is angry because he was not able to get a theater ticket. Usually he gets drunk when this happens. I was concerned that he would come back and forwent intensifying our activities. I persuaded her to leave and look for a quieter, undisturbed place." The women of his earlier dreams had always been only sexually seductive, anonymous figures with whom he jumped immediately into bed without much ado. In this dream, he encounters an anima figure for the first time who represents inner confrontation and individuation for him. By contrast his shadow with which he had been greatly inflated, the impulsive and primitively sentimental actor Hans Albers (*Hopla, Da Komm Ich*), has been separated from this dream-ego, and he seeks to avoid him. He can also postpone a sexual impulse in the dream in an ego-syntonic decision, which is a completely new achievement for him, and seek a quieter place. Following this dream he began to be approachable in terms of relativizing his harried pace and to develop more feeling, initially in isolated oases.

Observation of a dream series is, of course, the precondition for methodically working through these sorts of changes in the ego-complex. In an on-going analysis with a very busy analyst, this is not at all so simple. It would be demanding too much to ask an analyst to remember all the patient's dreams. But there are certain signals telling the analyst not to overlook those dreams that indicate clear changes in the dream-ego's modes of experience and behavior. For one thing, the dreamer often notices it and experiences this sort of dream as having a different significance, as important, lively, persistent, etc., even if it doesn't deal directly with archetypal material. Second, analysts should train themselves to pay attention to these processes. With sufficient attention one gets an impression of the dream-ego's typical patterns relatively quickly, just as we do for the conscious ego, and changes in these patterns, even of a slight degree, begin to be noticeable. Methodologically it is also helpful to emphasize these passages by drawing the patient's attention to them by directly asking whether or not he or she has ever before dreamt in this manner. Moreover, if the analyst takes no notes on the analytic hour, he or she should at least jot down the dreams so that these sorts of changes can be checked out.

My remaining task is that of briefly commenting on the problem of interpretation at the subjective level which seemingly gets neglected in this sort of procedure. In recent years Gestalt therapy (Pearls 1974) has taken up work at the subjective level with particular intensity. Patients are challenged to enter into the experience of other figures appearing in the dream, for example, significant others or even animals, and in doing so often have good success in gaining other possibilities for understanding and experiencing. Often the patient is very much impressed by this, but it must also be mentioned that many Jungians were doing this long before the advent of Gestalt therapy. In my experience with patients who have done Gestalt therapy before or during analysis, however, the effect produced is only transitory. Particularly when the neuroses are major, the ego very quickly resurrects its old boundaries and the method does not exempt one from laboriously and often tediously having to work through the meaning of dream symbolism on all levels.

On the other hand, the emphasis on the subjective level of interpretation in the therapeutic process seems to me always to be of significance when it is a question of the phases of reconnection with the Self and the establishment of the original wholeness in the sense of Edinger's "psychic life cycles" (1972). This brings about a strengthening of the ego functions that make it possible to relinquish defensive systems, to surrender, to make one's boundaries permeable, and to experience one's connection with the Self. In my opinion, methodologically this adds an additional facet to subjective-level interpretation and to active imagination on subjective-level dream contents in contrast to the old rule that the subjective level is to be approached only when interpretation on the objective level has been exhausted.

CHAPTER 9

The Method of Association and Amplification

First of all I would like to consider the differing emphases that the Freudian and Jungian schools place on association. Among Freudians and neo-Freudians free association is generally acknowledged as the primary method of obtaining material in psychoanalysis. According to Greenson, free association has "precedence over all other methods in producing material in the analytic setting" and is not used in anti-analytic (*zudeckenden*) or supportive therapies (1967, p. 46). In contrast to this, Jung did not work with "free association" but rather employed a method he called *amplification*. Jacobi writes:

> Free association, [Jung] believes, "always leads to a complex, but we can never be certain whether it is precisely this one that constitutes the meaning of the dream. . . . We can, of course, always get to our complexes somehow, for they are the attraction that draws everything to itself." But sometimes the dream points in exactly the opposite direction from the content of the complex, indicating on the one hand the natural function that may be able to free the dreamer from the complex and on the other hand a way the dreamer may follow. (Jacobi 1973, p. 84, citing Jung, *Kindertraumseminar*, 1938–39).

These two statements stand in absolute opposition to one another, for Jung's analytical psychology cannot be designated as an anti-analytic, concealing, or supportive therapy even in the most malevolent critical depiction. True, we must grant that Jacobi refers only to dreams, whereas Greenson speaks of the entire analytical material. This contradiction and simplification which one often encounters—i.e., that Freudian analysis is equivalent to the method of free association and Jungian analysis equals the amplification method—probably arose in that Jung, who had already demonstrated experimentally the dichotomy of consciousness and the unconscious in his association experiments published in 1904, and consequently was absolutely at home in the area of the methodology of association, also recognized its limitations. Most importantly we are dealing here with unconscious material that was never known to the patient and that consists first and foremost of contents of the collective unconscious which cannot be added to conscious by the method of free association. Even Freudians like d'Marmor (1970) have pointed to this problem. Thus C. A. Meier speaks consistently of the amplification method inaugurated by Jung when he states that it is suited less to each and every dream than "for those where the usual methods do not produce much that is satisfying" (1972, p. 21). Moreover, Meier continues, "amplification is limited to individual dream elements to which the dreamer can associate little or no personal experiences and that nevertheless play an essential role in the text of the dream. Amplification finds its classical application to those elements that have an impressively odd or strange character. The significance of such images, however, remains unrecognized because they are usually only allusions, pithy expressions, or fragmentary expressions."

Jung, well-known for his often biting remarks, once said at the time he introduced and defended his method of amplification that one could "just as well take a public notice or a sentence in a newspaper as associate to a dream" ("The Practical Use of Dream Analysis," C. W. 16, par. 320). But in another passage the same Jung also said, "The psychological context of dream-contents consists in the web of associations in which the dream is naturally embedded" (Psychology and Alchemy, C. W. 12, par. 48). It would be very difficult to understand how a researcher who had worked as extensively with the association method as Jung had and who, among other things, had also discovered an important signpost pointing to the manner and the contents of unconscious complexes, could have completely cast aside this method in order to make use solely of the method of amplification. In my opinion amplification is a most essential and significant methodological enrichment of the association method (which works only with the "free" associations of the patient) as well as one to be used relatively frequently. I myself know from personal experience that Jolande Jacobi (cited above) works with free association in the analyses she conducts, and I am of the opinion that there is scarcely an analyst of the Jungian school who utilizes a consistent and pure amplification method in analyses.

Although they are relatively well known, it seems to me worthwhile once again to describe these two approaches briefly. Free association is based on what occurs "spontaneously" to the patient; that is, the patient does not reflect in a conscious and logically rational way and then state a chain of ideas. Rather, alert, logical-rational thought is sidestepped and the feeling-toned images, fantasies, and memories that arise out of the unconscious are verbalized, regardless whether they appear logically consistent to the patient. This process has a certain similarity with the artist's creative fantasizing as Schiller once expressed it in a letter to Körner when he wrote that the guards posted before the doors of reason withdraw in order to let everything in the soul come forth unhindered. The analyst's standard question when employing the method of free association is, "What comes to mind in connection with this?" It makes no difference whether stated or posed in a different form. By means of a great number of such spontaneous responses the analyst obtains a chain of associatively cohesive elements that point toward a specific complex and ultimately can lead directly to a specific complex so that it can be raised into consciousness. Graphically this procedure can be schematized as shown in Figure 9.1.

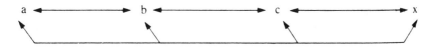

The individual letters of the chain of associations represent the individual "spontaneously" occurring ideas, memories, images, etc. "B" follows "A," "C" follows "B," etc., until finally the chain of associations reaches "X" and the complex being sought is discovered. The line below the chain of associations which moves directly toward "X" and is linked to the individual letters is intended to suggest that each individual association is essentially not "free" in the sense that it is arbitrary and separate and has absolutely nothing to do with the content of the complex. Rather, each association exists in some meaningful relation to the content of the complex which, to be sure, is not seen by the person whose complex it is. An example will illustrate the process.

A patient arrived very irritated a few minutes late for his session and began with a torrent of abuse directed at typical "women drivers" who did not start off fast enough when the light changed to green and who moped along in front of him so slowly that he could not get through traffic smoothly. After firing a few more choice salvos at this particular situation, he generalized the problem as he told me how greatly it upset him whenever he was confined or slowed down, whenever something impeded his progress and he could not quickly enough seize whatever opportunity might appear because of being hampered. Finally I raised a question: considering all that he had said, I wondered whether it might be possible that he was talking about his own situation in analysis, since during the previous hour he had spoken of the feeling of being hampered and getting stuck in the analytic process. The patient took up my question, and in connection with his anger it occurred to him that he found it extraordinarily difficult in session to express feelings that were negative or critical, or that had to do with irritation, although here he expressly had been given the "green light" to do so. Then in his further associations he expressed for the first time what disturbed him both in respect to my office as well as in regard to my attitude and behavior during his sessions, and the points and issues where he had sensed rejecting, critical, or angry feelings. In this way he was able to include negative and critical transference contents in the analytic process for the first time. Thanks to the possibility of freely associating in this area, he was able to broaden it, come to terms with it, and also to establish some connections between both it and genetic material as well as his relationship to the parental atmosphere. Many associations to the symbol of the woman who does not promptly move through the intersection on green occurred to the patient during this hour and thanks to the chain of associations, he was able to discover the possibility of an heretofore avoided, direct, critical confrontation with a paternal authority figure. In my opinion it would not have been appropriate to abandon the method of free association here and to insist on the method of amplification, which would also have been possible in principle. The symbol that the patient brought at the beginning of the hour embraced not only his angry affect toward being hindered; rather, it also had to do with a very specific symbolism, that of the automobile and of the woman in it. If I had proceeded here according to the method of amplification, I would have had to bring the patient's associations back again and again to the symbolism of the auto and the woman which perhaps would have lead to the issue of an anima problem enclosed in the persona. As I have shown in another study (Dieckmann 1976b), it is possible to garner countless amplifications of the symbol of the automobile, and many more can be compiled for the figure of an anima to which, of course, this collective image of an unknown woman who triggers a strong affect in the patient points.

In moving to a discussion of the procedure of amplification as such, it is first necessary to make some preliminary remarks. In analytic practice we find that the patient can give the most varied forms of association. The relevant associations can be subdivided into two large groups. First are the subjective associations among which we subsume all those spontaneous thoughts, memories, and feelings that refer to the personal life history and individual psyche of the patient. The chain of associations described above consists almost exclusively of this sort of subjective association. Of course, as the example also makes clear, subjective associations do not always have to lie in the distant or not-so-distant past. Rather, all current experiences including those that take place within the transference and countertransference constellation in the analytic hour or in regard to future plans and expected events belong here, too. Regarded as so-called "reality-based associations," these subjective associations related to the dreamer's memories of actually lived life hold the central focus in the analytic approach and in dream interpretation in Schultz-Hencke's (1949) neoanalytic school. The concept of reality-based associations that refer to actually lived life, however, is something decidedly problematic in the analytic setting and basically not very analytic. In the atmosphere of a specific situation constellated in the analytic hour, memories often carry an entirely different feeling-tone and are endowed with entirely different actions and experiences that belong elsewhere, or fantasies turn into memories of real events that never took place at all. The classical example of this is the error to which Freud succumbed in his theory of dreams in that he took the traumatic childhood sexual experiences that his patients reported for reality and as precipitating their illnesses whereas in fact, as it later turned out, they were symbolic expressions arising from the patient's psyche. Of course, the concretely minded person might have the unpleasant feeling here that actually there is no longer anything solid and certain to which one may cleave. But in analysis the positivistic enslavement to so-called objective reality experiences does not play the essential role. Rather, it is the patient's processes of emotional experience in a given situation that are critical, and much more depends on the symbolic events and the symbol-forming function of the psyche than upon the experience that took place concretely. As the reader will have already noticed, I did not treat the woman in the car at the stoplight as a concrete experience but rather understood it as a symbol. The change in, or the dynamics of, these kinds of symbolic processes of experience is an essential principle of analysis, and the goal of individuation lies in mediating a greater breadth of experience and the inclusion of the unconscious, symbolic background in external, concrete, daily experience. Here the symbolic processes supply the underlying motifs informing the forms of experience and of behavior. Through this inclusion of the unconscious, the external macrocosm and the psychic microcosm are brought into a mutual association in order to create a more comprehensive and more complete experience.

In the second group—that of the objective associations—we are dealing with spontaneously occurring thoughts, feelings, and memories that do not relate to personal material arising from the patient's psyche. In order to illustrate what is involved, I would like to offer another example. A woman patient had the following dream:

My parents had bought a house with my financial participation, circumstances permitting. It was situated on a lake. Unfortunately the lake could not be seen from the windows of the house, but a beautiful garden that ran down to the lake was visible. The only drawback was that the floors in the house were like a quagmire. It had been extraor-

dinarily rainy, but I thought the quagmire had to do with the slaugh-
terhouse nearby and that we would do better not to buy the house.
Oddly, both downstairs and upstairs were like a quagmire. I went into
the garden. On one side there was a low building, a great hall with
nothing but chairs, probably a club house. From this building you
could see the lake. I thought we should also try to buy this building.
This building had plank flooring. It was impossible to know whether
or not there was a quagmire under it.

The dreamer was in her thirties and worked in social services. Heretofore
she had lived very modestly on a relatively meager income, a "student's
existence," as she called it. Moreover, she had donated a considerable
portion of her income to social service institutions. At the time of this
dream she had come into a situation, due to a job change, in which she
could earn a considerable amount of money (for her) if she disregarded
her social service tendencies. Hence she was decidedly in a situation of
temptation and she had to come to terms with it.

For the sake of clarity I will not present her associations from that
session in their original sequence but rather in two groups. The first
group comprises her subjective associations and begins with her reporting the increase in her income and the possibilities that this opened for
her. Regarded genetically, she recalled an early fantasy when she had
wanted that sort of house on a peninsula and had imagined how she
would live there with a dog and lots of guests. She had often pursued this
fantasy but had forgotten it many years ago. Further she said that
recently her wish world had been awake to a much greater degree and
perhaps that was the origin of the old, forgotten fantasy that turned up
in her dream. Two days earlier she had visited an old colleague who had
the same position as she now did; he owned a nice house with valuable
antiques. The antiques in particular had attracted her because she had a
special weakness for them. She had imagined that she could now acquire
antiques like his if she wanted to. Although she had vowed not to accept
any social service obligations for the time being that did not remunerate
her at her new level, a task had been offered her where she could help in a
situation of decided need but which, she was certain, would cost her hard
work and earn her no financial rewards. She didn't have the heart to
refuse the task.

The two groups of spontaneous memories, thoughts, and feelings
comprise the objective associations that appeared amongst the subjective
associations and relate to two works by Bertold Brecht. In regard to the
house on the lake, she is reminded of "The Delayable Rise of Arturo Ui"
(Brecht 1976). In masked form the piece refers to the rise of National
Socialism in Germany. At the beginning of the piece a Hindenburg figure

is more or less bribed when he accepts a portfolio of stocks and a house on a lake. The parallel is very clear here. The patient senses that the demon, greedy for money and power, is rising up in herself, a demon who seeks to attain the goal of its drives inhumanly and without consideration for others. She encounters the Hitler in us and must come to terms with him. The slime of corruption from Brecht's drama reappears in her dream in the motif of the quagmirelike house that doesn't even have a view of the lake. It also seems very questionable whether or not the other building that they should also buy, and which has a view of the lake, may not be equally swampy under the beautiful floor boards.

The second association refers to the slaughterhouse that stands near the first house and which is the origin of the mire. In regard to the slaughterhouse she is again reminded of a piece by Brecht, "St. Joan of the Stockyards," with its depiction of an all-too-human situation of conflict, stated in the following verses:

> Humanity! Two souls abide
> Within thy breast!
> Do not set either one aside:
> To live with both is best!
> Be torn apart with constant care!
> Be two in one! Be here, be there!
> Hold the low one, hold the high one —
> Hold the straight one, hold the sly one —
> Hold the pair!
>
> (Brecht 1961, p. 256f)

These two objective associations set her personal conflict in the context of a collective human conflict which she had eluded heretofore by living in her own wish world and by leading her all-too-noble "student's life." She will have to bear this conflict her entire life long as one "torn apart with constant care." She needs to find a position in which she can unite both so that she can then remain "one."

In addition to these objective associations that the patient brings to the dream there is a whole tapestry of possible objective associations which the analyst should not be afraid to bring into the analysis when they contribute to understanding the patient's material. Thus the various underlying mythologems and treatments that the figure of Joan of Arc has received in the course of human history belong here, as do the figures of the great dictators and negative-demonic deities who depict the negative side of the father archetype. Likewise the problem of Goethe's Faust with his two souls belongs here, too, as well as the many mythological motifs of dismemberment and slaughter as preliminary steps to a process of renewal and transformation, such as Jung discussed in his "Visions of Zosimos" (*C.W.* 13) and I described in my interpretation of the "Handless Maiden" (Dieckmann 1967b).

Only after the archetypal content of the dream symbolism has been elucidated and enriched through a large number of objective associations does one attempt to expand this content by amplification. The translation of the word *amplificare*, of course, means "to broaden, expand, multiply, elevate, to place in a brighter light." Hence the method of amplification stays very much closer to the object—i.e., the dream or fantasy symbol that is to be amplified—than does the association method. Consequently amplification, as C. A. Meier (1972) expressed it, seeks not so much to bring the content of the dream into association with the consciousness of the dreamer as to remain in the unconscious; hence subject-object relationship poses no major problem for amplification. This sort of enrichment of the symbol gradually or suddenly leads to an illumination of the meaning which, for its part, can again spontaneously enter consciousness and thereby call forth a process of transformation. Rather, like assembling a jigsaw puzzle, amplification creates an entire picture from the parts of a picture and thus leads to the process of recognizing the symbol. Amplification is not a linear process like association, but rather a concentric one which leads back again and again to the same symbol. Jolande Jacobi (1943) has depicted this process in impressive drawings that we do not need to reproduce here.

In practice one, in fact, does get the impression that boundless association leads to stereotypes, that one runs up against the very same drives and primary processes again and again, that the method offers the patient very little help in mastering them and in working them through so that they become essentially transformative experiences. Siebenthal (1953) also discusses in detail the problem of whether or not one can say anything at all relevant about the structure of the dream by employing the method of free association. The method of amplification opens up the possibility of exploiting the symbol's capacity to transform energy and of bringing the transcendent function into action. Hobson (1971) pointed out that Jung's emphasis on amplification goes back to the year 1911 when he wrote *Symbols of Transformation* (*C.W.* 5) during his own creative crisis. In his autobiography, Jung (1962) then described how he discovered his own world and his own identity that was completely different from Freud's. In particular Hartmann's position in regard to the autonomous, creative, and compensatory function of the unconscious exerted a strong influence on Jung, especially since this function adjoined Jung's "number two" personality which did not live through an adapted persona in the positivistic sciences of those days.

By amplifying mythological images analogous to Miss Miller's fantasies, Jung also succeeded in arriving at a prognosis for the possible subsequent course of her psychological dynamics that was later borne out and verified (*C.W.* 5). In the foreword to that work, Jung pointed out what a comprehensive knowledge was required in order to adduce such analogies:

> As soon as these parallels come to be worked out they take up an incredible amount of space, which is why expositions of case histories are such an arduous task. But that is only to be expected: the deeper you go, the broader the base becomes. . . . For this a great deal of comparative material is needed, and it cannot be dispensed with any more than in comparative anatomy. Knowledge of the subjective contents of consciousness means very little, for it tells us next to nothing about the real, subterranean life of the psyche. In psychology as in every science a fairly wide knowledge of other subjects is among the requisites for research work. (*C.W.* 5, p. xxv–xxvi)

This knowledge from domains beyond the specialized analytic literature — that is, knowledge of mythology, ethnology, comparative history of religions, symbolism, fairy tales, etc. — is the necessary prerequisite for a fruitful application of the method of amplification since it gives the analyst a real understanding in depth of any given symbol. But from the standpoint of method, this sort of knowledge in depth does not suffice by itself. It must be explained to the patient, which is why the analyst should not be afraid to share such analogies with the patient; but in doing so it is of the greatest importance that those analogies fit the patient's situation and at the same time correspond to his or her momentary capacities to understand. Inherent in the method, of course, is the danger of inundating the patient with amplifications that he or she can no longer understand, which is why in practice I tend to offer them sparingly and carefully ponder the analogies to which the patient can establish a relationship with his or her feelings.

There is a beautiful legend of the Buddha that makes one pause to reflect and that illustrates the significance of this point. The legend tells that the Buddha had once stopped in a simsapa forest and had taken a handful of leaves. He showed them to his disciples and said to them that, just as the leaves in his hand were few in comparison to the leaves in the whole forest, what he had preached was only a fraction of what he knew, but he had intended to reveal to his disciples only as much as would be useful to them in attaining enlightenment. The analyst, too, should not give the patient more of the medicament of knowledge than is needed and can be metabolized and integrated in order to heal or solve the problem. "Overdoses" in this area can poison or inflate just as overdoses in organic medicine do.

In concluding our discussion we must raise yet one more question: To what psychic material can we apply the method of amplification? This is relatively easy to answer: to everything that consciousness can understand and incorporate as a genuine symbol. Here belong not only dreams, fantasies, hallucinations, active imaginations, meditative images, etc., but also memories, external objects, and empirical experiences in so far as they have symbolic character for the person concerned. In the first example, that of the woman at the green light, I noted that it was basically a genuine symbol in Jung's sense of the term, but that in this instance it did not seem opportune to enrich the symbol through amplification. This is not the place to discuss in greater detail what we understand as a symbol, and I refer the interested reader to Jacobi's *Complex, Archetype, Symbol* (1957), as well as to another paper of mine (Dieckmann 1972a).

Beside or beneath all that our consciousness experiences, a second level of psyche also expresses itself through the human unconscious; it speaks in another language, a symbolic language, and it is our task as analysts to learn to understand it. In the introduction to the first edition of *Collected Papers on Analytical Psychology* (*C.W.* 4), Jung designated the standpoint of his school as symbolic in contrast to the causal-reductive approach of Freud's psychoanalysis. The transcendent function is that symbolic function of the psyche capable of synthesizing the pairs of opposites. Here it is not a question of one of the basic functions such as thinking, feeling, intuition, or sensation, but rather of a complex function that is constituted of several factors and that makes possible the transition from one attitude to another. Whenever alert consciousness enters the process, seizes the symbol, and actually works it through to the point of altering consciousness, the transcendent function comes into play.

Not everything must be a symbol. Consciousness can pass by even great and significant symbols such as may be offered in a profound dream and neglect to ask their meaning. This creates the condition to which Jung makes an analogy to Parsifal (*C.W.* 14, par. 753). If the transcendent function comes into play, then even mundane events and objects can lead to profound experiences and transformations. In conclusion I will give an example of this.

The patient was in his late thirties and suffering from a relatively severe reactive depression when he came for therapy. In addition to the depressive component he also had strong compulsive characteristics. He was a very rationalistic, dry judicial official. The precipitating situation for his depressive moods was directly related to the problems of midlife and to his feelings of resignation that accompanied his having no more possibilities of promotion, of living the same married life in the same apartment, and of being able to calculate in advance the course of his life until he retired. After the patient had achieved some relaxation of his compulsive traits in the course of a prolonged analysis and his individuation had gotten underway, the following event took place immediately before one of his sessions. That year, after we had experienced a warm spell toward the end of April, we suddenly got another snowfall, followed, however, on the very day of this patient's session by warm weather and radiant sunshine. Thanks to these climatic events, the crocuses, primroses, and early tulips stood in full splendor in a covering of snow in the gardens of the suburb in which I live. The patient had viewed this panorama from a purely aesthetic standpoint on his way to his session and had found it beautiful, but suddenly, as he approached my door, he felt himself inwardly moved to stop and to stare as though transfixed at one single red tulip blossom. As he stood there he was seized — as he expressed it — by a very remarkable and deeply moving experience. Suddenly he felt himself identical with that blossom, and, with that feeling, the sense of meaninglessness and oppression that had long plagued him vanished. He had the feeling of again being alive and whole, as he put it, of being a complete human being who was capable of blossoming and passing away. Granted, after a few moments he tore himself away, chided himself for being silly and unreasonable, and rang my door bell.

But shortly after the beginning of the hour he changed his mind and decided to tell me of this event, albeit with distinct feelings of shame, and he was obviously greatly relieved that I took the experience seriously and did not cast it aside as unreasonable. Here, of course, I turned to the method of amplification. The patient himself thought of the symbol of the Blue Flower of German Romanticism and of the cowslip which, according to folk belief, is able to open heaven. I reminded him of Andersen's fairy tale of Thumbelina who was born from a tulip.

Then I reminded him of the symbolism of the Rosicrucians and of the history of that society which sought to reunite the natural-scientific and religious-mystical world views that at the time of the origin of the Rosicrucians were coming into ever greater contradiction. That brought us to speak of all those flowers — among others, the lotus birth of the Buddha — that are associated with the symbolism of the Self and hence with the totality of the personality so that the patient could gradually grasp that his individuation and his occupying himself with his unconscious had gradually led him to a place where, in a gnostic experience (knowledge through experience), he was capable of seeing his own Self, which in the East is understood as the Tao. Following this hour he was able to let this experience enter into his consciousness and to retain it, whereupon there followed a clear transformation and a significant improvement in his symptoms that gradually vanished completely in the further course of his analysis.

Through amplification the "meaning" of the symbol of this tulip came into relationship with the dreamer's consciousness, and the novel experience was able to have a consciousness-transforming effect for him. By its very nature, this effect is convincing for both the patient and the analyst who also experiences it, even if it is not completely comprehensible to consciousness. This particular analytic experience also seemed to me a convincing illustration of the value and the significance of using the method of amplification.

CHAPTER 10

Analytic Distance

Strictly speaking, the problem of analytic distance really belongs in the domain of transference and countertransference. But since analytic distance is a circumscribed, special issue that is much discussed yet little publicized, I treat it here in a separate chapter.

First of all, distance is a concept expressing the spatial separation between two objects. Only if there is distance is a vis-à-vis possible. Two objects that occupy precisely the same space cannot be juxtaposed but rather are fused with one another. Only the real juxtaposition in space between two people, be it ever so small, makes it possible for them to come to terms with each other at all. As long as this purely spatial vis-à-vis does not exist — as, for example, in the instance of a mother and her growing embryo — juxtaposition, coming to terms with each other, and differentiation permitting independent development of both parties is not possible. Hence concrete, spatial distance is quite simply a prerequisite if the process of independent maturation and development is to take place in an individual. This is quite obvious in concrete terms.

But when we enter the domain of psychic processes, the problem becomes incomparably more difficult. The psyche cannot be comprehended in spatial terms. Linguistically we use spatial concepts in this domain merely as analogies or metaphors. If, for example, we speak of "deep" levels or layers of the unconscious, we are indeed making use of a spatial concept, but we must always remember that this is purely metaphor. In the psyche there is no above and below, and hence neither deep nor high; rather, with these terms we circumscribe qualities of psychic experience accessible to consciousness with greater or lesser difficulty. Thus in the instance of "analytic distance" we must separate two realms: one is the realm having to do with empirical, concrete, physical distance between analyst and patient; the second is that field, much more difficult to grasp and describe, in which we utilize the concept of analytic distance as a metaphor for something purely psychic. With the latter we give the patient the free space Heyer described (1964), again an invisible, meta-phoric space that makes possible the flow of unconscious material.

Let us first briefly consider concrete, physical distance. Initially classical analysis created a very considerable, concrete, real distance by seating the analyst behind the patient. The patient cannot see the analyst and speaks in a different direction, which intentionally resembles soccer players who try to get the ball into their own goal rather than that of their opponents or partners. The greatest possible opportunity to make projections is granted the patient by avoiding any personal contact between analyst and patient and by the demand that the analyst exclude his or her own inner experiences and processes as much as possible from the analysis. When this is strictly enforced, it creates a considerable distance, and the analyst basically remains, for the duration of the treatment and even afterwards, a very distanced father or mother deity whose actual existence and reality the patient never experiences, whom the patient never knows but about whom he or she is always restricted to hunches and suppositions. Surely this classical, severe distance is hardly enforced nowadays. The insight that the objective, neutral analyst — who serves merely as a screen for projections — is an illusory fiction, as well as the many modern possibilities for variation in Freudian psychoanalysis in the therapy of the psychoses, borderline conditions, groups, families, etc., have greatly mitigated the severity of the original rule both in practice and in theory.

From the very beginning Jung's idea of analysis as a dialectical process between analyst and patient, which makes the analyst visible and transparent to the patient, has prevented the appearance of that sort of concrete, almost schizoid distance between the two persons involved. Granted, Jungian analysts' views of the optimal distance between analyst and patient vary considerably, and there is only a *consensus omnium* that one should avoid all-too intensive processes of merging. In my opinion no generally valid rules can be established in this area. It seems to me idle speculation to discuss in general whether, for example, taking a walk or going to the theater with the patient, touching the patient or letting the patient touch the analyst, etc., should be allowed. Generalizations of this sort are always wrong and what may be the worst thing in one situation — conclusively blocking an analysis or forcing a termination — can be the only thing possible and right in another case. The thing that seems to me important here is Christ's statement from the Apocrypha, cited by Jung: "Man, if indeed thou knowest what thou doest, thou art blessed" (1969, *Psychology and Religion*, par. 133). But since we do not know this in most instances, it is wiser to be extraordinarily cautious in regard to decreasing distance. Let me give an example.

I had a patient who, after considerable analysis, found himself in a situation that felt like a profound crisis. At the end of one analytic hour that had run a very dramatic course, I spontaneously put my arm around the shoulders of this weeping man who was the same age as I. However, I had overlooked the existence of his massive latent homosexual problem which he had not yet brought into analysis. It later turned out that my act contributed to intensifying his homoerotic and homosexual fears and consequently also his resistances against those tendencies so greatly that we were never entirely successful in clearing up the problem.

Perhaps a second example will make even clearer what is meant by the admonition, "If thou knowest . . . ." A very experienced older colleague (a Freudian, by the way) once told a small circle of professional acquaintances about her therapeutic work with a schizophrenic woman patient: in a very specific situation she (the analyst) had lain down beside the woman patient on the couch in order to let the patient feel some physical warmth. This act made it possible for the psychotic patient to enter into a real relationship with another human being for the first time ever in her life, and at this point in her treatment, the analyst had done precisely the right thing. A junior analyst who had just finished his training was present and was extraordinarily impressed with the success of this therapeutic intervention. Falling into the role of Goethe's sorcerer's apprentice, he shortly thereafter lay down on the couch beside a severe hysteric who expressed her difficulties with relationship in a similar way. Of course, the effect was correspondingly dramatic and the young analyst was able to free himself from the patient's embrace only by leaping back into his chair. I do not know how this treatment turned out, but in any event the old Latin proverb comes to mind: *Quod licet Jovi, non licet Bovi.*

In regard to this problem it again seems that the analyst must consider not only the patient's situation but also typology and psychological structure as well as his or her own issues and must be capable of taking all this into account. As everywhere in analysis, here, too, it depends not so much on what one does but rather on how one does it, and the how is always conditioned by the entire psychological background and by the unconscious of the persons involved. It can be wrong to prolong a session because one cannot say no and has separation difficulties; and it can be wrong not to prolong a session because one is too persona-bound and hence leaves too little room for the living process of analysis.

The entire issue of concrete analytic distance is important because it has very decisive repercussions on the problem of metaphoric distance. Hence we must first speak in greater detail of the problem of psychic distance, and, in order to do so, we do best to return to the *vas hermeticum* of the alchemists already mentioned in the Introduction.

Lao-Tzu says that the pitcher acquires meaning and function not by virtue of the clay of which it is made but rather by virtue of the emptiness the clay encloses. The image holds true for the mysterious *vas hermeticum* of the alchemists and for the metaphorical space that comes into being in analysis. For the patient in the analytic setting, an empty space must be present in which his or her fantasies can pour forth as free and unimpeded as possible and in which the symbols from the unconscious have the possibility of unfolding. Within this space, as in the alchemical process, transformation can take place and the *aurum non vulgum* can arise out of the *massa confusa* which, regarded analytically, corresponds to the process of transformation of the libido via the symbol as Jung has described ("On Psychic Energy," *C.W.* 8). As a concept, the *vas hermeticum* plays a major role in alchemy. One imagines this vessel as a sort of retort or oven, as a container for the substances to be transformed, but the descriptions the various alchemists give of the nature of this *vas* soon correct one's notion:

> It is a kind of matrix or uterus from which the *filius philosophorum*, the miraculous stone, is to be born. Hence it is required that the vessel be not only round but egg-shaped. One naturally thinks of this vessel as a sort of retort or flask; but one soon learns that this is an inadequate conception since the vessel is more a mystical idea, a true symbol like all the central ideas of alchemy. Thus we hear that the *vas* is the water or *aqua permanens*, which is none other than the Mercurius of the philosophers. But not only is it the water, it is also its opposite: fire. (Jung, *Psychology and Alchemy, C.W.* 12, par. 338)

Hence this vessel confronts us with a spiritual or psychological process of the unconscious such as I described in my discussion of the Arabic fairy tale, "The Fisher Who Found the Bottle" (Dieckmann 1977).

The relationship that the vessel has to the opposite elements fire and water and especially to the alchemical Mercurius presents a rather differentiated and complicated problem. Jung characterized Mercurius thus:

> (1) Mercurius consists of all conceivable opposites. He is thus quite obviously a duality, but is named a unity in spite of the fact that his innumerable contradictions can dramatically fly apart into an equal number of disparate and apparently independent figures.
>
> (2) He is both material and spiritual.
>
> (3) He is the process by which the lower and material is transformed into the higher and spiritual and, vice versa.
>
> (4) He is the devil, a redeeming psychopomp, an evasive trickster, and God's reflection in physical nature.
>
> (5) He is also the reflection of a mystical experience of the artifex that coincides with the *opus alchemicum*.

(6) As such, he represents on the one hand the self and on the other the individuation process and, because of the limitless number of his names, also the collective unconscious. (Jung, *C.W.* 13, par. 284)

We can easily translate this characterization of Mercurius to the analytic space that arises through distance. First, in point one Jung speaks of Mercurius as consisting of all conceivable pairs of opposites that separate dramatically into many figures, yet he is always designated as a unity. If we transfer this description to the analytic *vas*, we know it is not only the patient's fantasies that pour forth into the space between analyst and patient but also the analyst's fantasies, thus creating a duality or a pair of opposites. As Blomeyer's (1971) and my (Dieckmann 1971d) studies of concurrent fantasies of patient and analyst demonstrated, however, these fantasies are always meaningfully related to one another and consequently one can again speak of a unity. The disintegration into various figures then corresponds to the process of unconscious symbol formation which, of course, also appears as countless different figures within the analytic process.

In point two it is clear that we are dealing with a process both physical and spiritual since we have already discussed in detail the problem of the real, external distance in contrast to the invisible, metaphorical, and psychic distance that, so to speak, forms the compass of the container.

According to point three the analytical *vas* makes possible the transformation of the lower into the upper and vice versa, which is clearly expressed in the processes of the transformation of libido in analysis. Here, too, the expressly mentioned physical aspect is included since significant psychosomatic processes may run their courses in analysis and the libido, bound up in them — as, for instance, in a tetanus attack, asthma, or an ulcer — is transformed into the upper. However, upper psychic energy can be brought into the physical realm as a somatization, increase in blood supply, and elevated sensitivity. In a successful analysis changes in the areas of kinesthetics, overall body feel, and increased sensory perceptiveness usually take place.

It is a fact known to every analyst that the unconscious can be a devil, a savior pointing the way, as well as a divinity, and an evasive trickster that has both analyst and patient at its mercy; the various methods of final-prospective and causal-reductive work on the unconscious as well as the compensatory function of the unconscious correspond to this state of affairs.

Many rationally oriented scientists will certainly have difficulty swallowing the idea that the analytic space is a mirror image of a mystical experience. The processes of emotional development that may — not must — arise between two persons in the close relationship which analysis can be remains a mystery resting on a *deo concedente* regardless of all the analyst's art. As an analyst one can learn to be open to admitting these processes of development; one can stimulate and encourage them, but one cannot force them to take place by using technical tricks. Ultimately let us hope that it remains this way and that we be spared the perfect technicians of the soul who see in the soul nothing but an object of natural science that one can change arbitrarily. Here ends the often-heard comparison with surgery — that is, that one finds certain objects in certain places and, in so far as they are malignant, one can remove them or implant the corresponding prosthesis. Nothing can be removed or surgically excised from the human psyche in the analytic process; rather, psychic change has to do with transformation, growth, or maturation, and something artificial neither can nor should be inserted. Thus the experience of the analytic process within this *vas* also represents the Self and the path of individuation in which, along with the personal unconscious, the collective unconscious is also included.

I would now like to mention some practical examples that illustrate how one can deal with analytic distance in individual cases. The first example is that of a woman patient in her early thirties who sought analytic treatment because of a painful delusion in regard to relationship. During her first analytic hours she dreamed that she was in the animal show of a circus with her little six-year-old daughter and was watching the wild animals. Suddenly she realized that the cage of a large tiger was open and it was threatening to leave its cage. Only after a prolonged, anxious attempt to flee and a long search did she succeed in finding an attendant who then took care that the tiger got back into its cage again and that the cage was securely closed.

Without going into this dream and the patient's issues in detail, the dream does make impressively clear at the very beginning of analysis that the patient experiences the unconscious in the form of a wild, extremely dangerous tiger, and not only the patient herself but also her daughter are in mortal danger. Methodologically it does not make any sense to say to this woman, "Your fear is deluding you with something that really is not there at all. Neither the analysis nor your own unconscious is a wild tiger that can annihilate you and your daughter." For one thing, this woman would not understand such a statement since she is not, in the least, in a position to bring this animal into a real relationship with her analysis or with her own unconscious; and second, for the patient this tiger is an inner reality that simply must not be outmaneuvered. The analyst must clearly recognize that he or she is actually dealing with an intrapsychic tiger that brings a high level of fear and flight impulse into the relationship. For the time being this animal is more powerful than both analyst and patient and must first be brought into a protected and closed place in order that it not exert purely destructive effects. Since the tiger also represents or governs the patient's inner nature which is linked with the elements of warmth, closeness, and penetration, it is necessary in this case to maintain a relatively great distance at first. This distance can be managed both externally as concrete and internally as metaphoric.

I have intentionally chosen as my first example that of a relatively extreme case—a psychosis—because the issue of analytic distance is often clearest and most impressive in these sorts of conditions. As a consequence of very great fears and feelings of being endangered that proceed from the unconscious, patients with psychotic and borderline conditions can tolerate very little closeness at the beginning of therapy. To the extent that the analyst attempts to establish closeness through too frequent sessions or through strong empathy and getting too close too fast, extremely violent anxiety and flight reactions, which are very difficult to clear up later, are mobilized in these patients. Hence it is much more sensible to offer such patients the greatest possible degree of distance and to wait calmly until, through a slow process of habituation, the patient loses his or her fear of "getting closer." With these sorts of patients the analyst should not be deceived by the underlying addictionlike longing for closeness which is naturally present as a compensation in such isolated people. In practice it is often advisable to begin therapy with a psychotic patient by seeing him or her only once weekly or once every two weeks or even once a month until the anxiety has diminished to the extent that he or she can tolerate the "closeness" of two or three sessions per week. Granted, in the case described above this was not necessary; rather, the analysis could begin with two sessions per week which was supported by the prospective element in the dream where the attendant succeeds in getting the tiger back into the cage. But in spite of this it was a long time until enough "inner closeness" could develop that the patient was at all capable of bringing her sensitive delusion into analysis. She did so only after something more than one hundred hours of analysis.

A schizophrenic patient in his mid-thirties found himself in similar straits. His treatment, like the one described above, began with infrequent, widely spaced sessions. In the course of his therapy, four years passed before he was finally able to experience a personal, felt sense of closeness and to risk showing any personal interest in me. At the beginning of a session he regularly pushed his chair one or two yards back before he sat down and thereby indicated the distance he needed to maintain between us. Only when the phase began in which he was able to permit closer personal distance did he leave his chair in the same place where it stood when I saw other patients, and in the further course of time he even moved his chair closer to me from time to time. Previously he had rejected or responded with very strong irritation and confusion to every ever-so-cautious emotional overture on my part for more personal closeness and relationship.

I believe that these two examples alone distinctly show how singularly difficult it is to respect this *vas hermeticum* that contains the analytic space and also how lively and dynamic is the energy it contains since it changes again and again not only in the course of extended periods of treatment but also within individual sessions as it becomes more distant and expands or comes closer and constricts.

In the case of another patient, by contrast, a completely opposite situation prevailed. At the beginning of her analysis she had taken the couch, and the entire first phase of her therapy was characterized by her creating a relatively close feeling atmosphere (she was an extraverted feeling type), but she excluded all feelings of disappointment, irritation, rage, etc. These emotions were, for all practical purposes, completely repressed and, by repressing these dark feelings which she experienced as negative, she was able to maintain a close, womblike atmosphere in the analytic relationship. Then she dreamt that young men who were swinging on a platform were taught how to work with high-tension lines which initially frightened her greatly when one of the men came in contact with one of the lines. But then she told herself that nothing could happen since he did not have his feet in contact with the earth. Following this dream she realized that something was amiss in the whole situation. She had brought a high level of libido into analysis which, however, posed no danger since she was not grounded and which could not lead to any sort of transformation either, but rather presented only a training field for beginners who were not yet in a position to deal with these high-tension currents. Up until the time of this dream she had obviously also needed this sort of situation, and initially her analysis had to be a sort of practice field in which her genuine feelings did not have to be exposed because they were dangerous.

Shortly afterward, she dreamt that she was standing on the shore of a turbulent sea and suddenly a wave washed over her that did not sweep her into the water but only got her wet so that she was able to move up to a higher level in order to dry off. Directly following this dream, very intense and rather strongly aggressive feelings entered into the transference and countertransference constellation which, regarded genetically, arose from a negative father-daughter relationship. During the sessions when these feelings rose up in her, she also spontaneously sat down and assumed the position of the opponent, no longer that of someone containing everything. Although the distance between us grew larger inwardly, the analytic relationship gained in vitality and in personal content which, compared to the previously prevailing rather lukewarm, boring atmosphere, was a beneficial contrast. In this case one is very distinctly reminded of the above-mentioned pair of alchemical opposites, fire and water, of which the *vas hermeticum* is supposed to consist. The patient had brought a bit too much fire (positive transference libido) into the analysis of which the high-tension lines in her dream are reminiscent. In contrast to this, it was necessary that the other constituent of the *vas hermeticum*, the water, be mobilized in the symbolism of the stormy sea which brought about a real participation of the dream-ego and subsequently of the conscious ego-complex. In the preceding dream the dream-ego was still an uninvolved spectator who did not get in touch with the current; the dream-ego was able to accept only the stormy wave as an unpleasant but yet very much involved encounter with the inner forces.

Graphically one can represent analytic distance also as a dynamic process in the form of two circles, bound together in such a manner that they resemble a figure 8 (Figure 10.1). In regard to each other, they then form a relatively unmoveable unity, actually touching only at one point, **S**. However, a force or current would flow unhindered through both circles.

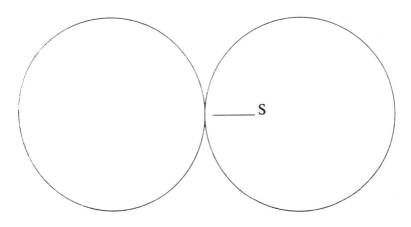

That would mean that a stimulus or excitation—or in the case of a relationship, a piece of information—flows immediately from any point in the system throughout the entire system unimpeded, and that every disturbance or movement (**E**) affects both circles every time simultaneously and in toto, as Figure 10.2 attempts to represent.

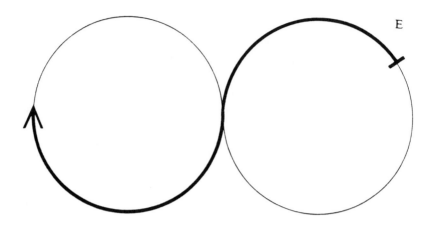

In a relationship, this signifies the condition of *participation mystique* (Lévy-Bruhl 1959). We find ourselves in a relationship of this sort — for example, in the extreme case of the fetus *in utero* — as part of one single circuit that is firmly attached at one point, thus everything that touches the one touches the other in the very same way. Fundamentally there is no distance in a relationship of this sort, and distance can be created only when the connection between the two circles is broken and they move apart as totally separate systems existing isolated from one another, as represented in Figure 10.3.

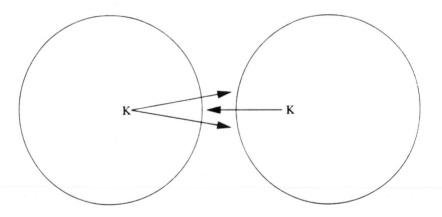

We experience this situation very frequently in interpersonal relationships when, for example, a condition of total *participation mystique* has been obtained for a period of time between two lovers and misunderstandings then arise between them due to the existing different natures of the two persons. Extraordinarily intense, affectively charged mutual reactions then take place that lead to a break in the relationship, internally if not externally, and to the feeling of being suddenly not understood, completely isolated, and far distanced from the other.

The more mature model of relationship that also leaves room for both individuation and the differences of the two personalities corresponds to the image of two overlapping circles (Figure 10.4).

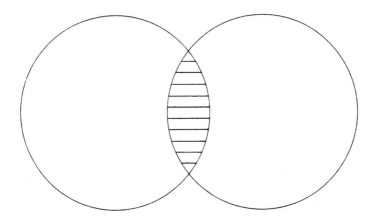

In this diagram there is only a certain domain—here indicated as shaded—in which the commonality of *participation mystique* takes place while another part, which can be far larger, is not shared in common but rather is reserved as an individual sphere containing the necessary distance between the two circles. In contrast to the previous models, this one is moveable since the shared portion can be enlarged or diminished, depending on the needs of the two persons and on the momentary exigencies of their situation (see Figures 10.5 and 10.6).

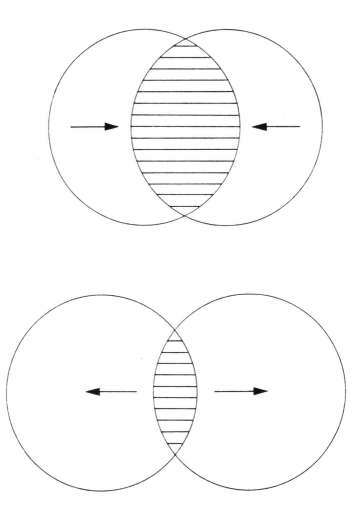

In conflict situations, some degree of commonly shared content can be preserved in this model and the situation does not necessarily have to lead immediately to total isolation or to a total break in the relationship. Rather, only an increase or a decrease in the mutual distance arises. Hence the possibility of individuation is preserved on the one hand and, on the other, the danger of a total rupture with complete isolation from one's partner is avoided.

Of course, models of this sort represent the extremely complex inter-action in the analytic space only to a severely limited degree. My sole concern was that of illustrating that we are dealing with a dynamic process here, and the inner *vas hermeticum* in which analysis runs its course is not a rigid, closed space. As Erich Neumann pointed out in his essay on the psychological significance of rite (1953a), creation of the analytic situation and of the analytic relationship, resting upon both specific, fixed, external rules as well as a corresponding inner distance, signifies the necessary protection for patients so that they can expose themselves to the archaic world and to the primordial experiences of the unconscious which then effect the processes of transformation and renewal. The primal peoples, exposed as they are to the danger of inundation by unconscious contents due to the weak development of their consciousness and to a relatively unstable individual ego, must enforce especially strict taboos here, particularly when it is a question of ceremonies that are intended to mobilize certain inner powers as do the *rites d'entrés* preceding the hunt, war, tilling the field, and (especially) religious ceremonies. Consequently violations of taboo and deviations from ritual that are often necessary for the continued existence of consciousness vis-à-vis often superior natural forces are usually punished with extreme severity, sometimes even with the death of the offender. We, too, work with powers of this magnitude and should be aware that very deep and powerful affective forces lie beneath the cover of our rational consciousness, powers that can be healing and constructive only if we are not inundated by them and if we do not sink into a commonly shared unconscious state. Seen from this vantage point, distance is an unconditionally necessary element in the methodology of analysis, particularly in regard to the deep, unconscious layers, and especially to the collective unconscious.

Simultaneously, however, analytic distance is also the model of the distance between the ego-complex and the unconscious, and everything we have said about analytic distance and the analytic space can be translated from the transference-countertransference situation directly to the relation between the ego and the non-ego. To the extent he or she succeeds, the patient experiences the creation of just this sort of meaningful but also distanced relationship between his or her conscious ego-complex and his or her own unconscious contents in the analytic process. They also retain this knowledge beyond the analysis so that it now empowers them to maintain the relationship with their unconscious after termination of treatment and neither to let themselves be flooded by contents that arise from the unconscious nor to get into the situation of being isolated from them. Hence the whole secret, in fact, lies in knowledge of the hermetic vessel which embraces the conscious and the unconscious and in which the transformation and the vitality of the inner life is maintained, just as was expressed in the quote from Maria Prophetissa: "One becomes two, two becomes three, and out of the third comes the One as the fourth" (Jung, *CW* 9ii, par. 237).

I am well aware that everything I have said here represents only a very pitiful abstraction of the inexpressible and intangible situation we call the analytic atmosphere, and that this inner atmosphere is the metaphoric space in which analysis runs its course and is the decisive criterion that nothing external can supplant. In borderline cases or psychoses, too, where a greater closeness is necessary (Balint 1968, Sechehaye 1955), literal, concrete closeness can never serve as a substitute for the other. From personal experience with a number of analysands and numerous control cases of other colleagues, I have determined that too marked a reduction of the real distance between analyst and patient usually arises from the helplessness of the analyst who ultimately is not able to make the process more effectual. In alchemy there is a figure that is very characteristic and correctly perceived intuitively. This is the so-called *soror mystica* whose presence many alchemists regarded as necessary when working on the opus. As a rule the *soror mystica* was a young girl or woman who had to stay continually with the alchemist in his laboratory while he was working on the opus but whom he must not touch. Her effect consisted solely in the presence of her *fluidum* and her atmosphere. The *soror mystica* is the alchemist's anima; applied to the analytic process, it is the anima or the animus of the analyst. To the extent that the anima and the animus represent a personification of the relationship to the unconscious (Jung, "Relations Between the Ego and the Unconscious," *C.W.* 7), their continual presence within the process is necessary. Their presence represents a living interest and empathy for the unconscious contents that are constellated, but at the same time also represents the necessary distance that hinders acting out the *coniunctio oppositorum* and furthers the creation of an inner union of these opposites.

CHAPTER 11

Transference and Countertransference

In every psychotherapeutic treatment a certain form of relationship between physician and patient arises that is embedded in the rituals of the methodology applied or school followed. This particular form of relationship is distinguished from all other customary human relationships in a specific way. From the beginning it arises from both partners and usually continues to exist long after the end of the treatment. In our technical terminology, we designate this form of relationship as transference and countertransference, in regard to which analytical psychology — in contrast to the early Freudian concept — makes no sharp distinction between neurotic transference and countertransference phenomena and so-called "normal" relationships. As early as 1946, when countertransference phenomena had received little or no discussion in psychoanalysis, Jung gave probably the most comprehensive presentation of that emotional relationship network that binds physician and patient in psychotherapy in his *Psychology of the Transference* (*C.W.* 16). In his schema of the "cross-cousin marriage" (which I reproduce here in slightly altered form in Figure 11.1), Jung described the possibilities for transference and countertransference.

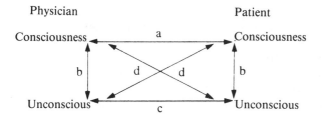

In this diagram, we see how "normal" conscious communication takes place between patient and analyst along vector **a** running from the consciousness of the analyst to that of the patient. That is, the physician or the patient verbally imparts some conscious content to the other which the other's consciousness receives. Vector **b** represents the relation between the consciousness of the physician and his or her own unconscious or, in the other half of the diagram, between the patient's consciousness and his or her unconscious. Unconscious contents pass along this vector into consciousness and are then shared with the other along vector **a**. From the patient's standpoint, this can be dreams, fantasies, or "spontaneous" ideas; from the physician's standpoint, they can likewise be fantasy contents or "spontaneous" ideas, memories, etc., that occur in regard to the patient. An additional vector, **d**, extends from the physician's unconscious to the patient's consciousness as well as from the patient's unconscious to the physician's consciousness. The physician observes, for example, the patient's unconscious material along this line and, at the appropriate juncture, shares the observation with the patient. Vice versa, the patient's consciousness can also observe the physician's unconscious contents, as, for example, slips of the tongue or certain stereotyped behaviors of which the physician is unconscious.

The last vector, **c**, represents the relationship between the unconscious of the two persons. It is the most interesting and certainly the most important therapeutically since this is the locus of the unconscious *participation mystique* between the psyches of analyst and patient that plays a role in every encounter between persons. Making this interaction conscious in the analytic process is of the greatest importance. Since all vectors can function simultaneously—i.e., contents can fall from consciousness into the unconscious as well as rise from the unconscious into consciousness—we have a total of twelve various pathways along which the consciousness and the unconscious of doctor and patient can communicate with each other.

In his *Psychology of the Transference*, published in 1946, Jung was still of the opinion that these intimate transference and countertransference relationships between doctor and patient did not manifest in all cases but rather only in far-reaching analyses while there were other instances in which the transference ran a "milder" course or was either not present at all or played no role. Today we know that that standpoint was erroneous and that transference and countertransference reactions begin from the first moment of meeting between analyst and patient. Freud also held the opinion that, for example, narcissistic neuroses displayed no transference (Freud, *S.E.* vols. 8 and 10), a view that today has also been refuted, particularly by Kohut (1971). On the contrary, we know today that, from the outset, it is precisely in the narcissistic neuroses and the psychoses that extremely violent, intense transference phenomena appear that, to be sure, are withheld from the outside world. It is also by no means the case that these transference and countertransference phenomena play a role only in analysis; rather, they are present in every form of psychotherapy, and consciously or unconsciously they play a role in every psychotherapeutic treatment method, even in the so-called "brief psychotherapies" such as hypnosis, autogenic training, guided imagery, etc., and should at least be better known and noted by the therapist when employing such methods. In order to illustrate this better, I would like to mention a brief example that came to my attention recently at a conference.

The topic of the conference was one of the methods of brief psychotherapy. Fortunately, one afternoon was dedicated to presenting failed cases and to discussion of the causes underlying the failure. One colleague presented the case of a young woman who, following termination of a pregnancy on medical advice, developed neurotic symptoms and entered treatment. Hers was most certainly not a case where an acute exacerbation of underlying chronic neurotic condition developed; nevertheless, no therapeutic gains were made. Rather, her symptoms became worse with each treatment so that finally her therapy had to be terminated. Only then did a certain degree of relief from her symptoms appear. Fantasies that the woman patient shared with her male therapist in treatment showed extremely violent and terribly threatening aggressive contents directed against both others and masochistically against herself. Neither doctor nor patient found any way to get into her murderous and destructive aggression. What underlay this problem?

After a period of discussion, the following information came to light. The colleague involved was also an expert consultant for termination of pregnancies and had given this very same woman a consultation recommending termination. On the basis of his recommendation, termination of her pregnancy had been approved. Since the child had been unwanted or impossible, the patient's ambivalence vis-à-vis her pregnancy — that is, especially the positive pole of her ambivalence — had been repressed into the unconscious. From the standpoint of consciousness, the colleague was, of course, her helper and benefactor. But the situation looked quite different from the vantage point of the unconscious. Moreover, since the entire sequence of events took place in a Catholic district, the patient's unconscious experienced this physician as the murderer of her child or as the accomplice of her own culpable deed tabooed by her superego. Before any sort of therapeutic method whatsoever could have any chance of success with these two persons, the issues surrounding the termination of her pregnancy would have had to be analyzed in detail, and I doubt that the problem could have been solved analytically.

Between 1969 and 1974, a study group in Berlin conducted investigations of countertransference phenomena (Blomeyer 1971, 1972; Dieckmann 1971d, 1973a, 1974c, 1976c; E. Jung 1973). Our methodology was that of noting down not only the patient's but also the analyst's associations and fantasies during an individual analytic hour, without, of course, telling the patient. The study group then analyzed and discussed these two series of associations, taking into account the preceding and the following analytic hours. In these studies, comprising a total of fifty-four cases, we were able to demonstrate that the extraordinarily dense interweaving of transference and countertransference that Jung assumes in *The Psychology of the Transference* was in fact present to a degree we had not expected. Some of the principal results of these investigations were the discovery of an almost complete correspondence between the patient's and the analyst's associations at the sensory level, a clustering of synchronicity phenomena when the analyst observed his or her own unconscious, and the recognition that patients' resistances in analysis were at least 50 percent determined by a resistance from the unconscious of the analyst. This last phenomenon in particular may well have played a considerable role in the case described above. In these investigations it proved expedient not only for purposes of scientific differentiation but also from the standpoint of practical therapeutic management to differentiate these transference and countertransference phenomena once again at another level into four distinct pairs of opposites according to the form and manner in which they appeared.

The first form in which transference and countertransference phenomena occur is projection. Unconscious material or unconscious figures are projected from one person onto the other, and the other is treated as if he or she were the projected person or were identical with the projected content. Basically this corresponds to the familiar, old transference neurosis of which Freud spoke, wherein, for example, a patient projects his father onto the analyst and then treats the latter as though he were his father. However, we should disabuse ourselves of the illusion that, vice versa, the analyst has no projections on the patient. This is never the case. The analyst has an unconscious, too, and projecting its contents into the world about us or onto other persons is an ever-present function of the unconscious. Consequently in the analytic situation it is important and necessary again and again for analysts to ask themselves what is being projected onto the patient, to become conscious of these projections and to work them through. For a long time—and one still encounters this notion in the literature today—projective countertransference was viewed only from the standpoint of its negative and destructive effects in regard to the analysis, while the projective transference of the patient was recognized early on as a valuable therapeutic force. But one should clearly recognize that projective countertransference not only poses a danger for the analysis, but also, as the psychoanalyst Heimann (1950) pointed out, can be used as a tool for understanding the analysand. Other authors such as Winnicott (1958), Gitleson (1952), Weigert

(1952), and Racker (1968) have explained that positive transference reactions of this sort contribute to enlivening the analytic situation and have signal character for the activation of deeper complexes. The projective countertransference in Jung's sense shows the alteration of the analyst that arises through affinity (i.e., through the elements that draw the two personalities together), and consequently it can have not only a dangerous but also a prospective-dynamic character to the extent that it becomes conscious and can be worked through in the course of the process. In this sense, not only the patient's projective transference to the analyst (whose experience of the analytic interaction and its interpretation forms an important therapeutic aid in analysis) but also the analyst's projected countertransference is an important therapeutic aid in analysis. In our study group we frequently found that the analyst's incompletely worked-through childhood fears played a sizeable role in the analytic work even of seasoned analysts, not only as hindrances but also in the sense that they led to fruitful dialectical exchanges between patient and analyst and brought with them an emotional vivification. In this way the analyst's repeated question, "What am I really projecting on my patient?" becomes a most essential technical and methodological resource in the analytic process. Moreover, posing this question and maintaining a continual awareness of one's own incompleteness and imperfection can protect the analyst from slipping into a wrong-headed role of omniscience toward the patient, or, what is even more dangerous, from becoming inflated by the patient's projection of the Self onto the analyst, a projection that every patient has on his or her analyst. Just as in the instance of transference projections, of course, it is an essential precondition for the therapeutic usefulness of countertransference projections that the analyst be able to become aware of his or her counterprojections and, second, be capable of withdrawing them or working them through. In spite of this, one should always be conscious of the fact that here, too, a certain residue remains and that no analysis is ideal.

Borrowing from Fordham (1957), there is a second level which we shall designate as objective transference and countertransference. The objective transference and countertransference consist simply of one's objective perception of existing psychic contents or conditions in the other and of sharing that perception at the right moment. The art of analytic interpretation rests essentially on the objective countertransference which perceives and recognizes psychic contents in the patient just beyond the patient's threshold of consciousness. In both the psychoanalytic literature and in that of analytical psychology, there has been a great deal of discussion about interpretation and its techniques and methods so that I need not go into detail on it here. Perhaps I should emphasize one point in this context, however: when making interpretations in analysis, it is important not only that the analyst grasp a psychic condition correctly but also—and this is especially important—that the interpretation come at the correct time and in a form acceptable to the patient. This point is best expressed by the Greek word *kairòs*, i.e., that the right thing be done at the right time and the right place. However, no method or technique can tell the individual analyst at what point the right thing should be said; rather, *kairòs* is always embedded in the emotional transference and countertransference situation that exists between the patient and the analyst at a given moment. When and how an interpretation is to be expressed is something the analyst can decide only with the aid of his or her intuitive function which, at a given moment, imparts the feeling that an interpretation is appropriate and how it can be formulated.

The patient's objective transference to the analyst is heeded and discussed in the literature to a significantly lesser degree. This objective transference has to do with the patient's conscious or unconscious perception of objectively present aspects of the analyst's personality which the patient brings up in the analysis. I would like to give an example of this from my experience. In the early years of my analytic practice, I had a patient who stuttered, the roots of which lay in a negative father complex. During one certain phase of his analysis, he brought a series of dreams having quite authoritarian and severe teacher figures, and it soon became apparent that he transferred this teacher to me. I interpreted this situation to him and he was able to accept it fully. My interpretation illuminated certain of his modes of experience and behavior in analysis, which he then was able to alter. But the teacher dreams remained and showed only a very minor decrease in frequency which began to irritate me. Then I reviewed the dreams of my other patients and found there, too, a relatively high percentage of similar teacher transference dreams. Now I recognized that unconsciously I was introducing a pedagogic and certainly authoritarian power element into my analyses. The resolution of this problem surely did not lie in repressing or suppressing one's pedagogic inclinations. Since analysis is a process of emotional learning, there is also a positive side to the analytic teacher. The analyst will find a sensible solution only if he or she becomes aware of this personality component, utilizes it consciously, and is able to discuss it with the analysand. When I was able to do this in the case mentioned, my patient's teacher dreams disappeared promptly.

I hope that this example illustrates how the transference figure of the "authoritarian teacher" arises from two roots. In part it is a projected figure arising from the patient's personal history and can be traced back to a father problem. This component is projected as transference as discussed above. However, the second root arises from the correspondence between an aspect of the analyst's personality with an internalized figure from the collective unconscious of the patient. From this stand-point it is no longer a projection but rather hits upon an existing aspect of the relationship between the patient and the analyst of which both were initially unconscious. In the instance of the second root, the transference is objective. Objective transference can, of course, take place without an overlapping projective transference. From the standpoint of method, it seems to me essential to examine carefully transference figures appearing in the dreams of my patients in terms of my own personality. Whenever clear transference figures appear in patients' dreams, the analyst should scrupulously examine the extent to which the unconscious is not perhaps right in this instance, negatively or positively, and whether or not the experience and behavior depicted in the transference figure corresponds to an unconscious experience and behavior on the part of the analyst in the analysis. Of course, the reverse of this is also true, and analysts should carefully observe what they dream of their patients since these dreams can give valuable insights into the momentary status of the objective transference and objective countertransference in the analysis.

During the last two decades, analysts as well as, for example, sociologists have become increasingly interested in the roles that are played out between partners in interpersonal relationships. To a certain extent, one party usually "suggests" a certain role quite unconsciously, assumes one part, the thesis, so to speak, and projects the antithesis onto the other party who fits the role in this form. The constellating power of the projection then usually coerces the other person, likewise quite unconsciously, to assume the role and to participate in the game. Probably best known and analytically most valuable are the descriptions of these sorts of games that Berne (1964) has given. By no means should we overlook the reality that these sorts of games are also played out on both sides to a relatively great degree in the analytic situation between doctor and patient. Often these games are more conscious, particularly on the analyst's part, and are accepted and played out with full or partial consciousness for long periods during the analysis. I have chosen the term "antithetical transference and countertransference" to designate this form in which transference and countertransference interlock so that a mutually compatible game arises.

Now the question immediately arises whether or not one should delineate antithetical games between patient and analyst from projections since they always rest on projection on at least one party's part. There are a number of very dangerous shadow roles that can sneak into the relationship between analyst and patient via the analyst, as Guggenbühl-Craig (1971) has described. On the other hand, there are forms of games that do not have such a negative accent, but rather, can be regarded as thoroughly worthwhile and legitimate aids to therapeutic work. For a long period in analysis and without hesitation I can consciously direct a good, maternal side of my personality to a patient who has been extensively deprived of good maternal attention at a feeling level during early childhood. That can give this sort of patient the opportunity to find the good, nurturing, and protective side of the mother archetype within so that, on that foundation, he or she can come to terms more effectively and more skillfully with a negative and frustrating mother. The same can hold true when the analyst assumes the role of the understanding but stern and resolute father, vis-à-vis a degenerate patient, thus first offering help in finding her- or himself. An approach of this sort—i.e., the analyst's more or less conscious collaboration in assuming an assigned role—should be included in the category of neither projective nor objective transference. The same holds true when, in order to mobilize latent functions in a patient in the sense Meier (1972) has in mind, the analyst responds in the countertransference with a function other than the patient's leading function. For example, it can be necessary and therapeutically fruitful when the analyst expresses more introversion and more of the feeling function in order to address the patient's inferior functions and to make them comprehensible when the patient is an extraverted thinker and works in analysis predominantly with extraverted thinking. Although it is tempting to work in terms of the concept of persona and much in interpersonal games and roles corresponds to persona functions, I would prefer to utilize the concept of antithetical transference and countertransference when dealing with games and roles that involve analyst and patient since the latter concept goes beyond persona functions. If, for example, a woman patient transfers her animus to the analyst and the analyst responds with a necessarily partial compliance or collaboration in the projection by responding in his countertransference with the help of his anima, this antithetical game or role play goes beyond the limits of persona.

Taking the case of a 25-year-old woman patient, I would like to illustrate briefly the problems that can arise between analyst and patient in this sort of situation as well as their methodological and therapeutic applicability. The patient, the youngest of four siblings, had grown up in the family of a minor industrialist who, in the years after 1945, had built up his own flourishing business with much initiative and activity. Although he had died a few years prior to the beginning of her analysis, my patient still had an extraordinarily intense inner relationship to her father. Without a doubt he had been an impressive and extremely successful man, but in my patient's characterizations of him, he also had very strong authoritarian characteristics. He ruled the entire family; even the smallest of his directives were followed to the letter; and the authoritarian atmosphere went so far that even father's hints were promptly executed by the mother and children. The entire familial atmosphere did not have the quality of an open, negative-brutal authoritarian dictatorship but rather was simply taken for granted in a positive sense. In addition to her formal studies, my extremely distinctive, vitally engaged patient had a number of other areas of interest to which she dedicated herself with much enthusiasm. From the beginning, she brought a very considerable fascination with her into the analytic relationship and transferred the image of an idealized father figure to me. This figure resided more in the realm of the spirit and had its predecessors in her philosophical and religious interests from the period when she was fifteen to twenty years old. In the beginning phase of her analytic therapy, I was forced to recognize that, vis-à-vis this woman, I behaved differently in that I got much more involved than with other patients. I tended to make many more interpretations than I usually did, engaged in conversations, and soon could not avoid admitting that I had fallen somewhat in love with her. Granted, that is not methodologically and scientifically correct, but nevertheless a fact that I had to take into account. Her capacity for enthusiasm and her lively interest had obviously appealed strongly to my anima with whom I always have loved to converse. First of all, I pondered that this game in which I assumed the role of a spiritual father-animus while she embodied that of a juvenile part of my anima was not particularly beneficial for the patient. Through this game, she got more attention than others, was spoiled, and fell into the role of the favorite child which she certainly had not been at home. Consequently I resolved consciously to assume a more distanced stance and to curtail my active intervention. Unfortunately I succeeded in keeping my good resolutions for only two or three sessions. Then to my chagrin I was forced to admit that I was behaving just as I had previously and that I was not keeping my own well-advised methodological intentions. Since I have gradually learned in the course of my analytical activity that the unconscious is more intelligent than consciousness, I decided to give up the attempt to react to this woman patient with a consciously forced analytic persona and simply to wait and see how the situation would develop. This decision brought with it a certain degree of relief and relaxation of the atmosphere, and, contrary to my skepticism, it turned out that the patient was able to continue extremely positively in a condition of oral anticipation. With lots of initiative she began actively to deal with her areas of anxiety and fear and to delve into them. It was not very long before she entered into a relationship with a man of her own age and was thereby able to extricate herself from a relationship with a considerably older father-figure, a man who was also married. As she took up her new relationship, her excessively strong fascination with analysis, which had totally consumed her up until then, vanished; after I laid my own jealousy to rest in the countertransference, the remainder of her analysis ran its course along the customary channels.

In retrospect I would now say that, at the beginning of her analysis, the patient's unconscious had latched onto precisely that element in the transference-countertransference situation which was absolutely necessary to get her development and individuation started. A prerequisite for her pulling together the courage to take the initiative and undertake independent development was a positive father-daughter relationship in which the father-figure, in contrast to her personal father, exercised no authoritarian control over her and who insisted on her taking the initiative, often much to her consternation since she would rather have been led as she had been at home. One additional element in this transference-countertransference game was that, in the countertransference, the father-animus was considerably more interested in the physical dimension than were her sublime spiritual heroes of late- and post-puberty. That was also necessary since her relationship to her body was severely underdeveloped in contrast to the rational domain.

I hope to have shown with this example how assuming these sorts of roles for a certain length of time in the analysis can have a significantly productive influence on the analytic process in so far as they are genuinely constellated by the unconscious. Again and again I have had the experience that the whole thing does not work if one assumes that sort of role more or less artificially, for example, out of wrongly understood sympathy for the patient. Moreover, with this example I wanted to illustrate that becoming conscious of these sorts of antithetical role constellations is by no means always enough to bring them to an end, and that altering the emotional climate in the transference and countertransference by main force has little effect. This may also be a tip for those who still believe one can do analysis with the aid of technical schemes anchored in the persona.

Here I want to mention another fundamental analytic problem that, in my opinion, falls within the scope of these sorts of antithetical transferences and countertransferences. All analysts are always enmeshed in the cultural canon surrounding them by the collective dominants of their consciousness. Consequently whether they will or not, they cannot avoid responding to those "patterns" corresponding to the customary cultural canon with a feeling of normalcy and reassurance while other constellations that do not correspond to the usual realities of the culture tend to evoke uneasiness and the feeling of the unusual or abnormal. To a greater or lesser extent, we all fall into experiencing the latter situation as pathological, neurotic, or infantile although in the domain surrounded by infantilisms lie only those first glimmers of consciousness that actually are urgently needed to compensate a collective consciousness which has become one-sided. But we must enter into these glimmerings and they must be developed. Vis-à-vis the patient, the analyst is now and then inclined to assume the role of representative of the collective consciousness while the patient represents the collective unconscious. If the analyst, who usually has greater leverage than the patient, succeeds in this sort of situation, the patient may indeed develop an adapted persona but what remains is a person who at his or her core is immature and unindividuated and who can again fall victim at any time to psychic or psychosomatic symptoms or develop a character neurosis. If the analyst does not succeed, the analysis is usually broken off. The patient keeps his or her symptoms and thereby loses the chance for real development, change, and maturation that by no means always follow the channels of traditional, collective norms. This is a problem concerning not only contents critical of society (as it might seem at first glance) but rather involves many forms of relationship that are disposed of all too easily with pathologizing catch words such as, for example, the relationship of an older woman to a much younger man that is usually very quickly and uncritically pigeonholed as an "unresolved bond to the mother."

These issues already lead over into the area I have called archetypal transference and countertransference situations. In the archetypal transference and countertransference, physician and patient face a constellated archetypal image and must come to terms with it. In attempting to do this, both parties move within the archetypal field on the basis of their own store of experience and the mutual processes of identification. Underlying the above-mentioned roles in the antithetical transference and countertransference, we always discover archetypes, such as mother-child, father-son, physician-patient, etc. But there the archetype is usually more in the background while the constellation of shared experience within an archetypal space contrasts with the roles assumed in games, since in an archetypal space the ego complexes of the two participants encounter, or struggle to come to terms with, the constellated archetypal image in the form adequate to each. Here both parties are partners in the process and together seek the best possible form for a collectively valid, empirically existing psychic problem. A typical confrontation with the archetypal background takes place especially often, for example, with depressive patients. As Wilke (1974) has demonstrated, one very often finds the great mother in her negative elementary character in the underlying process of the depressive patient. If the elementary negative character is constellated in the transference and countertransference situation and if it appears clearly in the foreground, especially laborious and difficult transferences and countertransferences arise. This is also difficult for the analyst, who will need a special reserve of energy in order to penetrate the darkness of the depression and to master the anxiety and fear it arouses. But only if this comes to pass is it possible in the analytic process to motivate the depressed patient's ego-complex to enter into the depressive area and to face the anxieties and fears bound up there. Severe ambivalences in the analyst's unconscious in regard to this destructive and anxiety-provoking negative elementary character often hamper the uncovering of these issues in the analysis of depressives and make themselves felt as countertransference resistances.

I would like to present one somewhat more extensive clinical example of this sort of archetypal transference and countertransference constellation. This is the case of a young woman patient with a multitude of schizoid-paranoid symptoms who entered treatment with me and who would be classified as borderline. At the beginning of her analysis, I was quite skeptical and did not have high expectations for her therapy, but then it developed surprisingly well. The young woman, who at age 21 was practically unable to act or work due to the severity of her illness and whose life was an unmitigated chaos, completed her G.E.D. and commenced university studies in the course of her therapy. In the 280th hour she reported to me that she had seen a hallucinatory image of a streetcar standing in a forest. This streetcar in the forest, she told me with horror, had been such a "terribly ruined sight." Berlin is surrounded with forests where, in fact, streetcar lines used to run. Consequently, in the past, a streetcar in the forest was a very commonplace image for every Berliner, a natural sight. Hence I was somewhat surprised at her agitation. In the course of the hour she began, as frequently happened, to speak of the streetcar repeatedly in stereotyped terms using the same few words, but always with new shades of feeling. Her stereotyped repetition gradually induced in me a *participation mystique* in her image, and a memory arose in me.

Years before, I remembered, a friend and I had driven through the Taurus Mountains in Asia Minor, a very sparsely populated area devoid of people. One afternoon we had been driving for hours without seeing a single house or person and we felt as though we were the only people on earth. In this mood we rounded the shoulder of a cliff and suddenly in the road before our car there stood three men in black suits wearing top hats. One of them had a double bass, the second an accordion, and the third a trumpet. This unexpected, grotesque image, so foreign and unadapted to the situation, almost struck us dead. As we found out later, these men had, of course, come from a nearby village and were on their way to play at a marriage or a funeral.

This memory, however, helped me begin to understand my patient and enabled me to communicate with her feelings. At the very moment the memory had risen up in me, my patient stopped her stereotyped litany — without, of course, my having told her anything of what was transpiring in me — and said with the greatest agitation: "I can't adapt to this ruined world! I will suffer it and I will slip away! If ever I get strong enough to stand it, I'll no longer see it nor suffer from it either."

Now I was reminded of another young woman patient who once had told me a very impressive dream from her puberty. This was her dream:

I was on the street that led to our school. Perhaps thirty feet from me a crowd of people had collected. In the middle of the crowd stood a young girl of my age. She was completely naked and her whole, scarcely developed, body shivered. Foaming at the mouth, the crowd standing around her were sticking needles, pens, toothbrushes, and nails into her naked body. With the nails they were carving rules and regulations into her trembling body. It broke my heart to see her, and I stared at the spectacle with burning tears in my eyes. Then she slowly raised her head, turned her blood- and tear-streaked face toward me, and I screamed. I screamed as loud as I could, for this girl was me.

I believe that this dream captures my patient's experience better than any abstract description of it and delineates the background of the adapted, adult world with its commandments and prohibitions, a background that I, too, have not overcome but must endure without screaming.

In any event, I understood my patient at the end of the session, and it was obvious that she noticed that she had been understood. Following this session she had two dreams that clearly indicated how processes of liberation and mastery of her anxiety set in after our shared experience in analysis. This is the dream that immediately followed the hour just discussed:

I am in a concentration camp. A man there wanted to help us escape. When we tried, we ended up in a room that had stalls, like a large toilet. But these stalls were arranged so that each had a bench and on each bench lay a person who looked dead. They had all gotten injections for their liberation. I, too, got an injection in my arm and was terribly afraid I would not be the same afterwards.

Her second dream came after the next session:

A reddish-lilac colored bus was standing in a forest; it looked like a double-decker bus. It was standing between two orange colored houses that looked like pop art. Then I was taken to East Berlin and there I went up a mountain. Everything was very beautiful, the weather was magnificent and the atmosphere was pleasant. Then I was with a 20-year-old boy in a forest. The boy was giving music lessons. In the forest, he spoke with an old man who was very smart.

After this conversation, he no longer needed to be afraid like I was. For my part, I had walked away because the conversation was too boring.

The patient felt that this dream had been entirely different than the earlier one with the derelict streetcar which had been more of a "horror trip" for her.

I shall not interpret these dreams in detail but rather only mention that, in the first dream, liberation and transformation were still experienced with fear, yet the motif did appear; in the second dream, the streetcar is replaced by the youthful, pop colors and the bus which allows civilization and nature to be conjoined and accepted. In my essay on the auto as dream symbol (Dieckmann 1976b) I discussed in detail that the self can appear in this symbolic form, something that also happens in this dream where a possibility of wholeness is sketched symbolically in the union of natural vitality and color with the mechanical carrier of energy. Even if the ego in the dream still finds the wise old man who can heal fears "too boring," the animus figure establishes a relationship with him which is encouraging.

But let us return to the 280th hour we were discussing and consider what took place in terms of transference and countertransference. I rather suspect that the patient's "penetrating," emotionally toned, stereotyped litany constellated the archetype of the *puer aeternus* or the *puella* in the analyst's unconscious, and that brought the corresponding images into consciousness. As M.-L. von Franz (1970) has written, this archetype possesses a peculiar sort of spirituality having very close contact with the unconscious. It rejects conventional situations, poses deep questions, and has the tendency to penetrate directly to the kernel of truth.

The young person who identifies with this archetype is still much closer to the vitality of the world which we all once experienced and rightly resists surrendering this vitality in favor of a process of adaptation. But this archetype is also feared because of its instability, its deficient insight into reality, and its destructive potential, and it evokes fear, which is probably why the intensity of the stereotyped litany was necessary to awaken it in me. The patient was not able to take further developmental steps until emotion mobilized this archetype in the countertransference and it, as well as the patient's words and emotions, confronted my ego complex. This archetype certainly lies closer to us than that of the child, but probably it is also more feared because of its enthusiastic power of attraction and its inflationary tendencies. This may contribute to many analysts' reluctance to do therapy with young people, to adjudge them unsuited for it, or to find it especially difficult to keep them in therapy. Constellating this sort of common experience within an archetypal space is something fundamentally different from a shared game with assigned roles or the process of projection of personal transference and countertransference material. I hope to have made this clear with this example.

There is not too much to be said in regard to the methods by which one can deal with archetypal transferences or countertransferences in the analytic setting. In the face of the constellated archetype, no specific patterns help; rather, to deal with it corresponds more to that multitude of different possibilities we find in the fairy-tale hero's confrontations and battles as he seeks to fulfill his task. Everything that contributes to success can be correct, and in the most varied situations, the exact opposite is occasionally necessary. However, the example presented above may still point to an essential methodological principle that must come into play if the therapeutic process is to continue to be fruitful. Here it is crucial that the analyst also come to terms with the constellated archetypal core of the complex and be prepared to renounce his or her analyst persona in that sort of situation. Only if this transpires in the countertransference can the problem truly be taken up and worked through. If the analyst does not dare encounter the energies of these images with all their feelings, the patient's ego-complex cannot fully come to terms with them either, since the patient is, of course, dependent on the analyst to accompany him or her on the journey. Granted, time and again there are instances in which this poses too great a demand either on the patient or on the analyst, a demand that must be avoided for the moment. In these kinds of cases, it is sometimes right to avoid confronting the problem and, as we also know from fairy-tale motifs, to resort to a magical flight until the core of the complex has lost enough of its destructive potential so that it is possible to confront it and come to terms with it.

In concluding this chapter I consider it very important to build a bridge between the transference and countertransference processes and our shared human forms of relating. We cannot help but see that all the forms of transference and countertransference described here also continually play a major role in all interpersonal relationships. In all the other forms of relationship that we know, we project onto one another. We experience objective qualities of character in the other that we do not yet know, or we discover ways of experiencing and acting that are new to us. We play definite "games" involving specific roles with each other. And last but not least, at the high points and times of crisis in our relationships, we are exposed to archetypal constellations. But it is characteristic for the analytic relationship between physician and patient that two persons come together according to specific rules and arrangements in order to reflect upon and understand the processes of their relationship while expressly including and emphasizing the unconscious. This sort of reflective understanding is possible only on condition that analytic distance be maintained. In this regard, the analytic relationship differs from all other forms of human relationship that we know. But basically, analytic distance has the same value, authenticity, and dignity of every human relationship; only its form is artificial, not its content. The words transference and countertransference, as mentioned at the beginning of this chapter, are nothing other than necessary technical terms; unfortunately this is forgotten all too often. Everybody who has experienced analysis takes something of this sort of relationship into his or her later human relationships and more attentively heeds the unconscious, just as we all always take something of our earlier relationships into subsequent relationships as long as we are alive.

CHAPTER 12

Problems of Interpretation in the Analytic Process

It is regrettable that, in contrast to the psychoanalytic literature, very little has been written about the methodology of interpretation in analytical psychology. Aside from the remarks found in Jung's *Two Essays on Analytical Psychology* (*C.W.* 7), there is really only the paper by Fordham (1975) on interpretation. Granted, Jung himself referred again and again to the importance of this problem. The aversion of analytical psychologists toward taking a stand on methodological and technical questions has caused them to neglect this area. Certainly one additional reason comes to light in Bradway's studies (Bradway 1964), namely that the first and second generations of persons who turned to Jung's analytical psychology were predominantly strong intuitive types. This obviously prevented exploration of these sorts of questions on a larger scale. Moreover, Jung justifiably demanded of analysts that they find their own style and consequently their own method. Despite the justification of these demands to discover one's own style and method, there are, in addition to the personal problems involved, also a number of general problems in analytical psychology in the area of techniques of interpretation that at least should come up for discussion even if they do not immediately become standardized method.

First of all it seems to me important that we find a definition of what we mean by "interpretation" and that we differentiate the concept of analytical interpretation from the multitude of interactions that take place between analyst and patient. Obviously this definition is not at all simple, and there are analysts who ascribe at least an interpretive quality to the therapist's every verbal utterance, sometimes including even the "um-hum" that acknowledges or inquires. The question now arises whether, say, an amplification or question directed toward the content of a complex is to be understood as an interpretation and where one should speak of interpretation and where of verbal interaction. Agreement probably exists only in conceptualizing the process of interpreting an unconscious content as always taking place at the verbal level; but here we must emphasize that, fundamentally, we are not dealing with a process that is only verbal.

It seems appropriate first of all to attempt to define what we mean by a *complete* interpretation. We must immediately qualify this: in practice, this never takes place in a single analytic hour but may often extend over very long periods of time. I would understand this sort of complete and successful interpretation as a conscious, emotionally laden verbal act on the part of the analyst which leads to bringing to consciousness a previously unconscious complex as well as the resistance and the systems of defense that have held this complex fast in the unconscious. A complete and successful interpretation should embrace the three tenses — past, present, and future — and should describe both the contents and the emotional cathexes. Likewise, it should give information about the personal contents and the archetypal core of the complex. In this context, "past" signifies the genetic component of the complex, that is, answers the questions of when and under what conditions did the complex develop and why was it absolutely necessary in the development of this particular patient to suppress and to repress the contents, feelings, and affects of precisely this complex. To the present belongs first and foremost the interpretation of the effects that these complex contents evoke within the transference and countertransference situation between analyst and patient, and beyond that, of course, also those distorted situations that arise through projection of the unconscious complex contents in the current life situation of the patient as well as in interpersonal relationships in general. "Future" refers to the "final" element contained in every unconscious complex that presses into consciousness, and which I have discussed in detail elsewhere (Dieckmann 1969, 1972b). The final component — i.e., the tendency toward meaning and purpose that arises when drive and image are linked and in which the possibilities of resolution and of development are contained — must be brought to consciousness or made conscious, and consciousness must judge it, that is, accept or reject it.

Basically the same thing holds true for the resistance and for the systems of defense. The interpretation should explain how this particular system of defense developed genetically and why at the time it was what proved to be the most meaningful way of mastering the situation. Further, the interpretation should expose what situational distortions arise when this earlier form of defense is maintained in current situations differing completely from the original situation. Again, the analytic transference and countertransference constellation is eminently suited to this end. Lastly, from the final viewpoint an interpretation should say something about the fate of the defensive systems; in this connection, the interpretation should be guided by the conscious and in part unconscious contents of the systems of defense since nobody can live without defenses. I do not want to equate the concept of the persona with that of systems of defense but rather point out that the formations of the systems of defense are located in the persona and the ego-complex, and that ultimately the significance of the process of interpretation cannot and must not lie in dismantling or overriding healthy and functional components of the persona and of the ego. Were this the case, instead of being a dialectical and synthetic process taking place between consciousness and the unconscious, the processes of interpretation would lead to a condition in which consciousness would merely be cathected by heretofore unconscious contents which would be acted out. An example of this would be the oft-discussed problem of strong, latent homosexual complex components that are then manifested meaninglessly and in a manner not in keeping with the whole personality.

Having given this very extensive definition of interpretation, I would like first of all to delve into the details of the process of interpretation and into the analytic bases upon which the interpretive process rests in order to illustrate how an interpretation looks in practice. Lastly I would like to share some reflections on the extremely difficult problem of timing interpretations in the analytic setting. In order to understand the first issue correctly, it is necessary at the outset to grasp that each analytic interpretation has two goals: first, to create an opening in consciousness that permits unconscious contents to enter, and, second, to enable the patient to understand unconscious contents symbolically. The first goal is intimately related to the treatment of resistances and defenses, and the analyst should always keep in mind Jung's warning (*The Psychology of the Transference, C.W.* 16) that the vulnerable needs resistances for its protection and they must not be prematurely or forcibly broken down. This does not prohibit us from including interpretations of, and attempts to make conscious, resistances and defensive formations, but they should be offered only at a point in time when both analyst and patient have developed the knowledge that continued adherence to them is no longer necessary.

We will frequently return to this pair of opposites comprised of resistance and defensive systems on the one side and the content of the complex on the other. But first of all let us turn our attention to the content of the complex. Given all the validity that analytical psychology ascribes to dreams and the process of dream interpretation, we should keep clearly in mind that the unconscious content of complexes is expressed not only in dreams and should be interpreted not only from the vantage point of dreams. Consequently as a matter of principle the interpretation of the unconscious contents should be oriented toward the actual complex and should take into account the greatest possible range of the complex's manifestations. In addition to noting the patient's dreams, associations, and amplifications, one should, when garnering unconscious contents, also attend to the important role played by the patient's nonverbal expressions, the way experiences are described, behaviors in the environment, day dreams and active imagination, just as one attends to the patient's experience and behavior in the analytic transference and countertransference setting, a point to which we will return later. In the process of interpretation, we should pay attention to and utilize not only the dream but the totality of all expressions of a specific, unconscious complex behind which, in my experience, there is almost always hidden an archetypal core. This approach does not compromise the dignity of the dream as the *via regia* to the unconscious, but I consider every form of one-sidedness — be it an orientation toward interpreting only dreams or only the transference — as detrimental. Every one-sidedness on the analyst's part gradually evokes a one-sided orientation in the patient also, which does not do justice to the multiplicity and diversity of life's processes and ultimately leads to narrowness. In the verbal form of what we say to the patient about his unconscious contents it also seems to me important, as Jung pointed out in his "Seminar on Children's Dreams" (Jung 1938/ 1941), that we use the patient's own images and stay as close as possible to those images. As Jung said, the elephant means something different to each person, and we must assume that there exists in nature not only a chance chaos, but also that images are contained in the world of natural law and that causality, not only pure arbitrariness, exists. Of course, this does not relieve us of the necessity of formulating abstract hypotheses; but within the analytic process imaginal thinking, which embraces a greater degree of completeness, plays a more important role than abstract thought (Dieckmann 1960).

The first prerequisite for interpreting unconscious contents is the creation of a relatively stabile ego-component which is in a position to enter into a genuine dialectical process with those unconscious contents. In his discussion of this problem, Whitmont (1969) reports a very impressive Jewish legend having to do with the crossing of the Red Sea. According to this legend, Moses commanded the Red Sea to part, but nothing happened until the first man stepped into the water. Only then did the waters yield. Of course, the images arising from the unconscious call for understanding and interpretation. But as Heyer (1931) elaborates, at the very beginning of this sort of dialectical process, experience teaches us that the greatest possible caution is called for, and it is often better to let the past explain itself by what the patient later tells. According to Heyer, all excessively one-sided conceptualizations (that could lead to panic) must be carefully corrected. Whoever wants to explain too much does not aid the fantasy activity that we are aiming to encourage but rather only breeds new intellectual opinions. It often takes a long time until the analysand has progressed far enough in his inner transformation that he can use his consciousness and his will in the right way — functions that of course must be enthroned as fabulous achievements of the human spirit since, after all, they alone have led us out of the primitive's mythical bondage to all things. But since we moderns as a whole have lost contact with nature, with the primitive, and with the animal in us to too great a degree, and our thought, our consciousness, and our will hang in mid-air, our development must first take a reductive path. Until we have again established our connection with the darkest depths of our being — which takes place in just those movements and earthquakes of the soul that appear to us as fantasy — our thought remains an empty intellectual exercise, spirit is dead and deadening *ratio*, indeed a hybrid outrage . . ., and consciousness finds itself in a perpetual spasm. But if the connection "downward" as a regression into our animal foundations has again been established, thus again giving us to nature and nature to us, then the new ascent toward a solar consciousness can begin; indeed, it must be this way, for by itself it would again be an outrage, an outrage against culture. (1931, p. 107)

Every interpretation must necessarily be preceded by an often laborious process of gathering information which, on the analyst's part, must be accompanied by processes of identification and of empathy. Here, again, it is not a question of purely rational information but of information that makes the processes transpiring in the patient also emotionally comprehensible to and replicable to the analyst. The meaning of this process is, again, that of comprehending or dialoging with the unconscious, repressed contents and systems of defense in the most complete way possible. The analyst must become conscious of both aspects — repressed material and systems of defense — as he or she gets to know the patient; this involves a broad range of facts, impressions, and affective expressions or allusions. In general, to the extent that the patient's spontaneous material does not suffice, the analyst's questions support this process. But by "questions" we do not mean the goal-directed questioning as in Schultz-Hencke's neo-analytic anamnesis (Schultz-Hencke 1970) which aims at eliciting information concerning very specific areas of inhibited drives. Questioning in analytical psychology serves rather to expand and to circumambulate the image the patient presents (as a sort of amplification) in order to be better able to grasp its meaning. Take, for example, the question, "What comes to mind when you call yourself a cold fish?" This question might lead one patient to report that she had eaten fish yesterday; another might share a childhood memory; a third might compare it to another animal; and a fourth might even refer to the symbol of Christ as fish. It is only the multiplicity of these sorts of amplifications and contexts that make it possible for the analyst to understand the meaning and the momentary emotional cathexis of a symbol.

The process of gathering information serves not only to comprehend the body of meaning of unconscious contents but is also necessary in order to experience the form of relationship in which the content and the resistance are juxtaposed. In my experience we have here three different possibilities, each of which we should scrutinize carefully. The first possibility is that the unconscious opposition to the conscious attitude is totally repressed and completely unconscious. If we take the example of aggressive or hostile feelings associated with an authority complex which is linked with an underlying negative father archetype, this feeling quality would be totally unconscious vis-à-vis obedience to, understanding for, and idealization of authority figures. Becoming conscious only of hostile feelings can already lead to a significant expansion of consciousness. The second possibility is that the patient is indeed conscious of hostile feelings toward authority figures, but because he or she is unconscious of the core of the complex, those hostile feelings stand in perpetual opposition to the attitude firmly integrated into consciousness. This results in continual ambivalence that often swings back and forth between hate and love.

The third possibility, one lying relatively close to the second, is that the opposing positions are not in conflict but rather exist independently side by side. In this case the hostility is, as a rule, projected onto remote objects and the authorities close at hand remain oddly bland and emotionless. But thanks to unconsciousness of the cores of the complexes, two things are lacking in all three possibilities: first, the archetypal images that constitute the core of the complex; and second, the ability to form uniting symbols that alone are capable of resolving the conflict and working it through in an appropriate way.

The process of gathering information described here and the corresponding questions that can be asked must be distinguished from the actual interpretation, nor should the analyst's pointed questions be called interpretations. Nevertheless, this process already creates and expands consciousness. We must clearly recognize that interpretation is by no means the only method by which we bring unconscious contents to consciousness. New contents pertaining to a specific problem are continually added to consciousness as we gather information, and unconscious material continually surfaces that is integrated into the patient's virulent problems like pebbles into a mosaic. Hence, as Heyer mentioned, much the patient has said is explained only by what the patient subsequently relates. Many hours when the analyst asks only one or two questions can be fundamentally more fruitful for the patient than the hour in which the analyst offers an ill-timed interpretation or explanation.

Having delved in some detail into the content of complexes and the formation of resistance and defensive systems in the patient, I want to discuss now something that is prerequisite for an effective interpretation and must transpire in terms of the analyst's processes of awareness and recognition. Of course, this is closely related to the problem of the countertransference and I have accorded it partial treatment in the chapter on transference and countertransference. Here I shall discuss only those aspects that pertain especially to the conditions necessary for a verbal interpretation.

In his article, Fordham (1975) establishes six categories of features that an interpretation should have. We need not repeat them in detail here since many of them are implicit in what has already been said or in what will follow. As his fifth point, Fordham mentions that an effective interpretation is always represented by an affect whose roots lie in the analyst's unconscious; the affect carries an element of spontaneity which itself constitutes the efficacy of the interpretation (1975, p. 87). This corresponds to our definition mentioned above in which we stated that the conscious, verbalized interpretation must always be an emotionally charged process. The emotional charge arises from the transference and countertransference constellation. It cannot be contrived or willfully produced; rather, it constellates of itself within the analytic process. Freud's early demand for a mirroring stance is, in my opinion, an attempt at repressing this element since the psychic fields of physician and patient in the analytic setting must interact at an affective and emotional level in any case. In 1929, Jung (*Psychology of the Transference, C.W.* 16) emphatically pointed out that the relationship between doctor and patient was a personal relationship in the impersonal setting of medical treatment and unavoidably the product of mutual influence involving the entire personalities of both the patient and the physician; both were two irrational quantities composed of the conscious and the unconscious. Whitmont also describes this condition in similar words:

Their psychic field patterns interact. Something happens, something clicks one way or another and their unconscious patterns "arrange" themselves relative to each other in a typical fashion whether they know it or not, or care to or not; the less they are aware of it, the more compulsive the effect of the occurrence will be. In this field, this energic configuration, they both share. (1969, p. 299)

The countertransference studies of the Berlin group (Blomeyer 1971; Dieckmann 1971d, 1973a, 1973b; E. Jung 1973) yielded a very impressive picture of this arrangement of psychic fields and their mutual interpenetration. Those studies demonstrated that the analyst's unverbalized associations were always meaningfully linked with the associations the patient was verbally expressing. Of course, the question arises whether it would be more correct to exclude this sort of emotional participation voluntarily and to state verbal interpretations in an atmosphere of factual, cool objectivity, or whether one makes use of these emotional processes and includes them in one's interpretations. In contrast to Freud, Jung pointed out the importance of spontaneity on the analyst's part very early on which, of course, should not be taken to mean that the analyst uncontrollably buries the patient with emotions; rather, while preserving an analytic tension, the analyst lets his or her emotions show only where the patient can meaningfully work them through. From my practice I can confirm that emotionless interpretations have little or no effect on the patient; at best, they remain on a rational, superficial level, while those interpretations in which the emotions constellated in the analyst clearly resonate gain considerably in their effectiveness and are the only ones suited to "getting under the patient's skin."

Of course, the necessary precondition is that, gradually over the course of time, the analyst has gained the most precise and accurate knowledge of the momentary state of the on-going processes taking place between him and the patient. Hence the analyst must have sufficient inner emotional clarity to grasp that here and now the patient has, for example, a mother projection on the analyst and that the problem of a negative mother-imago has been constellated between analyst and patient. Further, the analyst must understand which genetic factors from the patient's past contribute to this negative mother-imago, what archetypal image is active in the background coloring the patient's entire environment, and finally what hints at a resolution of the situation are possibly available from the symbols of previous dreams and fantasies. This is easily said, but in practice it is extraordinarily difficult.

For example, I recall the case of a young woman patient whose negative mother-imago had a Medea-like image as its archetypal core, a mother who kills and devours her own children. Certain data from her personal past had activated this image. Her natural mother had left her in the hospital and, shortly after her birth, had vanished without a trace. My patient grew up in a foster family that had pronounced oral features as well as symptoms of a depressive nature. Actually this situation was easy enough to comprehend from a purely rational standpoint, but it took us well over 100 analytic hours filled with mutual feelings of resignation before analyst and patient could face this image at an emotional level. Only then did dreams and fantasies develop in which the patient's ego-complex no longer needed to flee her problem and, with the protection of the analytic relationship, only then was it at all possible for her to become conscious of this image of mother. We simply must realize that as analysts we also get scared if we meet a Medea face to face who, as we well know, has the full force of reality intrapsychically, and that not only the patient but we, too, need a considerable length of time in order to be able to approach that sort of opponent. But generally this is to be understood not purely as timidity, cowardice, or as an impediment; rather, it is simply more intelligent to very carefully study an opponent who is superior in many ways, to learn as much as possible about them, and to discover their weak points before risking a direct confrontation. Hence we should be aware that, as I have stated in earlier studies (Dieckmann 1971d), fifty percent of the resistance is the therapist's. Preparing an effective interpretation also involves becoming conscious of one's own resistance, taking the time necessary to become familiar with it, and finally overcoming it. Only as this entire process runs its course does the analyst lay the emotional foundation which can make an interpretation given at the right moment truly effective for the patient.

Now the question arises, "How does this look in practice?" Is the sort of "complete" interpretation described earlier really possible? As we said, it should contain a verbal description of the content of the complex, as well as the resistance and the defensive systems built up around it in terms of its genesis, the current life situation, and the final, prospective development. In the analysis, say, of a somewhat complicated mother complex this would constitute a monograph all in itself. In a real sense a "complete" interpretation can actually be given only when the analyst has stepped out of the fire of transference and countertransference, that is, only after the termination of the analysis when it is pondered in retrospect. Here, as in many other cases, the demand for a "complete" interpretation turns out to be an ideal, something utopian, that cannot be achieved in practice. Of course, one could say that this is sufficient reason to abandon this sort of theory, to limit oneself to the data actually present in the analytic process and to what is possible in practice, and to seek a theory of interpretation that does justice to the concrete facts. But that approach and that sort of theory would eliminate the prospective, final viewpoint and the synthetic aspect that is so vitally important in analytical psychology. Renouncing utopia leads not only the scientist but also humanity in general to brutal castration and enslavement to the concrete facts. Ernst Bloch discussed this point very profoundly in his book, *Das Prinzip Hoffnung (The Principle of Hope)*. In one passage he says,

> Wherever the prospective horizon has been left out, reality appears only as what has come into being, as dead, and there the dead — the naturalists and the empiricists, that is — bury their dead. Wherever the prospective horizon has also been envisioned as thoroughly as possible, reality appears as what it actually is: as a network of dialectical processes taking place in an unfinished world, in a world that would be absolutely unalterable without its gigantic future and the real possibilities latent in it. (Bloch 1976, p. 257)

Aristotle already knew this when he wrote in his *Metaphysics*, "Everything that develops out of nature or art has matter, for every thing that becomes is capable of being and of not being . . ." (Aristotle, *Metaphysics* VII, 7). If we proceed along these lines, the theoretical ideal demanded trains one to develop possibilities; it furthers the process of becoming and hence the process of becoming conscious and of realization both in the analyst and in the analysis.

We must ask ourselves a question: What possibilities exist in practice that would do justice to a theory of interpretation which differs from the other interactions that take place between analyst and patient? First of all, it is important to recognize that a "complete" interpretation is a process that extends over long periods of the analysis and that can never take place within the limits of a few sessions. Rather, like a mosaic made up of all sorts of small pebbles, the process of interpretation pieces together individual, incomplete interpretations that circumambulate and amplify the actual unconscious complex. As this takes place, the individual pebbles of the mosaic are not assembled in a linear sequence; rather, even after the analyst has come to know the complex, the unconscious still guides the process, and the individual components of the interpretation are attuned to the material the patient offers. Here the analyst must decide the direction of the interpretation from moment to moment — whether to focus on the unconscious contents or on the defenses. And, in my experience, one can never say unequivocally that the resistance must be interpreted before the unconscious material or vice versa. Rather, they do and must take turns. Thus, for example, in one session a patient's repressed sexual fantasy activity can emerge into consciousness as an unconscious part of a specific complex to the extent that the patient can speak of it and the analyst can interpret it, while in the following hour the process is not continued or further worked through but rather the old defenses take over again or new defensive strategies are developed. When this happens, the analyst should let well enough alone until the material again comes within close range of the patient's consciousness. In practice this means that either the patient remarks that he or she is defending against something or has the vague feeling that the analytic process is stagnating. Only after interpreting the resistances can one again examine the contents arising from the unconscious. Rather than being overwhelmed by it in this process, the patient's unstable ego-complex samples the unconscious material in order to assimilate and integrate it. In regard to transference and countertransference, we must remind ourselves that the process is mutual and that analyst and patient together are involved in working on an unconscious constellation between them. Hence the sexual fantasies mentioned above can initially exert a strongly erotic effect on the analyst's countertransference which can manifest as countertransference resistance. But when this transpires, every analyst should admit without feeling guilty that he or she also needs time to understand and to integrate what is constellated in him or her by the patient's virulent, intense, emotionally laden psychic material.

We cannot repeat often enough that interpretations must be offered to the patient as hypotheses, not handed down as dicta. Only that interpretation that the patient can also accept is correct; it is left to the analyst's capacity for empathy and abilities to identify with the patient to recognize the extent to which acceptance of an interpretation is genuine and results in an increment of consciousness, or whether the interpretation was accepted simply out of compliance. Compliance poses the great danger inherent in hasty and premature interpretations, since the patient gains knowledge which does not at all correspond to inner reality. Then the patient erects a sort of analytic persona with which he or she erroneously believes it is possible to see into his or her own heart and into the heart of his or her environment. The patient attempts to impress others as a sort of initiate or sage without noticing that he or she actually knows nothing at all and still has symptoms. Thanks to our magico-mythic roots and psychic background, we fall into the trap of word magic much more often than we are aware of when we confuse the name of a thing with understanding or integrating it. The use of technical terms belongs in this domain. I myself have found that it is better to avoid using even very current and commonly used terms such as "frustration" in favor of simply asking the patient whether he or she tends to react to a disappointment by feeling sad, dull, downcast, irritated, enraged, or just downright disappointed. The verbal formulation of the interpretation should always be oriented to the patient's own verbal imagery, indeed, less to the imagery of the patient's conscious language which contains a good many defensive components than to the primordial and vital language of fantasy images, whether from dreams, daydreams, fantasies, or active imagination. This also holds true for the analyst's amplification of archetypal materials to the extent that these amplifications not only confirm and support already conscious contents but have interpretive character and are intended to raise a previously unconscious aspect of an archetypal imago into consciousness. It is not our task to make patients into mythographers; rather, we must resonate with what patients know and what is current for them. We must also be able to understand what sorts of connections exist between a Tarzan (Hänisch 1974) or a Superman of science fiction (M. Kadinsky 1969) and the archetypal figures of the mythologies of our culture.

I mentioned above that an interpretation should be offered to the patient, and what I have found works best in my experience is the verbal expression of a hunch or question. At first glance, a question would seem to contradict the above—that questions belong to the process of giving information. However, there are two sorts of questions, those that actually serve to elicit information and are intended to fill a genuine lacuna, and those of a Socratic nature such as we know from Plato's dialogues. Posing a Socratic question aims in a very specific direction and surmises, at least in general outline, the possible answer. I will attempt to elucidate the difference between the informative and the interpretive question with the help of an example.

At the beginning of his analysis, a patient told me that he had experienced the death of his father without much emotion and actually with a certain degree of satisfaction. His spontaneous comments on the image of his father were predominantly negative at the beginning of his analysis, and he depicted his father as severe, quick to anger, and rigid. Only in the further course of his analysis did he gradually mention a number of situations he could recall when his father had responded to him with understanding in a benevolent, comradely way. Initially the patient recounted these experiences as something only he had experienced, omitting his father's reactions. For example, he told me how worried, terrified, and anxious he was at having to go home when he had gotten bad grades one year at school and had not been promoted to the next grade. When I asked about his father's reaction, he suddenly recalled that in this instance his father had reacted with extraordinary understanding and had even tried to console him. My question did not imply an interpretation but rather only sought information since—considering his previous characterizations of him—I certainly was in no position to suspect that the father he had depicted only as rigid and severe would suddenly reveal a completely different side of his personality. An entirely different picture of his father arose in the further course of his analysis, a picture in which the initially very one-sided, conscious father-imago came to include positive and valuable features, too, as we all know from experience. Only then was a different situation constellated, one in which I could get a felt-sense of the significance of this father's death, a situation in which I could see in the patient's demeanor that the positive feelings of love and affection for his father lay just below the threshold of consciousness. When he mentioned the death of his father again, I asked, "Might it be that his death stirred up a lot of grief, disappointment, and pain, and that your indifference toward that experience is only a sort of wall intended to prevent these feelings from rising up in you?" This question evoked a very strong emotional reaction in the patient; he agreed and for the first time he was able to cry about his father's death. Following this session it was possible to make a series of interpretations related to the suppression of his feeling-toned complex dominated by the negative father archetype. I would call this entire process informative although, as mentioned above, it included a growth in consciousness. In my view, only the last question was interpretive; it was posed at a point in time when I, as analyst, had not only comprehended the situation rationally but also was emotionally able to experience his father's death in the sense of empathizing and of sharing his feelings, and when the patient's feelings about his father's death were so close to the surface that they could be expressed.

Not only purely verbal interpretation and the distinction between information and interpretation, but also the various levels at which one can offer interpretations belong within the area of the form of interpretation. Three pairs of opposites must be distinguished here:

1. interpretations on the objective and the subjective levels;
2. prospective and reductive interpretations; and
3. transference and countertransference interpretations.

I believe it is important that we be clear about the different possible levels at which we can interpret so that we can utilize the various levels or steps at the right time and place.

In regard to interpretation on the objective and the subjective levels, Jung's general rule of thumb ("General Aspects of Dream Psychology," *C.W.* 8, par. 509ff) still holds true: exhaustive interpretation on the objective level should precede interpretation on the subjective level. Granted, this is not always valid, and Jung himself often undertook subjective-level interpretation particularly for those patients for whom uncovering and relating to their own inner world and to their fantasies was more important than problems of relating to the world around them or than transference projections on the analyst. As a rule, it is the patient who indicates the level at which the interpretation should focus, albeit not always within a single analytic hour. Whether the subjective-level or the objective-level interpretation is chosen, the analyst should be guided by the patient's emotional situation and by his or her associations. Here, too, the patient's agreement with and acceptance of an interpretation is achieved most readily if the analyst remains flexible. Nevertheless it is important to avoid one-sidedness. Indeed, there are some patients who live their entire fantasy activity and their inner possibilities of experience more at the subjective level and other patients who do so more at the objective level. But it is necessary for both to get acquainted with the other modality, and this is closely linked with patients' becoming familiar with their inferior function.

Strongly neurotic marital relationships typify this last point. Not infrequently the analyst sees patients who have an overcaring attitude with underlying inclinations to dominate, or with messianic pretensions to heal, the other. These patients frequently enter relationships with severely disturbed partners, e.g., with addicts, pre-psychotics, or other severely disturbed persons. As a rule, the analyst must first work at the objective level to clarify the preconditions in the patient's development that have led to this situation and have influenced the particular choice of partner. Likewise the reality of the disturbed partner must be brought out through the process of interpretation, and it takes a long time before the patient is able to experience the partner as he or she really is and to accept the inertia of his or her disturbance. Only when this process has been concluded and the patient has resolved either to maintain or to dissolve the relationship is it possible analytically to withdraw the anima or animus projections at the subjective level and let the patient discover through the analyst's interpretations the extent to which the addict or the psychotic belongs to the patient's own psychic ensemble and to his or her pantheon of archetypal possibilities. In another paper (Dieckmann 1978c) I discussed this problem in detail in regard to addiction. Of course, guidance of these processes follows the lead of the unconscious. This means that object-level or subject-level interpretations in these sorts of cases do not come about in the form of a rigid process preprogrammed by the analyst's consciousness. Rather, the levels can overlap, and in certain cases it may be more sensible to interpret at the subjective level prior to the objective level, although as a rule this happens rather infrequently.

Let us now consider "reductive" and "prospective" interpretations. There is a very profound Indian saying that the most beautiful lotus blossom has its roots deep in the slime. Whenever we make a reductive interpretation in terms of the underlying drives and drive motivations, we should always be aware that we always have the entire plant before us in every psychic phenomenon and that the root does not consist only of one single tendril. In my opinion, an interpretation that traces a specific psychic experience causally and reductively to only one drive, under the motto "That's nothing but . . .," is too one-sided and always wrong. For example, analyzing the underlying motives for choosing the medical or nursing profession can uncover an identification with a parental wish regarding career, a longing to heal oneself, a seriously ill relative, or even a voyeuristic interest in the human body. Particularly when the underlying motives are relatively intensely cathected with libido, this can be profoundly unsettling and lead to feelings of insecurity if the analyst does not clearly realize that the causal-reductive interpretation grasps only one of the totality of conditions that lead to a condition or event. The analyst must also make this clear to the patient. The reductive method has its domain, especially in the area of the personal shadow. It goes without saying that the shadow must be uncovered and that the patient must confront it in all honesty; but analysts must be scrupulously mindful not to let this analytic instrument maneuver them into the role in which they attempt to unmask the patient, unfortunately an error made frequently by beginners or when analysis is misunderstood.

The discovery and elucidation of the prospective-finalistic aspect of the complex must be credited to analytical psychology. Since I have given a detailed elaboration of the possibilities offered by prospective interpretation of the complex and of dream contents elsewhere (Dieckmann 1972b, 1978a), I will limit myself here to a practical, methodological problem.

The prospective element has the seductive danger that the analyst may employ it too quickly or too soon and thereby attempt to avoid or circumvent exploring a dark and difficult underlying psychic condition. This can be studied most clearly when dealing with the motif of death and rebirth. It is very difficult for everybody to confront death genuinely in all its profundity and extent. Consequently one can catch oneself again and again thinking immediately of rebirth when the death motif appears in dreams, fantasies, and ideas of suicide, etc., and observe how this "saving fantasy" slips in in some form or other. I think that Hillman (1964) has very incisively demonstrated the extent to which one can and, in my opinion, really must approach this problem seriously without attempting immediately to rob death of its power through symbolization. Only when this process has run its course and genuine, emotionally cathected rebirth motifs emerge from the unconscious can the prospective interpretation commence. But precisely at these points one must pay special attention that the patient does not feign acceptance of a prospective interpretation due to fears, longings, wishes, or hopes and thereby avoid a deeper problem.

Particularly under Melanie Klein's influence, Freudian psychoanalysis has placed more and more emphasis, in part exclusively, on interpretation of the transference neurosis in recent years, while analytical psychology has remained oriented more toward understanding unconscious contents. Kirsch (1977) spotlighted this situation: when the analyst appears in patients' dreams and fantasies, we may consider him or her intrapsychically as symbolizing the physician or healer in the patient's psyche, or interpersonally as a real vis-à-vis. Only in the late 1950s did the problem of the systematic treatment of transference and countertransference again come under discussion in analytical psychology through the work of the London group (Fordham 1974a, 1974b; Plaut 1974; Kraemer 1974). At the end of the 1960s, the Berlin Study Group, as already mentioned, published a number of papers, and Gugenbühl-Craig (1971) in Zürich drew attention to the countertransference constellation. At every stage of the analytic process, the analyst must pay attention to, and keep account of, the level on which transference and countertransference is taking place. But I am not of the opinion that it makes sense and is necessary, as is believed in Freudian psychoanalysis, to refer all or even most interpretations to the transference-countertransference. Here, too, the essential criterion for an interpretation seems to me that of a correct assessment of the entire situation and of the relevant pointers offered by fantasy materials. Of course, this does not mean that a transference interpretation should be offered only when the figure of the analyst actually appears in the patient's dreams. The analyst and the relationship to him or her can appear from the unconscious in symbols or in projections onto other, often archetypal, figures. Nevertheless, dreams and life situations usually give sufficient indication that transference is intended. And, in my experience, this cannot be limited to a specific phase of analysis. Many analysts believe that transference interpretations should be given only when an adequately stable transference relationship between analyst and patient has developed. Not infrequently I have had the experience that right at the beginning of an analysis transference interpretations have arisen from the constellation that related both to illusionary expectations and to fears. Only after such interpretations were made was it possible for the historical background and the archetypal ground to unfold.

Jung preferred to use the well-known metaphor of the Chinese rainmaker when speaking of the analyst. If we take the countertransference results of the Berlin Study Group into account, according to which fifty percent of the resistance always belongs to the analyst, then countertransference is still used in interpretations too seldom or with too much hesitation. Since every complex that is constellated between the analyst and the patient in the course of treatment also constellates a corresponding complex in the unconscious of the analyst, it is important to observe this area in its own right. From these observations one can then often formulate possible interpretations that can show the patient what effects and experiences his or her behavior evokes in other persons. Accordingly it is also advisable for the analyst not only to observe his or her own dreams in which the patient appears but also, when an intense problem has been constellated in analysis, to relate the dream to that problem when the dream pursues it. Of course, it would be wrong to share personal unconscious material with the patient directly, but corresponding emotionally cathected insights often derived from dream materials can be worked over and included in interpretations.

In conclusion let us take a very brief look at the very problematic question of the timing of interpretations. In general, Jungian analysts, as Schmaltz (1955) has pointed out in detail, take the standpoint that timing is best left to the analyst's intuition and corresponding sense of appropriateness. Schmaltz correctly points out that the appearance of a felt-sense of appropriateness which is supposed to precede an interpretation is, from the standpoint of a science based on psychodynamics, a thoroughly legitimate means that does not open the door to chaotic arbitrariness. More recently, Fordham (1975) attempted to work out certain criteria for timing. Among them what stands in the foreground is the process of the analyst becoming emotionally and rationally conscious of a psychic content or defense as well as an identical, relatively highly developed process in the patient so that the analyst's verbalized interpretation resonates with an identical process lying just below the threshold of the patient's awareness. It is important that the patient has libidinally and emotionally cathected the unconscious content and that this content emerge into consciousness.

Certainly this is an apt characterization of the ideal, but one with which I cannot fully agree. In my opinion it takes too little account of the different psychological types. But I do adhere to the point that applies to the analyst. Every interpretation should be preceded by an epistemological process in which the analyst not only rationally grasps the particular content but also experiences it empathetically in his or her feelings. For example, when we have a patient in therapy whose only developed function is thinking, and that only to a modest degree, it is often impossible to approach unconscious contents at all except via this function. Then, of necessity, the patient must first grasp certain processes rationally in thinking terms before he or she can deal with the feeling or the intuitive dimension. Hence, in this sort of case, the purely rational understanding of an interpretation would not function as a defense to block but rather would facilitate the feeling aspect. Vice versa, the same, of course, holds true for the feeling type and for the intuitive or the sensor, and it does not seem to me possible — at least with the means now at our disposal — to make a generally correct determination of the right point in time to offer an interpretation without violating the variety of individual typologies. Again and again, in my own work with patients and as supervising analyst, I have found that it is absolutely necessary to leave the timing of an interpretation in the hands of the individual analyst who, with the help of intuition and empathy, must decide when and where an interpretation can best be made.

CHAPTER 13

Active Imagination

Active imagination has gradually become one of the classic methods in analytical psychology, employed by a multitude of patients in the course of the analytic process. There are a great number of publications concerned with the theoretical, the methodological, and the practical discussion of active imagination. The various authors hold differing views on many points, particularly in regard to 1) the participation of the ego-complex in active imagination, 2) the point in analysis when commencing active imagination is indicated, and 3) what should be called active imagination. When it seems important I will, in the course of this chapter, take up the points on which the various authors differ.

First I shall describe the procedure as such since the method of active imagination is still relatively unknown outside the field of analytical psychology. There are a great number of introspective, meditative procedures — e.g., catahymic imaging (Leuner 1970), the upper level of autogenic training (Schultz 1976), and Buddhist meditative practices, as well as certain processes that took place in medieval alchemy — that closely resemble active imagination and are frequently confused with it.

The signal characteristic that distinguishes active imagination from all other meditative practices and techniques is the basic fact that in active imagination the practitioner addresses only his or her own inner images and does not introduce external elements — as, for example, in guided imagery where one starts with a consciously chosen image or in other meditative practices where one works with a particular mantra. In active imagination, a process takes place between the conscious personality and the subjective, inner world of images. It is a process that fundamentally avoids introducing any other symbols whatsoever from outside that might form the basis for introspection or meditation.

In principle, active imagination proceeds as follows. The patient is placed in the position of withdrawing his or her projections, of introjecting them, and of forming and shaping them at the subjective level. Under these conditions the ego-complex is brought into a living relationship with the archetypal imagos of the unconscious. In this process, the active participation of the ego-complex further shapes and develops these images *as inner events and happenings*. This can take the most varied forms of expression—meditative fantasies; automatic painting, sketching, or writing; conversations with an inner "other," such as shadow, anima, animus, etc.; and even as dance, music, or any other expressive form. If we regard active imagination as a positive regression in the sense of Jung's libido theory ("On Psychic Energy," *C. W.* 8), we recognize that young children are filled with processes of active imagination. The imaginal playmate, toyland, or other fabulous worlds of fantasy, which the child's ego actively enters and shapes, belong to the domain of active imagination. Hence as Fordham (1977) has discussed in detail, a close relationship exists between active imagination and the transitional object described by Winnicott (1965) that is so uncommonly important for the psyche's symbol-forming function.

Jung (1938–1940, vols. 3 and 4) also points out that in certain forms and variations active imagination has been employed since the earliest times by peoples of both primitive and highly developed cultures. For example, Egyptian priests gave their clients wonderously beautiful blue crystals in which they were supposed to observe their own fantasy images. The purpose was to approach the divine and to heal ailments of the soul or even of the body. Intuitively the Egyptians recognized the unconscious background of the psyche which was projected into the crystal sphere as well as the efficacy of these images. As C. A. Meier (1967) described in detail, similar processes took place in ancient incubation. As I described elsewhere (Dieckmann 1972b), primal peoples such as the American Indians also make use of these processes. Thus in elaborating its methodology in modern psychology, active imagination takes its place in the lineage of ancient human knowledge that runs throughout the entire history of humankind. Active imagination also played a great role in alchemy to the extent that many philosophical alchemists described their meditations as a dialogue with an invisible person: they conversed with God, with their protective spirit, or with themselves. The notion that it was possible to transform chemical substances through the powers of imagination and that intensive concentration impressed certain structures upon matter that led to transformation was also a part of the body of medieval alchemical thought.

The person wishing to do active imagination must concentrate on a fragment of inner fantasy and attempt to exclude all other influences that come from the external world and are irrelevant. The fragment of fantasy can come from a dream or may arise spontaneously; it can have to do with a mood or an affect, and thus with practically any emotionally charged inner experience. As a rule, by holding the inner image and concentrating one's attention on it, it gradually begins to change; the image may start to move, or the affect or mood may change into a moving image or picture. The decisive step in active imagination then comes when the individual doing the imagination enters into the image or engages in a dialogue with the figures that appear. At the beginning one often experiences the feeling that one is making up the answers or the inner figures oneself; only gradually as one gains experience does it become clear that the figures from the unconscious speak their own language and are autonomous. For example, a patient dreamed of a journey through an unknown, foreign land; he was part of a group guided by a leader dressed in foreign clothing who explained the surroundings. Since the patient was on the periphery of the group far from the leader, he could not understand what the guide said. Later, in active imagination, he approached the unknown figure and began to speak with him. Soon he realized that the explanations of the foreign landscape bore a relationship to a current conflictual situation in his life and that the leader's words brought up a side of the problem of which he had been previously unaware. He was now able to see the situation with different eyes and to deal with it better.

If forms other than that of meditative imagination — such as painting, drawing, modeling, etc. — are chosen for one's active imagination, it is still important that the unconscious have free play and the opportunity to take shape. Consider unconscious or automatic painting, for example. The conscious idea of wanting to paint something specific should be excluded and one should let the unconscious guide one's hand. The same holds true for other modalities in which the unconscious can express itself. A 45-year-old woman patient with relatively severe bouts of reactive depression, who previously had made only one spontaneously scribbled drawing, purchased clay and described the creation of her first sculpture in these words:

> The depression of recent days has still not passed, but it has gotten better. I feel as though I am in a cobweb. I had the intention of making something in clay and it took a huge effort to overcome my resistance to doing it, although I did sense that it would help me. I didn't know how to begin. At first I thought of the black man that had occupied my fantasies so very much lately, but he didn't want to come out. So I squeezed and kneeded the clay for half an hour between my fingers and observed the forms that arose. I saw heads of animals; I felt the cold clay and gradually stopped thinking. And then I saw how finally the figure of a child emerged out of the clay as if from the very earth. This child had a toothache and ran to its mother to lay its head

between her breasts. Thus the figure of a mother with her child gradually arose. (Dieckmann 1971c, p. 134)

This brief summary should serve to characterize the method; interested readers can consult Jung's works and the secondary literature for further details. I would mention two extensive discussions of active imagination that are of particular value, those by Rix Weaver (1973) and A. N. Ammann (1978). Although Jung undertook the first experiments with active imagination on himself as early as 1913 and, without mentioning the term, described them in 1916 as the transcendent function (*C.W.* 8), he published the latter essay only relatively late (1958). References to the method can be found scattered throughout his works. Jung spoke more extensively of active imagination in his seminars, and in his mature work, *Mysterium Coniunctionis* (*C.W.* 14), he published a detailed discussion.

In the context of the present discussion it is important first to discuss the role and the function of the ego-complex in active imagination, since certain stages of ego development are prerequisite indicators for employing this method and the intensity of the ego's participation as well as its relinquishing its defenses are essential for the success of active imagination. Weaver (1973) formulated the various positions the ego-complex can ideally assume in undertaking to do active imagination. She writes:

In summing up the positions on Active Imagination, I assume the following:

1. That to pay attention to moods, to autonomous fantasy fragments, to extend the meaning of dreams by fantasy, etc., is the first move of the ego to objectify in this regard, and this objectifying is in itself the beginning of ego participation.
2. That involvement can take different forms.
   (a) The ego can initiate fantasy to find meaning of dreams, etc.
   (b) That one can find oneself caught by fantasy that forces itself into consciousness much as the dream does. In such a situation the ego is not lost in a flight of fantasy, but watches in a way that has an objective attitude to the images. The ego is the *conscious* recorder.
   (c) That one can catch a fragment of fantasy, or *initiate* fantasy and enlarge it by participation and intervention. This would bring in a subjective attitude to the unconscious material. Being consciously involved in the material means it comes under a greater restriction from the ego.
   (Often in Active Imagination both processes (b) and (c) alternate as they do with the creative artist. . . .)

3. (a) That ego participation is in the work from the moment of objective interest.

   (b) That ego participation increases with the involvement in the drama.

   (c) That all is not Active Imagination that includes the ego as part of the recorded activity, and where the ego selects too arbitrarily or ritualistically.

4. That where the whole work is projected much as alchemical writings, and mostly this is at an advanced stage of psychic maturity, it is equally Active Imagination. Here one is in a realm that influences, but remains beyond, ego participation, which can be recorded as such. As referred to in (2)(b), one often discovers here the more universal and eternal symbols, myths of beginnings, immortality, etc.

5. That the most important criterion of what is Active Imagination is not so much that the activity of the ego is actually recorded in the work, but that the ego undergoes meaningful participation no matter which form of expression it takes.

6. That ego participation differs in different people. The introvert can have an objective attitude to the unconscious and the extravert a subjective attitude in this realm. Both are possible. Only the person who has done the work is the final judge of what is meaningful for him. Meaningful work is not an egotistical selection, but requires the capacity to acknowledge certainty and uncertainty at the same time. (Weaver 1973, p. 19f)

In light of these definitions, it is apparent that a relatively high degree of ego-stability is the prerequisite for using active imagination as a therapeutic method. Consequently the point in time when it is undertaken falls in a relatively late stage of advanced analytic work when ego-stability has been achieved and the dependency transference has been resolved. Henderson (1955b) also takes this position. He emphasizes that active imagination should be undertaken only when analysis of the dependency transference has been concluded, which does not occur until the fourth stage of individuation has been entered.

In contrast to Henderson's position, Adler (1961) and I (Dieckmann 1971c) have described patients who took up active imagination relatively early in their analyses; in these cases, a positively toned transference-countertransference situation offered the patients the temenos or magic circle, so to speak, in which they were able to conduct their confrontation with the symbols of their inner world of fantasy. Through the transference-countertransference constellation, both analyst and patient maintained the ego-stability that made it possible to do active imagination in these cases. In my experience, this is thoroughly possible in a very large number of cases and can lead to very fruitful results.

Doubtless the problem arises at that point where analysts' differing therapeutic styles tend more to stress the synthetic processes of individuation in the stricter sense or remain more at the level of rational interpretations or reductive processes. In my practical experience, however, these two levels always run concurrently from the very beginning of analysis, and there is no sharp separation between the more synthetic work of withdrawing projected, neurotic transferences and the uncovering of the primary and secondary processes of neurosis. On the contrary, even a certain aggressive potential that was inhibited and latent, and initially could not be channeled either into the transference or the environment, can be utilized to introduce the processes of genuine active imagination. This brings undeveloped personality components, abilities, and functions (especially often the sensation and the feeling functions) into consciousness and develops them synthetically while at the same time achieving a symbolic understanding of the archetypal level. Only much later does expression, integration, and the transformation of a large part of the aggression into productive activity gradually come about; in this process, active imagination can be the beginning of these sorts of productive activities. Then one frequently observes that the intensity the patient has invested in meditation, painting, or modeling in clay wanes and the analysis again takes on more the character of dialectical, verbal communication (Dieckmann and Jung 1977).

Obviously Ammann (1978) also holds this view, even if not explicitly stated. In his book, he lists thirteen possible situations where the use of active imagination is especially indicated. Among these are situations that fall within the early stages of analysis, for example, directly working through affects, developing the analysand's seeds of creativity, working over situations containing too little or too much fantasy or dream activity, and also working on disturbances in adaptation. In practice I, too, have no reservations about employing active imagination in a relatively early stage of analysis with patients suited to it. Granted, I do not believe that it is possible simply to follow a catalog of possible uses of active imagination that refer to individual analytic situations. There is a precondition that must be met if active imagination is to be used: not only must the patient's ego-complex be ready to cooperate in the method, the patient must be capable of doing so, and that depends on the degree to which ego functions are disturbed. As I have already emphasized earlier in this book, the relatively imprecise expression "ego-stability" by no means suffices to describe this very complicated phenomenon.

In the case of neurotic disturbances, the several ego functions can be disturbed in various ways and to differing degrees, and the question of where and when a method like active imagination can be used must take this, among other things, into account. If we regard the problem from this angle, the ability of the ego-complex to relax its functions of control and organization and to admit unconscious contents is an absolutely necessary precondition for using active imagination. Wherever these two functions are disturbed, the patient is completely incapable of undertaking active imagination. This holds true especially for severely compulsive patients who must maintain their control and organization in order to defend against the underlying anxiety. In these cases it will be necessary first to loosen the controls and the organization through a laborious process of analysis in order to approach and work through the underlying anxieties. The relative intactness of the organizing ego-function which establishes interrelationships and connections among psychic contents is another prerequisite. To the extent that this function is not present, the attempt to do active imagination runs the great risk of flooding the ego with unconscious contents that it cannot integrate and that can then lead to an inflation. Likewise there must be present a certain degree of control of mobility capable of controlling impulses and emotions from the unconscious and thereby providing protection from overpowering anxieties or outbreaks of affect. The defense mechanisms are also of fundamental significance. Excessively strong reaction formation, isolation, and/or rationalization, as well as excessive identification and idealization, can hinder or disturb active imagination or evoke dangerous inflations.

In respect to the defense mechanisms, one should be especially aware that, like every other therapeutic method, active imagination, too, can serve a defensive purpose. Hence it is extremely problematic to use active imagination exclusively in the absence of dreams. When this is the case, it all too often happens that the patient paints, sketches, or meditates but due to the defense that has created a block against dreams, the active imaginations that arise have precisely the character of a defense and their intensification prevents the patient from getting at the underlying psychic contents against which he or she is defending. Of course, this must not be overgeneralized. To the extent that the defense is no longer rigid and the underlying unconscious content is close to the threshold of consciousness, dream fragments that appear can be elaborated through active imagination and the previously unconscious psychic contents can be brought into consciousness.

One should also keep in mind that this method can be used only individually. In every individual case, the analyst must have a relatively precise image of which of the patient's ego functions are adequately stable and the degree of the patient's motivation and suitability for employing active imagination at a particular point in time.

Many patients spontaneously take up this method and attempt to express themselves in some sort of creative modality. Other patients have fantasies forced upon them with which they must come to terms. Here the question arises whether or not every process of giving form, shape, or expression in analysis that the patient undertakes is to be understood as active imagination. The views held by analytical psychologists on this point differ. In addition to Henderson (1955a) and Weaver (1973), mentioned above, Fordham (1957), J. Kirsch (1973), and von Franz (1972) regard active imagination as a distinct method that should be distinguished in analysis from other form-giving processes such as unconscious painting, etc. Fordham (1956) has suggested a sensible differentiation between "active imagination" and "imaginal activity." In the German language area, the concepts "active" and "passive" imagination are distinguished, which I prefer.

As long as the criteria mentioned above regarding the ego's participation in the inner fantasies are not fulfilled, I prefer to speak of passive imaginal processes and of active imagination only when the ego-complex actually participates actively. This sort of ego activity was very clearly expressed by the woman patient mentioned earlier who modeled the mother-and-child figure when she said how she consciously entered actively into forming the initially shapeless mass of the *prima materia* of her clay against strong resistance.

In conclusion, I would like to comment on the problem of aesthetic form in active imagination especially where it is a question of more or less artistically creative processes. From the therapeutic standpoint, it appears that aesthetic form in active imagination is a fundamentally significant issue. Jung makes a clear distinction between the aesthetic standpoint in regard to a form of psychic expression and the element of psychic involvement (*C.W.* 14). In practice, too, it happens relatively infrequently that we find a happy combination of successful artistic form and the search for the understanding or meaning of the unconscious content in patients' unconscious, creative representations, whether the modality is writing, painting, or sculpting. It is precisely those patients who lay special value on an external form who are often prevented from shaping truly creative expressions from the unconscious. The feeling of their own technical imperfection blocks them so thoroughly that they dare not make the attempt at such expressions. For the therapist who is interested first and foremost in the patient's healing, it follows as a matter of course that his or her entire interest centers on the symbolic form and not on the aesthetic aspects of the formal expression. Nevertheless it seems to me, as I have discussed at length elsewhere (Dieckmann 1971c), that aesthetic form does play a certain role.

I believe that all analytical psychologists working with these methods would corroborate how tremendously expressive these products from the unconscious can be, products into which even persons with absolutely no artistic gifts pour great amounts of libido. If they have some degree of artistic ability, they can produce decidedly fascinating pictures, poems, fairy tales, novellas. I have observed that active imagination is especially effective when a patient attempts to harmonize both the principles of psychic engagement and aesthetic expression, working at forming the material with intensely patient fascination. This libidinal process of development often liberates not only the libido from its fixation in the symptoms but can also lead the patient to a meaningful, creative activity that continues long after the conclusion of the analysis. In my analytic activity, I have been able to observe a great many patients who, in the course of their analysis and through engaging in active imagination, have developed artistic abilities that remained a source of enrichment for their lives. These persons were previously unaware of the presence of these sorts of abilities and the development of these latent possibilities remained a lasting value for them even many years after their analysis. It goes without saying that precisely in these sorts of cases one must be alert to the danger of inflation so that patients who discover certain creative abilities during analysis do not get into a state of narcissistic grandiosity where they consider themselves great artists who lack only the recognition of the rest of the world.

CHAPTER 14

Psychological Types in the Methodology of Analysis

Up until the decade of the 1960s, the majority of analytical psychologists utilized psychological typology primarily for diagnostic purposes, if at all. In 1972, Plaut published the results of an international survey of the members of the International Association for Analytical Psychology on the practical significance of the type concept and on the individual analyst's own typology which showed a similar outcome. Forty-six percent, a rather high percentage, of the questionnaires were answered and returned. In regard to the practical application of psychological types, the results showed that only somewhat more than one-half of all Jungians found the type concept helpful in the practical work of analysis. The development of the inferior functions and the application of the concept of types in the transference and countertransference constellation seemed not to be the focal point of Jungian analysts' interest in contrast to the interpretation of symbols as a therapeutic method. One of the reasons for this surely lies in the fact that 51 percent of the responding analysts considered themselves to be intuitives while only 8.5 percent said they were sensation types (Plaut 1972). This also corresponds to a study that Bradway (1964) conducted among twenty-eight Jungian analysts in California using the Gray-Wheelwright Test. Here, too, the results showed a very high number of introverted intuitives who obviously felt very much at home with Jungian psychology. A later study of ninety-two Jungian analysts conducted in 1976 confirmed these findings (Bradway and Detloff 1976). It would seem justified to infer that classification methods appeal less to the introverted intuitive types (who appear to comprise the majority of Jungians) than do symbol interpretation and work with fantasies.

Whenever one makes the diagnosis of a specific psychological type, the feeling of having established something objective naturally arises very easily although basically in the individuation process the movement among the various functions and the development of the inferior functions is indispensable. I must confess that at the beginning of my practice I felt the same way as did the majority of the Jungians who responded to the surveys. My first attempts to work with psychological types ran aground on certain difficulties that I only gradually came to understand. Thus my experiences with my first patients were similar to what Henderson (1955a) had described in his study of the inferior function. I found that at least a portion of my patients presented themselves in the analytic setting differently than they did in the outside world, and initially my diagnoses, based on the presentation of certain leading functions in analysis, were "wrong." For example, one woman patient, who I had classified as an extraverted feeling type, turned out to be strongly introverted; I had equated her intense relatedness in the transference to the analyst and to the analytic (or treatment) setting as extraversion. With other patients exactly the opposite occurred in regard to my diagnosis of their attitude type: persons who were strongly extraverted in their environment were able to shift over to the necessary introversion in the analytic setting (sometimes on the basis of a compliant attitude) to such a degree that they impressed me as introverts. I was also able to observe this phenomenon in regard to the function types, and only much later did I learn that presenting a certain typology in the analytic setting by no means depended only on the typology of the patient concerned but that two very important, additional factors played a role. The first is the analytic setting itself which offers the patient the opportunity of bringing forward the inferior function. The second is the analyst's typology to which the patient reacts unconsciously or with only partial consciousness, depending on the degree to which these typological features are distinctly present in the analyst.

I have also noted a similar phenomenon when supervising the case histories taken by analysts-in-training in regard to structural diagnoses. At the beginning of their analytic activity, analysts are partial to the components of their own structure in the patients whom they see; the patients themselves react correspondingly, since, as is well known, projections have a constellating effect. Much to the bewilderment of many analysts-in-training, something like a "rotation of structure" ensues when the supervising analyst reviews their work, and a patient who previously appeared compulsive now appears depressed, or a hysteric appears schizoid. Of course, in regard to psychological types, these sorts of diagnostic considerations are even more complicated since not only must three (or, among neo-Freudians, four) different structures be evaluated, but also eight different typological possibilities as well as the secondary functions.

However, since we do not intend to treat psychological types from the diagnostic standpoint but rather to explore their methodological significance in the analytic process, I shall mention one additional difficulty that, after some initial attempts, also moved me to employ the concept of psychological types as a therapeutic method either not at all or only peripherally for a number of years. Like Jung himself (*C.W.* 6), Jacobi (1943) and other authors point out that methodologically one must approach the inferior function by way of an auxiliary function, since the latter is less deeply anchored in the unconscious than the inferior function itself. Theoretically that sounds quite obvious, but in practice I ran aground attempting to ascertain which was the more intensely unconscious secondary function. Hence I was confronted with a question: In the case of a thinking type, should I attempt to develop sensation or intuition in order to get to the inferior feeling function? And for the other types I encountered the same dilemma. Of course, one can determine the inferior function with a test (such as the Gray-Wheelwright) and orient the treatment accordingly. But I soon noticed that cases in which I did this never really got moving. I became more pedagogic than analytic and, of course, harvested greater resistance, so that I soon relinquished my conscious attempt at developing auxiliary functions in my patients in order to get to their inferior function.

The typological constellation between myself and my patients became gradually clearer only as we undertook detailed studies of transference and countertransference processes. I discovered that especially favorable or productive analytic situations always arose with a contrasting type constellation in the transference-countertransference. My initially somewhat imprecise personal experience was then confirmed in a publication by C. A. Meier (1969) on the principle of typological rotation in analysis. In my opinion, typology can be utilized methodologically in the analytic process only when transference and countertransference are taken into account, just as Meier also proceeds from the transference-countertransference model that Jung discussed as the "cross-cousin marriage" ("Psychology of the Transference," *C.W.* 16) and which I elaborated upon in the chapter on transference and countertransference.

If one regards these two interacting psychic systems from the typological standpoint, a second model appears, according to Meier, in which both the two individual systems as well as the four functions (thinking, feeling, intuition, and sensation) are contained in differing arrangements. The psyches of the analyst and of the analysand are represented here by circles (Figure 14.1).

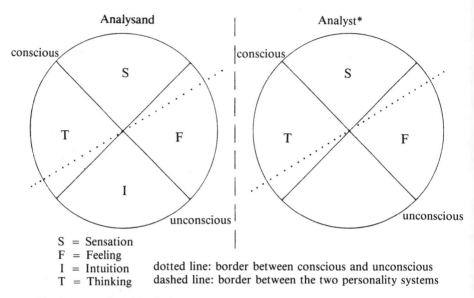

S = Sensation
F = Feeling
I = Intuition   dotted line: border between conscious and unconscious
T = Thinking   dashed line: border between the two personality systems

*in the case of an identical type

This offers an additional possibility of visualizing the reciprocal influence of the two systems on each other. In Figure 14.1, patient and physician are typologically identical, i.e., both have sensation as their conscious, leading function and thinking as their most highly developed secondary function. This diagram depicts two persons with highly rational orientations to the so-called "facts," the empirical phenomena and the logical interconnections among them that thinking can establish. To a great extent, feelings and intuitive ideas are excluded as "disruptive." In a typological constellation of this sort, very little if anything will transpire analytically, just as I described earlier in the case of my personal therapeutic experience involving different typologies. Whenever this sort of typological likeness exists, physician and patient find themselves in a harmonious relationship and merely expand the horizon of their knowledge. When it is not a case of two sensation types (such as described here) but of intuitives, it can happen that they get into certain kinds of inflations if analyst and patient "fire each other up" with "hunches" about the meaning of symbols. A real tension of opposites and hence a furthering of the analytic process can ensue only when an inferior function of the one is constellated vis-à-vis the leading function of the other. One should be able to expect that analysts would have developed all four functions to some extent in the course of their training analyses and that they would consequently be able to let their typological systems rotate. (In the example diagrammed above, the rotation would be toward increased feeling.) Only in this manner can analysis become a dynamic process and can a productive tension develop between the two systems. Here, of course, we must keep in mind that every function can also be used as a defense, as Zacharias (1965) pointed out.

As it runs its course in practice, every analytically assisted process of individuation naturally includes all four functions, i.e., the patient will respond to various situations that are constellated in the analytic process either *a priori* with various functions or will learn to do so in the course of the analysis so that the analyst will be continually compelled to let his or her own typological system rotate in order to maintain the process. If this does not happen, analyst and patient get stuck in certain phases of development or in shadow projections, and either a futile, pseudo-harmony or an incompatibility of personalities develops in which, unfortunately, the patient is usually the weaker party and consequently develops feelings of being too sick and incapable of making progress or having insights. Groesbeck (1978) demonstrated the clinical validity of this method on the basis of a series of clinical examples in which he showed how dream symbols, as a third force, effect a rotation of the typological mandalas of both analyst and patient.

Since, as a rule, the analyst assumes the role of advocate of the unconscious, he or she usually identifies with the patient's inferior function in the transference and countertransference constellation. Here identification in the sense of a conscious process means that the analyst assumes the compensatory function of the unconscious and introduces the compensatory, unconscious contents into the analysis in the course of making interpretations. In my experience, however, this sort of identification is made with the patient's inferior function and not with a secondary function in the great majority of cases. Contrary to theory—i.e., that the inferior function can be addressed only via a secondary function—it even happens that it is necessary in many cases to develop the inferior function to a limited degree before secondary functions can be differentiated at all.

For example, I am reminded of a patient, a distinctly introverted intuitive type, whose free-floating intuition was not linked to feeling or thinking. Consequently, during the first period of analysis, he inundated me with intuitive associations and amplifications of his dream motifs that were indeed extremely fascinating but so disconnected and polyvalent that they slipped out of my hands again and again like the mythological Proteus. Only when I began consistently to question the patient in regard to facts of both an inner and an outer nature did his analysis begin to assume a certain structure. What do you actually feel or sense right now? What really happened in the conversation with your wife? What did she say and what did you answer? Gradually the patient himself noticed how he ran away from every shred of reality with his intuition and began on his own to be more concerned with factual material, for example, by dwelling on certain dream symbols and concentrating on them or by finally telling me what the external actual reality of a situation was. Only after he was able to do this was he in a position to notice the accompanying feelings and to share them or to reflect logically on specific interrelationships and to develop a certain capacity for abstraction in addition to his purely imaginal thought.

A similar case, likewise rather extreme, was that of a schizoid teacher, an extraverted thinking type. He tried to keep his analysis on a purely rational plane. Among other symptoms, he suffered greatly from a difficulty in making verbal formulations when he was teaching and had attempted to overcome this problem with ever more rigorous and precise rational thinking which only added to his misery. For a period of time at the beginning of his therapy, he strove to fathom the therapeutic system which, in his view, I had to employ. His purpose in this endeavor, as later came to light, was to put it out of commission by following it slavishly just as he had done vis-à-vis his father. He was unconscious of his motivation which turned up only in his dreams in the form of magical personalities who exercised a mysterious and insuperable power on other persons. During the early hours I did not intervene but restricted myself to observing. Finally he got entangled in his rational explanations and his endless, complicated chains of causality and began sometimes to fall silent. During one of his pauses I said to him, "I have the feeling that you feel very helpless and abandoned now." The patient confirmed this and subsequently was able to surrender a piece of his resistance against the negative father and trace his feeling of helplessness and isolation back to childhood where it related to his mother and where it had become a basic survival feeling for him thanks to having been extended into the archetypal realm. Since he almost completely repressed his feelings and had attempted to override the helplessness and isolation with his very good intelligence and rationality, he was not really conscious of his basic feeling of being or not being in the world. In the following period, I tended either to address the patient's lacunae in feeling or to express feelings that emerged in me in the countertransference from under his rational surface. In addition to feeling, obviously this patient's inferior function, his intuition was least developed. Moreover, he defended against it with a rationalistic ideology that we approached only with great difficulty toward the end of his analysis. Not until near the end of his entire treatment was he able to let a part of his intuitive potential enter his consciousness and to accept it, which, however, he did only with the help of his essentially more developed feeling function.

I would like to present a short case history in order to show how the repressed inferior function appears relatively early on in a patient's dreams, to illustrate the stages through which it develops in analysis, and to point out what role the remaining functions play in treatment. The case was that of a 22-year-old male student of philosophy who had a depressive, schizoid structure. This patient had developed strongly and one-sidedly in the direction of thinking, both because of his family and by later introjecting his parental imagos. His auxiliary function was intuition, but his sensation and especially his feeling were almost completely unconscious. He suffered from major reactive-depressive mood swings and difficulties with work that were so extensive that sometimes he lay in bed the entire day unable to get up. The following recurrent dream that the patient had had since early childhood gave the impetus to seek analytic therapy.

I was in a shaft or well. Then something big and black came at me. I tried to get up out of the shaft and always awoke from the dream thrashing about so wildly that I often hurt myself on pieces of furniture.

The last time he had this dream before beginning treatment, he had smashed the glass top of a table (a rather thick and solid slab of glass) and severely cut his hand so that he had to be taken to an emergency room where he had stitches. He also suffered these sorts of unconsciously inflicted bodily wounds rather often when awake, which could be traced back to a strongly masochistically colored disturbance of his sensation function. At the beginning of his analysis, he had no body sense at all. Since he was very large, he thought of himself as awkward, was afraid of touching other people and squashing them with his strength, and generally had no idea what to do with his body.

Very early in his treatment — before the fourth hour — a dream appeared which played a key role in the rest of his therapy and offered access to his buried inferior function.

I am on a stage in a theater or auditorium that is brightly illuminated in the middle. The hall is only one-third filled with spectators. I am performing a skit: I enter the illuminated area; a rabbit is in front of me. I follow it in order to catch it and to roast it for a feast. The rabbit slowly escapes toward the other side of the stage. It does not want to be caught. Now I speak very softly; the spectators can hardly hear me. I explain to the rabbit that I really don't need him if he doesn't want to; that the feast would be just as good even without roast rabbit. As I speak, I walk backwards and the rabbit follows me, now also talking.

*He says that he wants to accompany me and come with me. He didn't
mean it like I took it.*

After the patient told me this dream, he reacted with a powerful shudder
and started to cry. Very intense feelings from his childhood arose in
regard to the rabbit, and among other things, he reported that he had
been sent to a children's home on a lake when he was five. There the
other children had taken away his dearly beloved teddy bear, a transitional object on which he was still strongly fixated, and had ripped out its
arm. Moreover, the childcare worker had then punished him because she
assumed he had done it. This event transpired right at the beginning of
his stay. He reacted to this with a period of mutism and did not utter a
single word for the remainder of his six-week banishment. He experienced an additional, very deep disappointment when he returned to his
grandparents' home since his father had meanwhile been hospitalized.
While he had been gone, his grandparents had given away the cat to
which he was very attached. When the patient was sent to school shortly
after that, he reacted again with mutism and consequently was taken to a
children's home or boarding school which at first inflicted another very
painful separation from his mother.

If we take this patient's childhood experiences as the basis on which to
measure how other persons — his significant others — dealt with his feelings at the time, we can imagine how strongly he felt compelled to
suppress any twinge of feeling. The dream was the first instance when he
could not kill the rabbit that, along with the teddy bear and the cat,
represented for him warmth, softness, and the vitality of the world of
feelings; rather, he could let it live and talk with it, which also corresponded to the strong eruption of feelings in his analytic hour.

As already mentioned, this patient's relatively well-developed secondary function was intuition, but he used it almost exclusively to defend
against feelings. Wherever anyone might have expected a feeling reaction
from him, or in situations in which feelings arose, he fled into grandiose
ideas and fantasies that, in accordance with his good intuition, were
indeed fitting, but remained very cool and distanced. As already seen in
his recurrent dream, his was a continual flight "upwards," into the so-
called "higher" regions, which found expression in a whole series of
dreams that again and again contained the same image. Wherever he got
into a dangerous or frightening situation, he developed the magical ability, thanks to this thoughts, of rising up into the air and flying away.

After his feeling world (depicted in the first dream of the rabbit and
expressed in the subsequent analytic hour) had been received with understanding, he brought another dream, full of feelings, about a month
later.

In a chapel I find two gigantic, stuffed brown bears that I take and carry around happily. They are about as big in relation to me now as my childhood teddy bear was when I was five. But I want to give back the bears, which are wrapped in pelts. I look for the boy to whom they probably belong and I want to tell him how much I like the bears. I go to the center of the chapel where a service is taking place. The boy I am looking for is wearing vestments and singing the liturgy. I stand beside him, waiting, but I do not want to disturb him while he is singing. I give him back the bear skins. Then I look for my belongings in a truck. They haven't been properly packed yet, and I don't yet see how much baggage I will have. I think that I will have to drag along a lot of stuff and proceed slowly with my packing. Now I get sad. I discover a device in a pothole next to the truck that lets you adjust a photo in a glass plate. I take it. Then I discover a wonderfully beautiful, almost completely naked girl on the glass of the photo. My sadness increases so much that I begin to cry. I sing a melody—an old children's song. As I am singing, tears of sadness roll down my cheeks.

In this dream the patient is able to discover a connection with the *intact* feeling world of childhood where the teddy bears have not yet been destroyed by the cruelty of the other children. But he is also able to give the childlike feelings back to the child in himself. Everything takes place within an archetypally positive maternal space, the chapel. It is characteristic that here he had to reach back to the archetypal symbolism of the collective unconscious in order to find the positive side of the mother archetype which he was unable to experience with his own mother who had not been particularly understanding. Finally, in this dream, he succeeds in opening to and experiencing both happiness and sorrow, something of which he had been completely incapable since early childhood. Simultaneously, he notices that he had never experienced his feeling side in any of his relationships, but had attempted to build relationships by including other persons in a commonly shared, great philosophical or religious idea (the chapel!). Of course that never worked, and his depressive moods were intensified when relationships were regularly broken off, especially with women, since an idea can never form a solid basis for an interpersonal, feeling relationship. Now, for the first time, he experienced the absence of his feelings in the external world as a lack and as a loss. This in turn activated his sensation function since with this *function réal* he was able to establish when and where this lack really existed.

In the further course of treatment, he experienced, first, a gradual development of his feeling and also of his sensation functions in the transference-countertransference constellation, ultimately giving him access to his own body. When his girlfriend, with whom he had formed a relationship during his analysis, got pregnant, they decided to get married and to have the baby. Toward his son, he experienced his emotions and bodily feelings in the outer world for the first time, especially when he let his little boy crawl around on his belly or his chest. Only after he had established a successful feeling relationship with his son was he gradually able to develop a more intense feeling relationship to his wife and to other significant adults in his life. Although this patient was and remained a thinking type, he had a decidedly rich and intense feeling world, a fact that is not at all so uncommon among thinking types, as Hillman (1971) has explicitly pointed out. In this patient's treatment, the inferior function first appeared in dreams. After he was able to accept and affirm the dreams, the inferior function began to develop and to emerge into consciousness more or less parallel with the unconscious secondary function, in this case sensation. He did not gain access to his inferior function via the secondary function; rather, he utilized his leading function and his most highly developed secondary function predominantly as a defense against his inferior function, and his unconscious secondary function was not the first function to enter his consciousness in analysis.

I have no intention of generalizing this phenomenon and am not of the opinion that we must alter the theory, because the easiest access to the inferior function can come about directly in most cases rather than progressing via the secondary function. What I do want to point out is the necessity for the analyst to remain flexible whenever working with typological concepts. Rigid adherence to very specific theoretical preconceptions can, in some cases, hinder access to the inferior functions, especially if the secondary function is enlisted in the service of defense. In every individual case, the analyst must decide by which path he or she can best approach the repressed, unconscious inferior function. In doing this, it is advisable, as in the example just given, to leave the guidance to the unconscious which is constellated in the transference and countertransference between patient and analyst.

Wilke (1969) describes a similar situation in which the unconscious was accessed directly by the superior function. His patient, an extraverted sensation type, altered his attitude type in analysis to the extent that he became able to introvert and utilize his introverted sensation for a more intensive observation of his dreams. This sort of observation and incorporation of individual dream images and symbols in all their gradations and subtleties of meaning gradually led to changes and transformations in the patient's personality. In this case, access to the unconscious came about due to a change of attitude in the leading function since it was not built into the defensive systems but rather proved to be the most important means for studying the unconscious.

The question now arises as to the role typology plays in the methods of the various psychological schools. Jung himself was an introverted intuitive thinker, and without a doubt his psychology reveals distinct characteristics of his typology. Consequently we can understand the results of Bradway's (1964) research which showed that the overwhelming majority of Jungians were introverted intuitive types since that sort of psychology appealed to them. If one carefully reviews the description of the various types that Jung presents in his work (*C. W.* 6), one cannot help but notice that the introverted thinking type and the introverted intuitive received most favorable treatment while the sensation type came off worst of all.

It is also certain, as I discussed in an earlier work (Dieckmann 1960), that, in contrast to Freud, Jung had a different way of observing the emotional object. The fundamental sources from which Jung developed his doctrine of the feeling-toned complex are the diagnostic association studies. In them, Jung established that certain disturbances in the association experiment were produced by psychic images that he called complexes. Each complex consists primarily of the central emotion, the vehicle of meaning or the core element, and secondarily of the associations clustered around the core element. The core of the complex itself is identical with an archetype. The entire concept of the complex is, therefore, not the most quantitative concept possible but rather predominantly a qualitative concept which only secondarily is energetically charged with emotion or affect. In Jung's writings, individual complexes present a graphic image, and one seeks to comprehend this sort of image as one moves toward a deepened grasp of the psyche. In this endeavor, the parts are understood from the perspective of the whole rather than the whole in terms of the parts.

This is a thoroughly legitimate way of viewing the object in nature. Here the object is seen as quality and form in its sensuously rich manifestation. To study it is to immerse oneself in the phenomena, and one seeks the interconnections among phenomena not mechanically and theoretically in the form of laws but rather graphically as type or *Gestalt*. Jaspers (1954) calls these two forms of scientific endeavor the "natural-mechanical" and the "natural-historical" world views, two different forms in which the object can be studied that began with Plato and Aristotle and continue throughout the whole of European intellectual history. Proceeding from the stormy development of the modern natural sciences, the natural-mechanical world view has gained ever greater dominance, especially in the course of the last century, and has been promulgated by its proponents as the sole scientifically acceptable approach. Only after the limits of the natural-mechanical world view began to become more and more apparent in recent decades, especially through discoveries in physics and mathematics, has the natural-historical world view with its more graphically and holistically oriented form of thought gradually begun to gain ground again. Basically both forms of thought, taken together, should be possible if one is to comprehend an object completely: on the one hand, the mechanically determined, calculable, predictable form patterned on the image of the machine, and on the other hand, the graphic form, shaped by the image or the type that is not determined or predictable but can be comprehended only within the framework of statistical probability.

Emphasis on the one form of thought that plays a leading role determines the character of the psychological school concerned. Dangers inhere in both forms, since too strong a bond to a specific world view that gains predominance can no longer do justice to the other side. In its extreme form, purely mechanical thought leads to a dead system that exists only for its own sake and ruthlessly annihilates anything living. In the worst case, the methodology that this sort of system produces corresponds to a Procrustes bed and is fixated in very definite, rigid forms and rules concerning what, when, and where things must be done. The overemphasis on graphic thought runs the danger of drifting away from form toward formlessness and of ultimately dissolving in an irrational vagueness. Corresponding to this, its methodology is imprecise, fuzzy, and irrational and leads to a dissolution of the necessary rituals and the form principle itself that alone make possible any and all analytic development.

One methodologically important problem in typology remains to be discussed, that of adaptation via the inferior function. We are a strongly extraverted culture, and the quiet introvert, who often creates a cooler, more distanced, and socially less adept impression, is not exactly highly valued. Often he or she is regarded as eccentric or even declared to be pathological or narcissistic. These terms should not be confused. The introvert's intercourse with external objects that are always held at a certain distance must not be equated with a narcissistic disturbance although that impression could arise on cursory external inspection. It is to Jung's merit to have pointed out differences in type and the uniqueness and good qualities of the introverted type, and hence to have freed introversion and the introverted type of person from our culture's pattern of downgrading. Knowledge of the unique qualities and the strong points of the introverted type, however, have not yet become common knowledge in our society, and both education in the parental home and the general social patterns of our civilization often influence the introvert to attempt to develop his or her inferior extraversion and try to use it to adapt to the world.

But introverts are not at all so uncommon in our society. In a study I conducted involving 87 of my patients in regard to the favorite fairy tale (Dieckmann 1975), the distribution of introverts and extraverts was nearly equal. (These patients had sought me out because of their problems without knowing what analytic school I followed.) Among these 87 patients, 42 were introverts and 45 extraverts; this indicates the small majority of extraverts was insignificant. We are fully justified in assuming that the distribution between extraversion and introversion in a larger population would shift in the direction of extraversion since among the patients that come to an analyst a certain, sometimes conscious, sometimes unconscious process of preselection takes place. Almost all patients — except, perhaps, for a few who are sufficiently informed about Jungian psychology — are primarily attuned to having to live extravertedly and to expecting to find in analysis the healing or improvement of their problems and difficulties through an improved, extraverted adaptation to the environment. It seems to me of very great methodological significance that these introverted persons become acquainted with their typology in analysis, accept it, and also come to feel at home in it.

Of course, this by no means excludes the development of inferior functions; rather, it only means that the original type as such can be accepted with its possibilities as well as its limits. I do not want to get into what I consider a futile discussion in regard to whether typology is genetically determined and conditioned (i.e., whether it falls within the domain of heredity and consequently is only minimally susceptible to practical influence), or whether we are dealing with something acquired relatively early on. Probably both factors play a role, and this is a problem similar to that in Freudian psychoanalysis in regard to developmentally early structures. The latter, too, cannot be totally dissolved and reversed in the course of the analytic process; rather, exactly like typology, a basic structure remains despite a completed analysis which only enables the patient to move about more freely within the given basic structure, as Argelander (1972) has discussed. The whole genetic question is certainly of great theoretical interest, but I do not want to enter into it in detail here since it has no great degree of relevance on the basis of the practical experience available to us. Analysis can enable the patient to loosen structures or typologies so as to move about more freely within his or her particular typology, diminish inhibitions, and help gain access to creativity and vitality. But analysis cannot create a completely different type of person.

To return to the problem of the primarily introverted patient who attempts to a large extent to adapt to the environment with inferior extraversion and has great difficulties doing so or who comes to grief trying, I believe that it is methodologically of great importance first of all to affirm these people in their introverted typology. For example, the introvert very often complains about feelings of inferiority and failure in groups or in social settings. In contrast to the extravert, introverts have difficulties reacting with adequate speed and spontaneity to the flow of thoughts or feelings in groups since they are not able to grasp intuitively what is going on in the room from moment to moment. They need distance from the object and orientation to the inner subject; consequently, they see the fitting answer or comment only when the group has disbanded. Often they also meet with rejection or experience other people as reserved when they do risk introducing their subjective factor since it frequently appears unusual or not fully suitable in the situation. But if the introvert recognizes his or her psychological typology and feels comfortable with it, he or she will often be able to discover that a good listener is far more sought after in our society than a good talker or narrator since most people in our culture would rather talk than listen. Consequently an attentive and interested listener is a person in great social demand. Moreover, the introvert can learn to introduce his or her subjectivity constructively, too.

A strongly introverted woman patient, who worked in a children's clothing shop and initially took very little part in the lively discussions that often took place there among parents because she was afraid to say anything, proudly told me one day that she had finally said something. Suddenly she had spoken up in a group meeting and told the others that, although externally everything looked harmonious, she had the subjective feeling that not everything was all right in the group and that there were subterranean tensions. Every time she went home after a meeting, she felt downcast although the discussion seemed successful on the surface. The other members of the group reacted initially with a moment of bewilderment, but then confirmed her subjective impression and discussed a number of subterranean tensions that they had previously passed over. I offer this as only one possible example of the essential and important sorts of things an introverted person has to share in smaller or larger groups to the extent that the introvert knows how to be comfortable with his or her typology.

Of course, the same phenomenon found in regard to attitude type holds true for function type, too. A clear and not at all uncommon example of this has to do with certain forms of compulsion neurosis. As a consequence of the almost complete repression of emotions that takes place in these illnesses, compulsive neurotics and patients with neurotically compulsive structuring are frequently regarded as having thinking or sensation as their leading function. What is overlooked here is the fact that these compulsive persons make feeling-toned, moralistic judgments since the judging component of the feeling function has moved into the collective unconscious or into the superego, and their pedantry and petty moral judgments are used as a defense against strong Dionysian elements in which the dominant feeling is contained in the unconscious. The thinking of these compulsives is actually a mixture of feeling and thinking, such as Jung described in regard to animus-possessed women. In the woman's animus, this mixture of feeling and thinking is perhaps more obvious and distinct than in compulsive men where it is disguised by an emphasis on factuality and rationality. Actually, here it is not at all a question of true, independent thinking that decides according to logical categories free from value judgments, but rather it is a sort of thinking constricted by the value judgments of a twisted or split feeling function which, as a consequence of its power, is feared and defended against.

Taking as his population a number of patients examined clinically, Göllner (1975) determined that Jung's old intuitive notion that women tended more to be feeling types and men to be thinkers no longer held true, at least today, and that the distribution was actually the other way around. In this sense, it is very important always to remember that a person's leading function is not the one that appears strongest to the observer, but rather is the function with which the person observed most often manages object relationships. Differentiation of the various functions and their relationship to other structural components — such as anima, animus, etc. — also belong in this initially more diagnostic domain, as Wolff (1959), von Franz (1971), Ulanov (1971), and Willeford (1974) have discussed. Viewed methodologically, this can lead to quite profound "Aha" experiences for these patients when they discover that their leading function is really not thinking but feeling, and, on the other hand, without ever having explicitly to tell the patient, a different and better therapeutic atmosphere arises in the countertransference when the analyst recognizes that the compulsively structured patient in front of her or him is a feeling type. Blomeyer (1971) and I (Dieckmann 1971) have discussed in detail the great degree to which this sort of inner countertransference attitude on the part of the analyst is significant and the extent to which an inadequate attitude can develop into a countertransference resistance. Of course, these sorts of considerations hold true also for the other function types, and it would be a desirable addition to the literature of analytical psychology if the relationships among the individual psychological and somatic illnesses and the various typologies could be worked out on a larger scale, since the pointers in Jung's typology (*C.W.* 6) are still in need of a thorough examination and possible revision. Wilke (1974) and U. Dieckmann (1974) have done preliminary work on this.

Scientific systems are the work of mankind, just as all analysts are human beings. Hence both kinds of thought—i.e., the "natural-mechanical" and the "natural-historical"—are burdened with all the imperfections that always cling to human creations. Consequently it is necessary to maintain a constant alertness to problems in one's own theory and methodology. This alertness to problems is necessary for analytical psychology and with the help of other functions, enables us to investigate what we have attained and repeatedly to formulate our questions anew. Thus, it is very interesting to observe that, among the predominantly introverted intuitive Jungians in recent years, more and more extraverted sensation types have turned up who express their views on things and who, since they represent the "inferior function," are regarded in part skeptically and in part are enthusiastically applauded.

Mattoon (1974) has pointed out that analytical psychology still has some lessons to learn from academic psychology: 1) the collection of data or facts that support Jungian hypotheses; 2) the collection of facts that speak against certain of Jung's hypotheses and would thus modify Jungian theory; and 3) raising questions, the answers to which would give analytical psychology a more comprehensive theory of personality. There exists an entire body of extra-analytic findings that can support or enrich Jungian hypotheses, particularly from the area of the psychology of animals and of instincts (especially Portmann 1953), as well as studies from experimental dream research and even from behaviorism.

Particularly interesting points of view emerge also from the research findings of the French school of structuralists. Lévi-Strauss (1973) and Piaget (1969) advance the hypothesis that the psyche has at its disposal preformed categories that make it possible for the human being to learn language and to develop similar forms of organization even in widely separated cultures. These elementary categories or combinations could well be an equivalent to the theory of archetypes. In this sense, a more strongly extraverted sensation function in the area of analytical psychology as a science would have to be concerned a great deal more comprehensively not only with intrapsychic findings but also, in keeping with Jung's tradition, in regard to the findings of other sciences whose researches offer essential support to or even modifications of our system. Paying this sort of attention to inferior functions in the entire scientific system could then, *nolens volens*, also lead to modifications and improvements in methodology.

Bibliography

Abraham, K. 1969. Ergänzung zur Lehre vom Analcharakter. *Psychoanalyatische Studien zur Charakterbildung* [Supplement to the study of the anal character. Psychoanalytic studies on character formation]. Frankfurt: Atheneum.

Adler, G. 1961. *The Living Symbol*. Bollingen Series LXII. New York: Pantheon Books.

Ammann, A. N. 1978. *Active Imagination*. Olten: Walter Verlag.

Andersen, H. C. 1987. *Fairy Tales*. New York: NAL.

Argelander, H. 1967. Das Erstinterview in der Psychotherapie [The initial interview in psychotherapy]. *Psyche* 21:34.

_____. 1972. *Der Flieger. Eine charakteranalytische Fallstudie* [The flyer: a characterological case study]. Frankfurt: Suhrkamp.

Aristotle. *Metaphysics*, VII, 7.

Artemidorus of Daldis. 1975. *The Interpretation of Dreams: Oneirocritica by Artemidorus*. R. J. White, ed. Park Ridge, N.J.: Noyes Press.

Balint, M. 1965. *Primary Love and Psycho-Analytic Technique*. London: Tavistock Publications.

_____. 1968. *The Basic Fault: Therapeutic Aspects of Regression*. London: Tavistock Publications.

Balint, M., and Balint, E. 1961. *Psychotherapeutic Techniques in Medicine*. London: Tavistock Publications.

Berne, E. 1964. *Games People Play*. New York: Grove Press.

Bernoulli, R. 1935. Seelische Entwicklung und Alchemie [The development of the soul and alchemy]. *Eranos-Jahrbuch*. Zürich: Rhein Verlag.

Bloch, E. 1976. *Das Prinzip Hoffnung* [The principle of hope]. Frankfurt: Suhrkamp.

Blomeyer, R. 1971. Die Konstellierung der Gegenübertragung beim Auftauchen archetypischer Träume. Falldarstellyng [The constellation of the countertransference with the appearance of archetypal dreams. A case study]. *Zeitschrift für Analytische Psychologie und ihre Grenzgebiete* 3/1:29–40.

_____. 1972. Uebertragung und Gegenübertragung in der Kindertherapie unter Gesichtspunkten der Analytischen Psychologie [Transference and countertransference in child therapy from the viewpoint of analytical psychology]. *Zeitschrift für Analytische Psychologie und ihre Grenzgebiete* 4/3:207–218.

_____. 1974. Aspekte der Persona [Aspects of the persona]. *Zeitschrift für Analytische Psychologie und ihre Grenzgebiete* 5.

Bornemann, E. 1973. *Psychoanalyse des Geldes* [Psychoanalysis of money]. Frankfurt: S. Fischer Verlag.

Boss, M. 1975. *"I dreamt last night. . . ."* New York: Gardner Press.

Bossard, R. 1976. *Traumpsychologie.* Olten: Walter Verlag.

Bradway, K. 1964. Jung's psychological types. Classification by test versus classification by self. *Journal of Analytical Psychology* 9.

Bradway, K., and Detloff, W. 1976. Incidence of psychological types among Jungian analysts classified by self and by test. *Journal of Analytical Psychology* 21.

Brecht, B. 1961. *Seven Plays.* E. Bentley, ed. New York: Grove Press.

_____. 1976. *Gesammelte Werke.* Frankfurt: Suhrkamp.

_____. 1981. *Gedichte von Berthold Brecht in einem Band.* Frankfurt: Suhrkamp.

Cahen, R. 1976. Abwesenheit und Rhythmus als therapeutische Faktoren [Absence and rhythm as therapeutic factors]. *Zeitschrift für Analytische Psychologie und ihre Grenzgebiete* 7.

Cooper, D. 1972. *Tod der Familie* [The death of the family]. Reinbek: Rowohlt Verlag. Original English edition, New York: Pantheon, 1970.

daVinci, L. *Tagebücher und Aufzeichnungen* [Diaries and notes]. Leipzig, 1953.

Desmonde, W. 1957. The origins of money in the animal sacrifice. *Journal of the Hillside Hospital* 6.

Deutsch, F. 1939. The associative anamnesis. *Psychoanalytic Quarterly* 7.

Deutsch, F., and Murphy, W. 1955. *The Clinical Interview.* New York: International Universities Press.

Deutsches Aertzeblatt. 1976. 73 (27), pp. 1833–1844.

Dieckmann, H. 1958. Die Einstellung Rainer Maria Rilkes zu den Elternimagines [Rainer Maria Rilke's attitude to the parental imagos]. *Zeitschrift für Psychosomatische Medizin* 5:51–57, 128–136.

_____. 1960. Die Differenz zwischen dem anschaulichen und dem abstrahierended Denken in den Psychologien von C. G. Jung und Freud [Differences between Jung's imaginal and Freud's abstract thought]. *Zeitschrift für Psychosomatische Medizin* 6:287–292, 7:58–65.

_____. 1961. Der Antisemitismus als personales psychologisches Problem [Antisemitism as a personal psychological problem]. *Wege zum Menschen* 13:8–17.

_____. 1962. Ueber einige Beziehungen zwischen Traumserie und Verhaltensänderungen in einer Neurosenbehandlung [Concerning some relationships between dream series and behavioral changes in the treatment of a neurosis]. *Zeitschrift für Psycho-somatische Medizin* 8.

_____. 1963. Ritualbildungen in der Therapie [Formation of rituals in therapy]. *Zeitschrift für Psycho-somatische Medizin* 9.

_____. 1965. Integration process of the ego-complex in dreams. *Journal of Analytical Psychology* 10.

_____. 1966. Mutterbindung und Herzneurose [Attachment to mother and heart neurosis]. *Zeitschrift für Psycho-somatische Medizin* 12:26–39.

_____. 1967a. Das Lieblingsmärchen der Kindheit und seine Beziehung zu Neurose und Persönlichkeitsstruktur [The favorite childhood fairy tale and its relation to neurosis and personality structure]. *Praxis der Kinderpsychologie und Kinderpsychiatrie* 17/8.

_____. 1967b. Zum Aspekt des Grausamen im Märchen [Concerning the element of horror in fairy tales]. *Praxis der Kinderpsychologie und Kingerpsychiatrie* 16:300–307.

_____. 1968. Das Lieblingsmärchen der Kindheit als therapeutischer Faktor in der Analyse [The favorite childhood fairy tale as a therapeutic factor in analysis]. *Praxis der Kinderpsychologie und Kinderpsychiatrie* 17:288–292.

_____. 1969. Magie und Mythos im menschlichen Unbewussten [Magic and myth in the human unconscious]. *Wege zum Menschen* 21/6.

_____. 1971a. *Probleme der Lebensmitte* [Problems of midlife]. Stuttgart: Verlag Adolf Bonz.

_____. 1971b. The favorite fairy tale from childhood as a therapeutic factor in analysis. In J. Wheelwright, ed., *The Analytic Process*. New York: C. G. Jung Foundation, pp. 68–84.

_____. 1971c. Symbols of active imagination. *Journal of Analytical Psychology* 16.

_____. 1971d. Die Konstellierung der Gegenübertragung beim Auftauchen architypischer Träume. Untersuchungsmethoden und -ergembisse [Constellating the countertransference when archetypal dreams appear]. *Zeitschrift für Analytische Psychologie und ihre Grenzgebiete* 3/1.

_____. 1971e. The favorite fairy tale of childhood. *Journal of Analytical Psychology* 16.

_____. 1972a. Das Traumsymbol in der Analytischen Psychologie [The dream symbol in analytical psychology]. *Zeitschrift für Analytische Psychologie und ihre Grenzgebiete* 3/2.

_____. 1972b. *Träume als Sprache der Seele* [Dreams as the language of the soul]. Stuttgart: Verlag Adolf Bonz.

_____. 1973a. Uebertragung, Gegenübertragung, Beziehung [Transference, countertransference, relationship]. *Zeitschrift für Analytische Psychologie und ihre Grenzgebiete* 4/3.

_____. 1973b. Transfert e Controtransfert [Transference and countertransference]. *Revista di Psychologia Analytica* 4/2.

_____. 1973c. Symbolism in the work of Chagall. Lecture to the Society of Jungian Analysts of Southern California.

_____. 1974a. *Individuation in den Märchen der 1001-Nacht* [Individuation in the fairy tales from 1001 Nights]. Stuttgart: Verlag Adolf Bonz.

_____. 1974b. *Das Lieblingsmärchen. Das Problemkind in der ärtzlichen Praxis* [The favorite fairy tale. The problem child in medical practice]. Munich: J. F. Lehmanns Verlag.

_____. 1974c. Der Traum und das Selbst des Menschen [The dream and the self of mankind]. *Zeitschrift für Analytische Psychologie und ihre Grenzgebiete* 5/1.

_____. 1974d. Transference and Countertransference. *Encyclopaedia Italiana.*

_____. 1974e. Das Lieblingsmärchen [The favorite fairy tale]. *Praxis der Psychotherapie* 19/1.

_____. 1975. Typologische Aspekte der Lieblingsmärchen [Typological aspects of the favorite fairy tale]. *Zeitschrift für Analytische Psychologie und ihre Grenzgebiete* 6/3.

_____. 1976a. Einige Aspekte zur Individuation der 1. Lebenshälfte [Some aspects of individuation during the first half of life]. *Zeitschrift für Analytische Psychologie und ihre Grenzgebiete* 7/4.

_____. 1976b. Das Auto als Traumsymbol [The automobile as dream symbol]. *Zeitschrift für Analytische Psychologie und ihre Grenzgebiete* 7/1.

_____. 1976c. Transference and countertransference. Results of a Berlin research group. *Journal of Analytical Psychology* 21/1.

_____. 1977. *Märchen und Symbole* [Fairy tales and symbols]. Stuttgart: Verlag Adolf Bonz.

_____. 1978a. *Umgang mit Träumen* [Dealing with dreams]. Stuttgart: Kreuz Verlag.

_____. 1978b. Kongressvortrag Rom 1977 [Address to the Rome congress, 1977]. *Zeitschrift für Analytische Psychologie und ihre Grenzgebiete* 9/2.

_____. 1978c. Einige Aspekte zur Persönlichkeitsstruktur des Suchtgefährdeten aus der Sicht der Analytischen Psychologie C. G. Jungs [Reflections on the personality structure of at-risk patients from the viewpoint of C. G. Jung's analytical psychology]. *Sucht als Symptom.* Stuttgart.

_____. 1978d. Sinn und Wertfragen vor und in der Lebensmitte [Meaning and questions of values before and at midlife]. *Praxis der Psychotherapie* 23.

_____. 1986. *Twice-Told Tales: The Psychological Use of Fairy Tales*. B. Matthews, trans. Wilmette, Ill.: Chiron Publications.

Dieckmann, H., and Jung, E. 1977. *Heiterentwicklung der analytischen (komplexen) Psychologie des XX. Jahrhunderts* (Further development of analytical psychology (the psychology of the complexes) in the 20th century]. Vol. 3, Munich: Kindler Verlag.

Dieckmann, U. 1974. Ein archetypischer Aspekt in der auslösenden Situation von Depressionen [An archetypal, precipitating element in depression]. *Zeitschrift für Analytische Psychologie und ihre Grenzgebiete* 5/2.

d'Marmor, J. 1970. Limitations of free association. *Archives of General Psychiatry*, p. 160–165.

Dührssen, A. 1972. *Analytische Psychotherapie in Theorie, Praxis und Ergebnissen* [Analytical psychotherapy in theory, practice and results]. Göttingen: Verlag für Medizinische Psychologie.

Edinger, E. 1972. *Ego and Archetype*. New York: C. G. Jung Foundation.

Elias, N. 1969. *Ueber den Prozess der Zivilisation* [Concerning processes of civilization]. Basel: Haus zum Falken, 1969.

Erickson, E. H. 1970. *Identität und Lebenszyklus* [Identity and the life cycle]. Frankfurt: Suhrkamp Verlag. Original English edition, New York: International Universities Press, 1967.

Fairbairn, W. R. P. 1958. On the nature and aims of psychoanalytical treatment. *International Journal of Psychoanalysis* 39/5.

Fenichel, O. 1941. Problems of psychoanalytic technique. *The Psychoanalytic Quarterly*.

Ferency, S. 1916. Pekunia Olet. *Internationale Zeitschrift für ärztliche Psychoanalyse* 4.

Fordham, M. 1944. *The Life of Childhood*. London: Kegan Paul, Trench, Trubner.

_____. 1955. On the origins of the ego in childhood. In *Studien zur Analytischen Psychologie C. G. Jungs*. Zürich: Rascher Verlag.

_____. 1956. Active imagination and imaginative activity. *Journal of Analytical Psychology* 1.

_____. 1957. *New Developments in Analytical Psychology*. London: Routledge and Kegan Paul.

_____. 1969. *Children as Individuals*. New York: C. G. Jung Foundation.

_____. 1974a. Notes on transference. In *Technique in Jungian Analysis*. M. Fordham, R. Gordon, J. Hubback, and K. Lambaert, eds. London: Heinemann.

_____. 1974b. Technique and countertransference. In *Technique in Jungian Analysis*. M. Fordham, R. Gordon, J. Hubback, and K. Lambaert, eds. London: Heinemann.

_____. 1975. On interpretation. *Aspekte der Analytischen Psychologie. Zum 100. Geburtstag von C. G. Jung. Journal of Analytical Psychology* 6:277-293.

_____. 1977. A possible root of active imagination. *Journal of Analytical Psychology* 22.

Freud, S. 1953-1974. *The Standard Edition of the Complete Psychological Works of Sigmund Freud.* J. Straachey, trans. London: Hogarth Press, 1969 edition.

Fromm, E. 1936. *Autorität und Familie* [Authority and family]. Alcan.

Fromm-Reichmann, F. 1950. *Principles of Intensive Psychotherapy.* Chicago: University of Chicago Press.

Gill, M., Newman, P., and Redlich, F. 1954. *The Initial Interview in Psychiatric Practice.* New York: International Universities Press.

Gitleson, M. 1952. The emotional position of the analyst in the psychoanalytic situation. *International Journal of Psychoanalysis* 33.

Glover, E. 1955. *The Technique of Psychoanalysis.* London: Bailliere, Tindall and Cox.

Göllner, R. 1975. Empirische Ueberprüfung einiger Aussagen über Einstellungs- und Funktionstypen von C. G. Jung [Empirical examination of some of C. G. Jung's statements on attitude and function type]. *Zeitschrift für Analytische Psychologie und ihre Grenzgebiete* 6.

Goethe, J. W. 1974. *Faust.* J. Prudhoe, trans. Manchester: Manchester University Press.

Greenson, R. 1967. *The Technique and Practice of Psychoanalysis.* New York: International Universities Press. German translation, 1975.

Groesbeck, C. 1978. Psychological types in the analysis of the transference. *Journal of Analytical Psychology* 23.

Guggenbühl-Craig, A. 1971. *Power in the Helping Professions.* New York: Spring Publications.

Hänisch, I. v. 1974. Tiefenpsychologische Aspekte der Tarzanfigur [Depth psychological aspects of the Tarzan figure]. *Zeitschrift für Analytische Psychologie und ihre Grenzgebiete* 5.

Hartmann, H., Kris, E., and Loewenstein, R. 1946. Comments on the psychic structure. *Psychoanalytic Study of the Child* 2.

Heigl, F. 1978. Behandlung von Neurosen. Prognose—Indikation [Treatment of neuroses. Prognosis—indications]. *Monatskurse für ärztliche Fortbildung* 28/4.

Heimann, P. 1950. On countertransference. *International Journal of Psycho-Analysis* 31.

Henderson, J. 1955a. The inferior function. *Studien zur Analytischen Psychologie C. G. Jungs.* Zürich: Rascher Verlag.

_____. 1955b. Resolution of the transference in the light of C. G. Jung's psychology. *Report of the International Congress of Psychotherapy, Zürich 1954.* Basel.

Heyer, R. 1931. Bericht über C. G. Jungs analytisches Seminar [Report on C. G. Jung's seminar on analysis]. *Zentralblatt für Psychotherapie und ihre Grenzgebiete* 4:2–6.

_____. 1964. *Seelenkunde im Umbruch der Zeit* [Psychology in times of radical change]. Stuttgart.

Hillman, J. 1964. *Suicide and the Soul.* Zürich: Spring Publications.

_____. 1971. The feeling function. In *Lectures on Jung's Typology.* M. L. von Franz and J. Hillman, eds. New York: Spring Publications.

Hobson, R. 1971. Imagination and amplification in psychotherapy. *Journal of Analytical Psychology* 16.

Horney, K. 1942. *Self-Analysis.* New York: H. H. Horton.

Hubback, J. 1974. Notes on manipulation activity and handling. *Journal of Analytical Psychology* 19.

Jackson, M. 1962. Chair, couch and countertransference. *Journal of Analytical Psychology* 7.

Jacobi, J. 1943. *The Psychology of C. G. Jung.* New Haven, Conn.: Yale University Press, 1973.

_____. 1957. *Complex, Archetype, Symbol.* Princeton, N.J.: Princeton University Press, 1959.

_____. 1965. *The Way of Individuation.* London: Hodder and Stoughton, 1967.

_____. 1971. *Masks of the Soul.* Grand Rapids, Mich.: Eerdmans.

Jänicke, M. 1977. Soziale und ökologische Bedingungen rückläufiger Lebenswerwartung in Industrieländern. *Mensch, Medizin, Gesellschaft.*

Jaspers, K. 1954. *Psychologie der Weltanschauungen* [The psychology of world views]. Berlin.

Jezower, I. 1928. *Das Buch der Träume* [The dream book]. Berlin: Rowohlt Verlag.

Jones, E. 1919. Ueber analerotische Charakterzüge [On anal-erotic character traits]. *Internationale Zeitschrift für ärztliche Psychoanalyse* 5.

Jung, C. G. 1938–1941. *Kindertraumseminar* [Seminar on children's dreams]. Mimeograph.

_____. 1938–1940. *Seminar: Modern Psychology.* Mimeograph.

_____. *The Collected Works of C. G. Jung.* Princeton, N.J.: Princeton University Press.

_____. 1962. *Memories, Dreams, Reflections.* A. Jaffe, ed. New York: Vintage Books, 1971.

Jung, C. G., and Kerényi, K. 1951. *Essays on a Science of Mythology.* Princeton, N.J.: Princeton University Press, 1971.

Jung, E. 1971. Der Grossinquisitor, ein Beitrag zum Archetyp des Grossen Vaters [The grand inquisitor: a contribution to the archetype of the great father]. *Zeitschrift für Analytische Psychologie und ihre Grenzgebiete* 2.

_____. 1973. Zur Gruppendynamik in einem psychotherapeutischen Forschungsteam [On group dynamics in a psychotherapeutic research team]. *Zeitschrift für Analytische Psychologie und ihre Grenzgebiete* 4.

Kadinsky, D. 1964. *Die Entwicklung des Ich beim Kinde* [The development of the ego in the child]. Bern: Verlag Hans Huber.

_____, ed. 1969. *Der Mythos der Maschine* [The myth of the machine]. Bern: Verlag Hans Huber.

_____. 1970. The meaning of technique. *Journal of Analytical Psychology* 5.

Kadinsky, M. 1969. Ueber Science Fiction [On science fiction]. In *Der Mythos der Maschine*, D. Kadinsky, ed. Bern: Verlag Hans Huber.

Kerényi, K. 1951. *The Gods of the Greeks.* London: Thames and Hudson.

Kirsche, J. 1973. *The Reluctant Prophet.* Los Angeles: Sherborne Press.

Kirsch, T. 1977. Dreams and psychological types. Remarks at the 7th International Congress of Analytical Psychology, Rome.

Klein, M. 1962. *Das Seelenleben des Kleinkindes* [The emotional life of the infant]. Stuttgart: E. Klett Verlag.

Kleitmann, N. 1963. *Sleep and Wakefulness.* Chicago: University of Chicago Press.

Kohut, H. 1971. *The Analysis of Self: A Systematic Approach to the Psychoanalytic Treatment of Narcissistic Personality Disorders.* New York: International Universities Press.

Kraemer, W. 1974. The danger of unrecognized countertransference. In *Technique in Jungian Analysis.* M. Fordham, R. Gordon, J. Hubback, and K. Lambaert, eds. London: Heinemann.

Kretschmer, E. 1922. *Körperbau und Charakter. Untersuchungen zum Konstitutionsproblem und zur Lehre von den Temperamenten* [Body type and character. Investigations of the problem of constitution and on the doctrine of the temperaments]. Berlin: J. Springer.

Laing, R. D. 1969. *Politics of the Family.* New York: Random House.

Leuner, H. 1970. *Katathymes Bilderleben.* Stuttgart: Georg Thieme Verlag.

Lévy-Bruhl, C. 1959. *Die geistige Welt der Primitiven* [The spiritual world of primitives]. Düsseldorf-Köln: Diederichs Verlag.

Lévi-Struass, C. 1973. *Das wilde Denken* [Savage thought]. Frankfurt: Suhrkamp.

Mattoon, A. 1974. The neglected function of analytical psychology. Paper read at the 6th International Congress of Analytical Psychology, London.

Meier, C. A. 1967. *Ancient Incubation and Modern Psychotherapy.* Evanston, Ill.: Northwestern University Press.

_____. 1969. Individuation und psychologische Typen [Individuation and psychological types]. *Zeitschrift für Analytische Psychologie und ihre Grenzgebiete.*

_____. 1972. *Die Bedeutung des Traumes* [The meaning of the dream]. Olten: Walter Verlag.

Neue Brockhaus-Enzyklopädie. 1973. Wiesbaden: F. A. Brockhaus.

Neumann, E. 1953a. On the psychological significance of ritual. *Quadrant* 9/2 (1976).

_____. 1953b. *Zur Psychologie des Weibleichen* [The psychology of the feminine]. Munich: Kindler Verlag.

_____. 1954. *The Origins and History of Consciousness.* R. F. C. Hull, trans. Princeton, N.J.: Princeton University Press.

_____. 1973. *The Child.* R. Manheim, trans. New York: C. G. Jung Foundation.

_____. 1974. *The Great Mother.* R. Manheim, trans. Princeton, N.J.: Princeton University Press.

Ovid. *The Metamorphoses of Ovid.* A. E. Watts, trans. San Francisco: North Point Press, 1980.

Pauli, W. 1952. Der Einfluss der archetypischen Vorstellunged auf die Bildung naturwissenschaftlicher Theorien bei Kepler [The influence of archetypal ideas on Kepler's scientific theories]. *Naturerklärung und Psyche.*

Pearls, F. 1974. *Gestalttherapie in Aktion.* Stuttgart: Klett-Cotta.

Piaget, J. 1969. *Nachahmung, Spiel, Traum* [Imitation, play, dream]. Stuttgart: Original edition, London: Routledge and Kegan Paul, 1951.

Plaut, A. 1971. Lerntheorie und Analyatische Psychologie [Learning theory and analytical psychology]. Paper read at the Seminar of the German Society for Analytical Psychology (DGAP), Berlin.

_____. 1972. Analytical psychology and psychological types. Comments on replies to a survey. *Journal of Analytical Psychology* 17.

_____. 1974. Transference phenomena in alcoholism. *The Library of Analytical Psychology* 2.

Portmann, A. 1953. *Das Tier als sociales Hesen* [The animal as social creature]. Zürich: Rhein Verlag.

Raabe, W. 1977. Vom alten Protheus. *Collected Works of Wilhelm Raabe*, vol. 4. Munich: Winkler.

Racker, H. 1968. *Transference and Countertransference*. London: Hogarth Press.

Reich, W. 1973. *Charakateranalyse* [Analysis of character]. Frankfurt.

Rycroft, C. 1968. *Critical Dictionary of Psychoanalysis*. London: Nelson.

Sanctis, S. de. 1896. *E sogni e li sonno nell'isterismo e nella epilessia*. Rome.

Schmaltz, G. 1955. *Komplexe Psychologie und Körperliches Symptom* [The psychology of the complexes and bodily symptom]. Stuttgart: Hippokrates Verlag.

Schultz, I. 1976. *Das Autogene Training* [Autogenic training]. Stuttgart: Georg Thieme Verlag.

Schultz-Hencke, H. 1949. *Lehrbuch der Traumanalyse* [Textbook of dream analysis]. Stuttgart: Georg Thieme Verlag.

_____. 1952. *Das Problem der Scshizophrenie* [The problem of schizophrenia]. Stuttgart: Georg Thieme Verlag.

_____. 1970. *Lehrbuch der analytischen Psychotherapy* [Textbook of analytic psychotherapy]. Stuttgart: Georg Thieme Verlag.

Sechehaye, M.-A. 1955. *Die symbolische Hunscherfüllung* [Symbolic wish fulfilment]. Bern: Hans Huber Verlag.

Seifert, T. 1978. Resignation und Hoffnung in Partnershaft und Ehe. *Praxis der Psychotherapie* 23.

Sheely, G. 1976. *In der Mitte des Lebens*.

Siebenthal. 1953. *Die Wissenschaft vom Traum* [The science of the dream]. Heidlberg: Springer Verlag.

Singer, J. 1976. *Worunter Menschen leiden* [Why people suffer]. Olten: Walter Verlag.

Spitz, R. 1960. *Die Entstehung der ersten Objektbeziehungen* [The origin of the first object relations]. Stuttgart: Klett Verlag.

Steckel, W. 1950. *Technique of Analytic Psychotherapy*. New York: Liveright.

Stone, L. 1961. *The Psychoanalytic Situation: An Examination of Its Development and Essential Nature*. New York: International Universities Press.

Sullivan, H. 1951. The psychiatric interview. *Psychiatry* 14.

Szent-Györgyi, A. 1970. *The Crazy Ape*. New York: Philos Library.

Toffler, A. 1970. *Future Shock*. New York: Random House.

Ulanov, A. 1971. *The Feminine in Jungian Psychology and in Christian Theology*. Evanston, Ill.: Northwestern University Press.

Verworn, M. 1928. *Kausale und konditionale Weltanschauung* [Causal and conditional world views].

von Franz, M.-L. 1970. *The Problem of the Puer Aeternus*. New York: Spring Publications.

_____. 1971. The inferior functions. In *Lectures on Jung's Typology*. M. L. von Franz and J. Hillman, eds. New York: Spring Publications.

_____. 1972. *C. G. Jung—Wirkung und Gestalt* [C. G. Jung—Influence and Person]. Stuttgart.

Weaver, R. 1973. *The Old Wise Woman*. New York: The C. G. Jung Foundation.

Weigert, E. 1952. Contribution to the problem of terminating psychoanalysis. *Psychoanalytic Quarterly* 21.

Wheelwright, J. 1968. Remarks at the 3rd International Congress of Analytical Psychology, Montreal.

Wheelwright, J., and Gray. 1944. *The Gray-Wheelwright Test*. San Francisco: Society of Jungian Analysts of Northern California.

Whitmont, E. 1969. *The Symbolic Quest*. Princeton, N.J.: Princeton University Press.

Whitmont, E., and Kaufmann, Y. 1973. *Analytical Psychology in Current Psychotherapy*. Ithaca, N.Y.: Peacock Publishers.

Wickes, F. 1938. *The Inner World of Man*. New York: Farrar and Rinehart.

Wilke, H.-J. 1969. Die Empfindung in der analytischen Arbeit. *Zeitschrift für Analytische Psychologie und ihre Grenzgebiete* 2.

_____. 1974. Neurosentheoretische Ueberlegungen zur Struktur und Dynamik depressiver Erkrankungen [Reflections on the theory of neurosis concerning the structure and dynamics of depressive illnesses]. *Zeitschrift für Analytische Psychologie und ihre Grenzgebiete* 5.

_____. 1978. Zur Problematik des depressiven Wahns [On the problem of depressive delusion]. *Zeitschrift für Analytische Psychologie und ihre Grenzgebiete* 9.

Willeford, W. 1974. Towards a dynamic concept of feeling. Paper read to the Berlin Study Group for Analytical Psychology, Berlin.

Winnicott, D. 1958. Hate in the countertransference. In D. W. Winnicott, *Collected Papers*. London: Hogarth.

_____. 1965. *The Maturational Process and the Facilitating Environment*. London: Hogarth.

_____. 1969. *Kind, Familie und Umwelt* [Child, family and environment]. Munich: Ernst Reinhardt Verlag.

Wolff, T. 1959. *Studien zu C. G. Jungs Psychologie* [Studies in C. G. Jung's psychology]. Zürich.

Wolfman. 1972. *Der Wolfsmann vom Wolfsmann* [The wolfman on the wolfman]. Frankfurt: S. Fischer.

Zacharias, G. 1965. Zur Rolle des Widerstandes in der Psychotherapie [On the role of resistance in psychotherapy]. *Spektrum Psychologiae. Festschrift zum 60. Geburtstag von C. A. Meyer.* Zürich: Rascher Verlag.

Zetzel, E. 1956. Current concepts of transference. *International Journal of Psychoanalysis* 39:369–376.

Zimmer, H. 1938. Die indische Weltmutter [The Indian world mother]. *Eranos-Jahrbuch* 6. Zürich: Rhein Verlag.

Index

221